Pro JavaScript for Web Apps

Adam Freeman

Apress®

Pro JavaScript for Web Apps

ISBN-13 (pbk): 978-1-4302-4461-5

ISBN-13 (electronic): 978-1-4302-4462-2

President and Publisher: Paul Manning
Lead Editor: Ben Renow-Clarke
Development Editor: Louise Corrigan
Technical Reviewer: RJ Owen
Editorial Board: Steve Anglin, Ewan Buckingham, Gary Cornell, Louise Corrigan, Morgan Ertel, Jonathan Gennick, Jonathan Hassell, Robert Hutchinson, Michelle Lowman, James Markham, Matthew Moodie, Jeff Olson, Jeffrey Pepper, Douglas Pundick, Ben Renow-Clarke, Dominic Shakeshaft, Gwenan Spearing, Matt Wade, Tom Welsh
Coordinating Editor: Jennifer L. Blackwell
Copy Editor: Kim Wimpsett
Compositor: Bytheway Publishing Services
Indexer: SPi Global
Artist: SPi Global
Cover Designer: Anna Ishchenko

Distributed to the book trade worldwide by Springer Science+Business Media New York, 233 Spring Street, 6th Floor, New York, NY 10013. Phone 1-800-SPRINGER, fax (201) 348-4505, e-mail orders-ny@springer-sbm.com, or visit www.springeronline.com.

For information on translations, please e-mail rights@apress.com, or visit www.apress.com.

Apress and friends of ED books may be purchased in bulk for academic, corporate, or promotional use. eBook versions and licenses are also available for most titles. For more information, reference our Special Bulk Sales–eBook Licensing web page at www.apress.com/bulk-sales.

Any source code or other supplementary materials referenced by the author in this text is available to readers at www.apress.com. For detailed information about how to locate your book's source code, go to www.apress.com/source-code.

Dedicated to my lovely wife, Jacqui Griffyth.

Contents at a Glance

Contents

About the Author

Adam Freeman is an experienced IT professional who has held senior positions in a range of companies, most recently serving as chief technology officer and chief operating officer of a global bank. Now retired, he spends his time writing and running.

About the Technical Reviewer

 **RJ Owen** is the lead experience planner at EffectiveUI, focusing on customer insight work, including ethnographic research, design validation, co-creation exercises, and expert design. RJ started his career as a software developer and spent ten years working in C++, Java, and Flex before moving to the design research and customer insight team at EffectiveUI. He truly loves good design and understanding what makes people tick. RJ holds an MBA and a bachelor's in physics and computer science. He is a frequent speaker at many industry events, including Web 2.0, SXSW, and Adobe MAX.

Acknowledgments

I would like to thank everyone at Apress for working so hard to bring this book to print. In particular, I would like to thank Jennifer Blackwell for keeping me on track and Ben Renow-Clarke for commissioning and editing this title. I would also like to thank my technical reviewer, RJ Owen, whose efforts made this book far better than it would have been otherwise.

CHAPTER 1

Getting Ready

Client-side web app development has always been the poor cousin to server-side coding. This started because browsers and the devices they run on have been less capable than enterprise-class servers. To provide any kind of serious web app functionality, the server had to do all of the heavy lifting for the browsers, which was pretty dumb and simple by comparison.

Over the last few years, browsers have got smarter, more capable, and more consistent in how they implement web technology and standards. What used to be a fight to create unique features has become a battle to create the fastest and most compliant browser. The proliferation of smartphones and tablets has created a huge market for high-quality web apps, and the gradual adoption of HTML5 provides web application developers with a solid foundation for building rich and fluid client-side experiences.

Sadly, while the client-side technology has caught up with the server side, the techniques that client-side programmers use still lag behind. The complexity of client-side web apps has reached a tipping point where scale, elegance, and maintainability are essential and the days of hacking out a quick solution have passed. In this book, I level the playing field, showing you how to step up your client-side development to embrace the best techniques from the server-side world and combine them with the latest HTML5 features.

About This Book

This is my 15th book about technology, and to mark this, Apress asked me to do something different: share the tools, tricks, and techniques that I use to create complex client-side web apps. The result is something that is more personal, informal, and eclectic than my regular work. I show you how to take industrial-strength development concepts from server-side development and apply them to the browser. By using these techniques, you can build web apps that are easier to write, are easier to maintain, and offer better and richer functionality to your users.

Who Are You?

You are an experienced web developer whose projects have started to get out of control. The number of bugs in your JavaScript code is increasing, and it takes longer to find and fix each one. You are targeting an ever-wider range of device, including desktops, tablets, and smartphones, and keeping it all working is getting tougher. Your working days are longer, but you have less time to spend on new features because maintaining the code you already have sucks up a big chuck of your time.

The excitement that comes from your work has faded, and you have forgotten what it feels like to have a really productive day of coding. You know something is wrong, you know that you are losing your grip, and you know you need to find a different approach. If this sounds familiar, then *you* are my target reader.

What Do You Need to Know Before You Read This Book?

This is an advanced book, and you need to be an experienced web programmer to understand the content. You need a working knowledge of HTML, you need to know how to write JavaScript, and you have used both to create client-side web apps. You will need to understand how a browser works, how HTTP fits into the picture, and what Ajax requests are and why you should care about them.

What If You Don't Have That Experience?

You may still get some benefit from this book, but you will have to figure out some of the basics on your own. I have written a couple of other books you might find useful as primers for this one. If you are new to HTML, then read *The Definitive Guide to HTML5*. This explains everything you need to create regular web content and basic web apps. I explain how to use HTML markup and CSS3 (including the new HTML5 elements) and how to use the DOM API and the HTML5 APIs (including a JavaScript primer if you are new to the language). I make a lot of use of jQuery in this book. I provide all of the information you need for each topic, but if you want a better grounding in how jQuery works and how it relates to the DOM API, then read *Pro jQuery*. Both of these books are published by Apress.

Books aside, you can learn a lot about HTML and the browser APIs by reading the specifications published by the W3C at www.w3.org. The specifications are authoritative but can be hard-going and are not always that clear. A more readily accessible resource is the Mozilla Developer Network at http://developer.mozilla.org. This is an excellent source of information about everything from HTML to JavaScript. There is a general bias toward Firefox, but this isn't usually a problem since the mainstream browsers are generally compliant and consistent in the way they implement web standards.

Is This a Book About HTML5?

No, although I do talk about some of the new HTML5 JavaScript APIs. Most of this book is about technique, most of which will work with HTML4 just as it does with HTML5. Some chapters are built purely on HTML5 APIs (such as Chapters 5 and 6, which show you how to create web apps that work offline and how to store data in the browser), but the other chapters are not tied to any particular version of HTML. I don't get into any detail about the new elements described in HTML5. This is a book about programming, and the new elements don't have much impact on JavaScript programming.

What Is the Structure of This Book?

In Chapter 2, I build a simple web app for a fictitious cheese retailer called CheeseLux, building on the basic example I introduce later in this chapter. I follow some pretty standard approaches for creating this web app and spend the rest of the book showing you how to apply industrial-strength techniques to improve different aspects. I have tried to keep each chapter reasonably separate, but this is a reasonably informal book, and I do introduce some concepts gradually over a number of chapters. Each chapter builds on the techniques introduced in the chapters that go before it. You should read the book in chapter order if you can. The following sections summarize the chapters in this book.

Chapter 1: Getting Ready

Aside from describing this book, I introduce the static HTML version of the CheeseLux example, which I use throughout this book. I also list the software you will need if you want to re-create the examples on your own or experiment with the listings that are included in the source code download that accompanies this book (and which is available free from Apress.com).

Chapter 2: Getting Started

In this chapter, I use some basic techniques to create a more dynamic version of the CheeseLux example, moving from a web site to a web app. I use this as an opportunity to introduce some of the tools and concepts that you will need for the rest of the book and to provide a context so that I can show better techniques in later chapters.

Chapter 3: Adding a View Model

The first advanced technique I describe is introducing a client-side view model into a web app. View models are a key component in design patterns such as Model View Controller (MVC) and Model-View-View Model. If you adopt only one technique from this book, then make it this one; it will have the biggest impact on your development practices.

Chapter 4: Using URL Routing

URL routing allows you to scale up the navigation mechanisms in your web apps. You may not have realized that you have a navigation problem, but when you see how URL routing can work on the client side, you will see just how powerful and flexible a technique it can be.

Chapter 5: Creating Offline Web Apps

In this chapter, I show you how to use some of the new HTML5 JavaScript APIs to create web apps that work even when the user is offline. This is a powerful technique that is increasingly important as smartphones and tablets gain market penetration. The idea of an always-on network connection is changing, and being able to accommodate offline working is essential for many web apps.

Chapter 6: Storing Data

Being able to run the web app offline isn't much use unless you can also access stored data. In this chapter, I show you the different HTML5 APIs that are available for storing different kinds of data, ranging from simple name/value pairs to searchable hierarchies of persisted JavaScript objects.

Chapter 7: Creating Responsive Web Apps

There are entire categories of web-enabled devices that fall outside of the traditional desktop and mobile taxonomy. One approach to dealing with the proliferation of different device types is to create web apps that adapt dynamically to the capabilities of the device they are being used on, tailoring their appearance, functionality, and interaction models as required. In this chapter, I show you how to detect the capabilities you care about and respond to them.

Chapter 8: Creating Mobile Web Apps

An alternative to creating responsive web apps is to create a separate version that targets a specific range of devices. In this chapter, I show you how to use jQuery Mobile to create such a web app and how to incorporate advanced features such as URL routing into a mobile web app.

Chapter 9: Writing Better JavaScript

The last chapter in this book is about improving your code—not in terms of using JavaScript better but in terms of creating easily maintained code modules that are easier to use in your own projects and easier to share with others. I show you some convention-based approaches and introduce the Asynchronous Module Definition, which solves some complex problems when external libraries have dependencies on other functionality. I also show you how you can easily apply unit testing to your client-side code, including how to unit test complex HTML transformations.

Do You Describe Design Patterns?

I don't. This isn't that kind of book. This is a book about getting results, and I don't spend a lot of time discussing the design patterns that underpin each technique I describe. If you are reading this book, then you want to see those results and get the benefits they provide *now*. My advice is to solve your immediate problems and then start researching the theory. A lot of good information is available about design patterns and the associated theory. Wikipedia is a good place to start. Some readers may be surprised at the idea of Wikipedia as a source of programming information, but it offers a wealth of well-balanced and well-written content.

I *love* design patterns. I think they are important and useful and a valuable mechanism for communicating general solutions to complex problems. Sadly, they are all too often used as a kind of religion, where every aspect of a pattern must be applied exactly as specified and long and nasty conflicts break out about the merits and applicability of competing patterns.

My advice is to consider design patterns as the foundation for developing *techniques*. Mix and match different design patterns to suit your projects and cherry-pick the bits that solve the problems you face. Don't let anyone dictate the way that you use patterns, and always remain focused on fixing real problems in real projects for real users. The day you start arguing about solutions to theoretical problems is the day you go over to the dark side. Be strong. Stay focused. Resist the pattern zealots.

Do You Talk About Graphic Design and Layouts?

No. This isn't that kind of book, either. The layout of the example web apps is pretty simple. There are a couple of reasons for this. The first is that this is a book about programming, and while I spend a lot of time showing you techniques for managing markup dynamically, the actual visual effect is very much a side effect.

The second reason is that I have the artistic abilities of a lemon. I don't draw, I don't paint, and I don't have a sideline business selling my oil-on-canvas work at a local gallery. In fact, as a child I was excused from art lessons because of a total and absolute lack of talent. I am a pretty good programmer, but my design skills suck. In this book, I stick to what I know, which is heavy-duty programming.

What If You Don't Like the Techniques or Tools I Describe?

Then you adapt the techniques until you do like them and find alternative tools that work the way you prefer. The critical information in this book is that you can apply heavy-duty server-side techniques to create better web apps. The fine implementation detail isn't important. My preferred tools and techniques work well for me, and if you think about code in the way I do, they will work well for you too. But if your mind works in a different way, change the bits of my approach that don't fit, discard the bits that don't work, and use what's left as a foundation for your own approaches. We'll both come out ahead as long as you end up with web apps that scale better, make your coding more enjoyable, and reduce the burden of maintenance.

Is There a Lot of Code in This Book?

Yes. In fact, there is so much code that I couldn't fit it all in. Books have a page budget, which is set right at the start of the project. The page budget affects the schedule for the book, the production cost, and the final price that the book sells for. Sticking to the page budget is a big deal, and my editor gets uncomfortable whenever he thinks I am going to run long (hi, Ben!). I had to do some editing to fit in all of the code I wanted to include. So, when I introduce a new topic or make a lot of changes in one go, I'll show you a complete HTML document or JavaScript code file, just like the one shown in Listing 1-1.

Listing 1-1. A Complete HTML Document

```html
<!DOCTYPE html>
<html>
<head>
    <title>CheeseLux</title>
    <script src="jquery-1.7.1.js" type="text/javascript"></script>
    <script src="jquery.mobile-1.0.1.js" type="text/javascript"></script>
    <link rel="stylesheet" type="text/css" href="jquery.mobile-1.0.1.css"/>
    <link rel="stylesheet" type="text/css" href="styles.mobile.css"/>
    <script>
        function setCookie(name, value, days) {
            var date = new Date();
            date.setTime(date.getTime()+(days * 24 * 60 * 60 *1000));
            document.cookie = name + "="+ value
                + "; expires=" + date.toGMTString() +"; path=/";
        }

        $(document).bind("pageinit", function() {
            $('button').click(function(e) {
                var useMobile = e.target.id == "yes";
                var useMobileValue = useMobile ? "mobile" : "desktop";
                if (localStorage) {
                    localStorage["cheeseLuxMode"] = useMobileValue;
                } else {
                    setCookie("cheeseLuxMode", useMobileValue, 30);
                }
                location.href = useMobile ? "mobile.html" : "example.html";
            });
        });
    </script>
```

```
</head>
<body>
    <div id="page1" data-role="page" data-theme="a">
        <img class="logo" src="cheeselux.png">
        <span class="para">
            Would you like to use our mobile web app?
        </span>
        <div class="middle">
            <button data-inline="true" data-theme="b" id="yes">Yes</button>
            <button data-inline="true" id="no">No</button>
        </div>
    </div>
</body>
</html>
```

This listing is based on one from Chapter 8. The full listing gives you a wider context about how the technique at hand fits into the web app world. When I am showing a small change or emphasizing a particular region of code, then I'll show you a code fragment like the one in Listing 1-2.

Listing 1-2. A Code Fragment

```
...
<title>CheeseLux</title>
<script src="jquery-1.7.1.js" type="text/javascript"></script>
<script src="jquery.mobile-1.0.1.js" type="text/javascript"></script>
<link rel="stylesheet" type="text/css" href="jquery.mobile-1.0.1.css"/>
<link rel="stylesheet" type="text/css" href="styles.mobile.css"/>
<meta name="viewport" content="width=device-width, initial-scale=1">
<script>
...
```

These fragments are cumulatively applied to the last full listing so that the fragment in Listing 1-2 shows a meta element being added to the head section of Listing 1-1. You don't have to apply these changes yourself if you want to experiment with the examples. Instead, you can download a complete set of every code listing in this book from Apress.com. This free download also includes the server-side code that I refer to later in this chapter and use throughout this book to create different aspects of the web app.

What Software Do You Need for This Book?

You will need a few pieces of software if you want to re-create the examples in this book. There are lots of choices for each type, and the ones that I use are all available without charge. I describe each in the sections that follow along with my preferred tool in each category.

Getting the Source Code

You will need to download the source code that accompanies this book, which is available without charge from Apress.com. The source code download contains all of the listings organized by chapter and all of the supporting resources, such as images and style sheets. You will need the contents of this download if you want to completely re-create any of the examples.

Getting an HTML Editor

Almost any editor can be used to work with HTML. I don't rely on any special features in this book, so use whatever editor suits you. I use Komodo Edit from Active State. It is free and simple and has pretty good support for HTML, JavaScript, jQuery, and Node.js. I have no affiliation with Active State other than as a happy user. You can get Komodo Edit from `http://activestate.com`, and there are versions for Windows, Mac, and Linux.

Getting a Desktop Web Browser

Any modern mainstream desktop browser will run the examples in this book. I like Google Chrome; I find it quick, I like the simple UI, and the developer tools are pretty good. Most of the screenshots in this book are of Google Chrome, although there are times when I use Firefox because Chrome doesn't implement an HTML5 feature fully. (The support for HTML5 APIs is a bit mixed as I write this, but every browser release improves the situation.)

Getting a Mobile Browser Emulator

In Chapters 7 and 8, I talk about targeting different kinds of devices. It can be slow and frustrating work dealing with real devices during the early stages of development, so I use a mobile browser emulator to get started and put the major functionality together. It isn't until I have something functional and solid that I start testing on real mobile devices.

I like the Opera Mobile emulator, which you can get for free from `www.opera.com/developer/tools/mobile`; there are versions available for Windows, Mac, and Linux. The emulator uses the same code base as the real and, widely used, Opera Mobile, and while there are some quirks, the experience is pretty faithful to the original. I like this package because it lets me create emulators for different screen sizes from small-screened smartphones right through to HD tablets. There is support for emulating touch events and changing the orientation of the device. You can run the examples in Chapters 7 and 8 in any browser, but part of the point of these chapters is to elegantly detect mobile devices, and you'll get the best results by using an emulator, even if it isn't the one for Opera.

Getting the JavaScript Libraries

I don't believe in re-creating functionality that is available in a well-written, publically available JavaScript library. To that end, there are a number of libraries that I use in each chapter. Some, such as jQuery, jQuery UI, and jQuery Mobile, are well-known, but there are also some that provide some niche features or cover a gap in browsers that don't implement certain HTML5 APIs. I tell you how to obtain each library as I introduce it, and they can all be found in the source code download that is available from Apress.com. You don't need to use the libraries that I like in order to use the techniques I discuss, but you will need them to re-create the examples.

Getting a Web Server

The examples in this book are focused on the client-side web apps, but some techniques require certain behaviors from the server. Most of the examples will work with content served up by any web server, but you will need to use Node.js if you want to re-create every example in this book.

The reason that I chose Node.js is that it is written in JavaScript and is supported on a wide range of platforms. This means that any reader of this book will be able to set up the server and read and understand the code that drives the server.

The server-side code is included in the source code download from Apress.com, in a file called server.js. I am not going to go into any detail about this code, and I am not even going to list it. It doesn't do anything special; it just serves up content and has a few special URLs that allow me to post data from the example web app and get a tailored response. There are some other URLs that create particular effects, such as adding a delay to some requests. Take a look at server.js if you want to see what's there, but you don't need to understand (or even look at) the server-side code to get the best from this book.

You will, however, need to install and set up Node.js so that it is running on your network. I provide instructions for getting up and running in the sections that follow.

Getting and Preparing Node.js

You can download Node.js from http://nodejs.org. Installation packages are available for Windows, Mac, and Linux, and the source code is available if you want to compile for a different platform. The instructions for setting up Node change often, and the best way to get started is by reading Felix Geisendörfer's beginner's guide to Node, which you can find at http://nodeguide.com/beginner.html.

I rely on some third-party modules, so run the following command after you have installed the Node.js package:

```
npm install node-static jqtpl
```

This command downloads and installs the node-static and jqtpl packages that I use to deliver static and templated content in the examples. The command will generate output similar to this (but you may see some additional warnings, which can be ignored):

```
npm http GET https://registry.npmjs.org/node-static
npm http GET https://registry.npmjs.org/jqtpl
npm http 200 https://registry.npmjs.org/jqtpl
npm http 200 https://registry.npmjs.org/node-static
node-static@0.5.9 ./node_modules/node-static
jqtpl@1.0.9 ./node_modules/jqtpl
```

The source code download is organized by chapter. You will need to create a directory called content in your Node.js directory and copy the chapter content into it. There isn't much structure to the content directory; to keep things simple, almost all of the resources and listings are in the same directory.

■ **Caution** There are changes in the resource files between chapters, so make sure you clear your browser's history when you move between chapter content.

You will also need to copy the server.js file from the source code download into your Node.js directory. This Node script is only for serving the examples in the book; don't rely on it for any other purpose, and certainly don't use it to host real projects. Once you have everything in place, simply run the following command:

```
node server.js
```

You will see the following output (or something very close to it):

```
The "sys" module is now called "util". It should have a similar interface.
Ready on port 80
```

If you are using Windows, you may be prompted to allow Node to communicate through the Windows Firewall, which you should do. And with that, your server is up and running. The script listens for requests on port 80. If you need to change this, then look for the following line in the server.js file:

```
http.createServer(handleRequest).listen(80);
```

■ **Caution** Node.js is very volatile, and new versions are released often. The version that I have used in this book is 0.6.6, but it will have been superseded by the time you read this. I have stuck to the more stable Node APIs, but you might need to make some minor tweaks to get everything working.

Introducing the CheeseLux Example

Most of the examples in this book are based on a web app for a fictional cheese retailer called CheeseLux. I wanted to focus on the individual techniques in this book, so I have kept the web app as simple as possible. To begin with, I have created a static web site that offers limited products to the user. The entry point to the site is the example.html file. I use example.html for almost all of the listings in this book. Listing 1-3 shows the initial static version of example.html.

Listing 1-3. The Static example.html

```html
<!DOCTYPE html>
<html>
<head>
    <title>CheeseLux</title>
    <link rel="stylesheet" type="text/css" href="styles.css"/>
</head>
<body>

    <div id="logobar">
        <img src="cheeselux.png">
            <span id="tagline">Gourmet European Cheese</span>
    </div>

    <form action="/basket" method="post">

        <div class="cheesegroup">
            <div class="grouptitle">French Cheese</div>

            <div class="groupcontent">
                <label for="camembert" class="cheesename">Camembert ($18)</label>
                <input name="camembert" value="0"/>
            </div>

            <div class="groupcontent">
                <label for="tomme" class="cheesename">Tomme de Savoie ($19)</label>
                <input name="tomme" value="0"/>
            </div>

            <div class="groupcontent">
                <label for="morbier" class="cheesename">Morbier ($9)</label>
                <input name="morbier" value="0"/>
            </div>
        </div>

        <div id="buttonDiv">
            <input type="submit" />
        </div>
    </form>
</body>
</html>
```

I have started with something basic. There are four pages in the static version of the web app, although I tend to focus on the functionality of only the first two in later chapters. These are the product listing and a basket showing a user's selections (which is handled in the static version by basket.html). You can see how example.html and basket.html are displayed in the browser in Figure 1-1.

Figure 1-1. The example.html and basket.html files displayed in the browser

You don't need to do anything with the static files, but if you look at the contents of basket.html, for example, you will see that I use templates to generate the content based on the data submitted via the HTML forms, as shown in Listing 1-4.

Listing 1-4. Using a Template to Generate Content

```
<html>
<head>
    <title>CheeseLux</title>
    <link rel="stylesheet" type="text/css" href="styles.css"/>
</head>
<body>
    <div id="logobar">
        <img src="cheeselux.png">
        <span id="tagline">Gourmet European Cheese</span>
    </div>
    <form action="/shipping" method="post">
        <div class="cheesegroup">
            <div class="grouptitle">Your Basket</div>
            <table class="basketTable" border=0>
                <thead>
                    <tr><th>Cheese</th><th>Quantity</th><th>Subtotal</th></tr>
```

```
                    <tr><td class="sumline" colspan=3></td></tr>
                </thead>
                <tbody>
                    {{each properties}}
                        {{if $value.propVal > 0}}
                        <tr>
                            <td>${$data.getProp($value.propName, "name")}</td>
                            <td>${$value.propVal}</td>
                            <td>
                                $${$data.getSubtotal($value.propName, $value.propVal)}
                            </td>
                        </tr>
                        {{/if}}
                    {{/each}}
                </tbody>
                <tfoot>
                    <tr><td class="sumline" colspan=3></td></tr>
                    <tr><th colspan=2>Total:</th><td>$${$data.total}</td>
                </tfoot>
            </table>
            <div class="cornerplaceholder"></div>
        </div>
        <div id="buttonDiv">
            <input type="submit" />
        </div>
        {{each properties}}
            <input type="hidden" name="${$value.propName}" value="${$value.propVal}"/>
        {{/each}}
    </form>
</body>
</html>
```

These templates are processed by the jqtpl module that you downloaded for Node.js. This module is a Node-compliant version of a simple template library that is widely used with the jQuery library. I don't use this style of template in the client-side examples, but I wanted to explain the meaning of those tags in case you were tempted to peek at the static content.

In the next chapter, I'll use some basic JavaScript techniques to create a more dynamic version of this simple app and then spend the rest of the book showing you more advanced techniques you can use to create better, more scalable, and more responsive web apps for your own projects.

Font Attribution

I use some custom web fonts throughout this book. The font files are included in the source code download available from Apress.com. The fonts I use come from The League of Movable Type (www.theleagueofmoveabletype.com) and from the Google Web Fonts service (www.google.com/webfonts).

Summary

In this chapter, I outlined the content and structure of this book and set out the software required if you want to experiment with the examples in this books. I also introduced the CheeseLux example, which is used throughout this book. In the next chapter, I'll use some basic techniques to enhance the static web pages and introduce some of the core tools that I use throughout this book. From then on, I'll show you a series of better, industrial-strength techniques that are the heart of this book.

CHAPTER 2

Getting Started

In this chapter, I am going to enhance the example web app I introduced in Chapter 1. These are the entry-level techniques, and most of the rest of the book is dedicated to showing you different ways to improve upon the result. That's not to say that the examples in this chapter are not useful; they are absolutely fine for simple web apps. But they are not sufficient for large and complex web apps, which is why the chapters that follow explain how you can take key concepts from the world of server-side development and apply them to your web apps.

This chapter also lets me set the foundation for some web app development principles that I will be using throughout this book. First, I will be relying on JavaScript libraries whenever possible so as to avoid creating code that someone else has produced and maintained. The library I will be making most use of is jQuery in order to make working with the DOM API simpler and easier (I explain some jQuery basics in the examples in this chapters). Second, I will be focusing on a single HTML document.

Upgrading the Submit Button

To get started, I am going to use JavaScript to replace the submit button from the baseline example in Chapter 1. The browser creates this button from an input element whose type is submit, and I am going to switch it out for something that is visually consistent with the rest of the document. More specifically, I am going to use jQuery to replace the input element.

Preparing to Use jQuery

The DOM API is comprehensive but awkward to use—so awkward that there are a number of JavaScript convenience libraries that wrap around the DOM API and make it easier to use. In my experience, the best of these libraries is jQuery, which is easy to use and actively developed and supported. jQuery is also the foundation for many other JavaScript libraries, some of which I'll be using later. jQuery is just a wrapper around the DOM API, and this allows the use of the underlying DOM objects and methods if it is required.

You can download the jQuery library from jQuery.com. jQuery, like most JavaScript libraries, is available in two versions. The uncompressed version contains the full source code and is useful for development and debugging. The compressed version (also known as the *minimized* or minified version) is much smaller but isn't human-readable. The smaller size makes the minimized version ideal for saving bandwidth when a web app is deployed into production. Bandwidth can be expensive for popular web apps, and any savings is worth making.

Download the version you want and put it in your content directory, alongside example.html. I'll be using the uncompressed version in this book, so I have downloaded a file called jquery-1.7.1.js.

■ **Tip** I am using the uncompressed versions because they make debugging easier, which you may find useful as you explore the examples in this book. For real web applications, you should switch to the minimized version prior to deployment.

The file name includes the jQuery version, which is 1.7.1 as I write this. You import the jQuery library into the example document using a script element, as shown in Listing 2-1. I have added the script element in the head section of the document.

Listing 2-1. Importing jQuery into the Example Document

```
...
<head>
    <title>CheeseLux</title>
    <link rel="stylesheet" type="text/css" href="styles.css"/>
    <script src="jquery-1.7.1.js" type="text/javascript"></script>
</head>
...
```

USING A CDN FOR JQUERY

An alternative to hosting the jQuery library on your own web servers is to use a public *content distribution network* (CDN) that hosts jQuery. A CDN is a distributed network of servers that deliver files to the user using the server that is closest to them. There are a couple of benefits to using a CDN. The first is a faster experience to the user, because the jQuery library file is downloaded from the server closest to them, rather than from your servers. Often the file won't be required at all. jQuery is so popular that the user's browser may have already cached the library from another application that also uses jQuery. The second benefit is that none of your precious and expensive bandwidth is spent delivering jQuery to the user.

When using a CDN, you must have confidence in the CDN operator. You want to be sure that the user receives the file they are supposed to and that the service will always be available. Google and Microsoft both provide CDN services for jQuery (and other popular JavaScript libraries) free of charge. Both companies have solid experience of running highly available services and are unlikely to deliberately tamper with the jQuery library. You can learn about the Microsoft service at www.asp.net/ajaxlibrary/cdn.ashx and about the Google service at http://code.google.com/apis/libraries/devguide.html.

The CDN approach isn't suitable for applications that are delivered to users within an intranet because it causes all the browsers to go to the Internet to get the jQuery library, rather than access the local server, which is generally closer and faster and has lower bandwidth costs.

So, let's jump right in and use jQuery to hide the existing input element and add something else in its place. Listing 2-2 shows how this is done.

Listing 2-2. Hiding the input Element and Adding Another Element

```
<!DOCTYPE html>
<html>
<head>
    <title>CheeseLux</title>
    <link rel="stylesheet" type="text/css" href="styles.css"/>
    <script src="jquery-1.7.1.js" type="text/javascript"></script>
    <script>
        $(document).ready(function() {
            $('#buttonDiv input:submit').hide();
            $('<a href=#>Submit Order</a>').appendTo("#buttonDiv");
        })
    </script>
</head>
<body>
    <div id="logobar">
        <img src="cheeselux.png">
            <span id="tagline">Gourmet European Cheese</span>
    </div>

    <form action="/basket" method="post">

        <div class="cheesegroup">
            <div class="grouptitle">French Cheese</div>

            <div class="groupcontent">
                <label for="camembert" class="cheesename">Camembert ($18)</label>
                <input name="camembert" value="0"/>
            </div>

            <div class="groupcontent">
                <label for="tomme" class="cheesename">Tomme de Savoie ($19)</label>
                <input name="tomme" value="0"/>
            </div>

            <div class="groupcontent">
                <label for="morbier" class="cheesename">Morbier ($9)</label>
                <input name="morbier" value="0"/>
            </div>
        </div>

        <div id="buttonDiv">
            <input type="submit" />
        </div>
    </form>
</body>
</html>
```

I have added another script element to the document. This element contains inline code, rather than loading an external JavaScript file. I have done this because it makes it easier to show you the changes I am making. Using inline code is not a jQuery requirement, and you can put your jQuery code in external files if you prefer. There is a lot going on in the four JavaScript statements in the `script` element, so I'll break things down step-by-step in the following sections.

Understanding the Ready Event

At the heart of jQuery is the $ function, which is a convenient shorthand to begin using jQuery features. The most common way to use jQuery is to treat the $ as a JavaScript function and pass a CSS selector or one or more DOM objects as arguments. Using the $ function is very common with jQuery. I have used it three times in four lines of code, for example.

The $ function returns a *jQuery object* on which you can call jQuery methods. The jQuery object is a wrapper around the elements you selected, and if you pass a CSS selector as the argument, the jQuery object will contain all of the elements in the document that match the selector you specify.

■ **Tip** This is one of the main advantages of jQuery over the built-in DOM API: you can select and modify multiple elements more easily. The most recent versions of the DOM API (including the one that is part of HTML5) provide support for finding elements using selectors, but jQuery does it more concisely and elegantly.

The first time I use the $ function in the listing, I pass in the document object as the argument. The document object is the root node of the element hierarchy in the DOM, and I have selected it with the $ function so that I can call the ready method, as highlighted in Listing 2-3.

Listing 2-3. Selecting the Document and Calling the ready Method

```
...
<script>
    $(document).ready(function() {
        ...other JavaScript statements...
    })
</script>
...
```

Browsers execute JavaScript code as soon as they find the `script` elements in the document. This gives us a problem when you want to manipulate the elements in the DOM, because your code is executed before the browser has parsed the rest of the HTML document, discovered the elements that you want to work with, and added objects to the DOM to represent them. At best your JavaScript code doesn't work, and at worst you cause an error when this happens. There are a number of ways to work around this. The simplest solution is to place the `script` element at the end of the document so that the browser doesn't discover and execute your JavaScript code until the rest of the HTML has been processed. A more elegant approach is to use the jQuery ready method, which is highlighted in the listing just shown.

You pass a JavaScript function as the argument to the ready method, and jQuery will execute this function once the browser has processed all of the elements in the document. Using the ready method allows you to place your `script` elements anywhere in the document, safe in the knowledge that your code won't be executed until the right moment.

Caution A common mistake is to forget to wrap the JavaScript statements to be executed in a function, which causes an odd effect. If you pass a single statement to the ready method, then it will be executed as soon as the browser processes the script element. If you pass multiple statements, then the browser will usually report a JavaScript error.

The ready method creates a handler for the ready event. I'll show you more of the way that jQuery supports events later in this chapter. The ready event is available only for the document object, which is why you will see the statements highlighted in the listing in almost every web app that uses jQuery.

Selecting and Hiding the Input Element

Now that I have delayed the execution of the JavaScript code until the DOM is ready, I can turn to the next step in my task, which is to hide the input element that submits the form. Listing 2-4 highlights the statement from the example that does just this.

Listing 2-4. Selecting and Hiding the input Element

```
...
<script>
    $(document).ready(function() {
        $('#buttonDiv input:submit').hide();
        $('<a href=#>Submit Order</a>').appendTo("#buttonDiv");
    })
</script>
...
```

This is a classic two-part jQuery statement: first I select the elements I want to work with, and then I apply a jQuery method to modify the selected elements. You may not recognize the selector I have used because the :submit part is one of the selectors that jQuery defines in addition to those in the CSS specification. Table 2-1 contains the most useful jQuery custom selectors.

■ **Caution** The jQuery custom selectors can be extremely useful, but they have a performance impact. Wherever possible, jQuery uses the native browser support for finding elements in the document, and this is usually pretty quick. However, jQuery has to process the custom selectors differently, since the browser doesn't know anything about them, and this takes longer than the native approach. This performance difference doesn't matter for most web apps, but if performance is critical, you may want to stick with the standard CSS selectors.

Table 2-1. jQuery Custom Selectors

Selector	Description
:button	Selects all buttons
:checkbox	Selects all check boxes
:contains(text)	Selects elements that contain the specified text
:eq(n)	Selects the element at the nth index (zero-based)
:even	Selects all the event-numbered elements (one-based)
:first	Selects the first matched element
:has(selector)	Selects elements that contain at least one element that matches the selector
:hidden	Selects all hidden elements
:input	Selects all input elements
:last	Selects the last matched element
:odd	Selects all the odd-numbered elements (one-based)
:password	Selects all password elements
:radio	Selects all radio element
:submit	Selects all form submission elements
:visible	Selects all visible elements

In Listing 2-4, my selector matches any input element whose type is submit and that is a descendant of the element whose id attribute is buttonDiv. I didn't need to be quite so precise with the selector, given that it is the only submit element in the document, but I wanted to demonstrate the jQuery support for selectors. The $ function returns a jQuery object that contains the selected elements, although there is only one element that matches the selector in this case.

Having selected the element, I then call the hide method, which changes the visibility of the selected elements by setting the CSS display property to none. The input element is like this *before* the method call:

```
<input type="submit">
```

and is transformed like this *after* the method call:

```
<input type="submit" style="display: none; ">
```

The browser won't show elements whose display property is none and so the input element becomes invisible.

■ **Tip** The counterpart to the hide method is show, which removes the display setting and returns the element to its visible state. I demonstrate the show method later in this chapter.

Inserting the New Element

Next, I want to insert a new element into the document. Listing 2-5 highlights the statement in the example that does this.

Listing 2-5. Adding a New element to the Document

```
...
<script>
    $(document).ready(function() {
        $('#buttonDiv input:submit').hide();
        $('<a href=#>Submit Order</a>').appendTo("#buttonDiv");
    })
</script>
...
```

In this statement, I have passed an HTML fragment string to the jQuery $ function. This causes jQuery to parse the fragment and create a set of objects to represent the elements it contains. These element objects are then returned to me in a jQuery object, just as if I had selected elements from the document itself, except that the browser doesn't yet know about these elements and they are not yet part of the DOM.

There is only one element in the HTML fragment in this listing, so the jQuery object contains an a element. To add this element to the DOM, I call the appendTo method on the jQuery object, passing in a CSS selector, which tells jQuery where in the document I want the element to be inserted.

The appendTo method inserts my new element as the last child of the elements matched by the selector. In this case, I specified the buttonDiv element, which means that the elements in my HTML fragment are inserted alongside the hidden input element, like this:

```
...
<div id="buttonDiv">
        <input type="submit" style="display: none; ">
        <a href="#">Submit Order</a>
</div>
...
```

■ **Tip** If the selector that I passed to the appendTo method had matched multiple elements, then jQuery would duplicate the elements from the HTML fragment and insert a copy as the last child of *every* matched element.

---

jQuery defines a number of methods that you can use to insert child elements into the document, and the most useful of these are described in Table 2-2. When you *append* elements, they become the last children of their parent element. When you *prepend* elements, they become the first children of their parents. (I'll explain why there are two append and two prepend methods later in this chapter.)

Table 2-2. jQuery Methods for Inserting Elements in the Document

Method	Description
append(HTML) append(jQuery)	Inserts the specified elements as the last children of all the elements in the DOM
prepend(HTML) prepend(jQuery)	Inserts the specified elements as the first children of all the elements in the DOM
appendTo(HTML) appendTo(jQuery)	Inserts the elements in the jQuery object as the last children of the elements specified by the argument
prependTo(HTML) prependTo(jQuery)	Inserts the elements in the jQuery object as the first children of the elements specified by the argument

Applying a CSS Class

In the previous example, I inserted an a element, but I did not assign it to a CSS class. Listing 2-6 shows how I can correct this omission by making a call to the addClass method.

Listing 2-6. Chaining jQuery Method Calls

```
...
<script>
    $(document).ready(function() {
        $('#buttonDiv input:submit').hide();
        $('<a href=#>Submit Order</a>').appendTo("#buttonDiv").addClass("button");
    })
</script>
...
```

Notice how I have simply added the call to the addClass method to the end of the statement. This is known as *method chaining*, and a library that supports method chaining is said to have a *fluent API*.

Most jQuery methods return the same jQuery object on which the method was called. In the example, I create the jQuery object by passing an HTML fragment to the $ function. This produces a jQuery object that contains an a element. The appendTo method inserts the element into the document and returns a jQuery object that contains the same a element as its result. This allows me to make further method calls, such as the one to addClass. Fluent APIs can take a while to get used to, but they enable concise and expressive code and reduce duplication.

The addClass method adds the class specified by the argument to the selected elements, like this:

```
...
<div id="buttonDiv">
    <input type="submit" style="display: none; ">
    <a href="#" class="button">Submit Order</a>
</div>
...
```

The a.button class is defined in styles.css and brings the appearance of the a element into line with the rest of the document.

UNDERSTANDING METHOD PAIRS AND METHOD CHAINING

If you look at the methods described in Table 2-2, you will see that you can append or prepend elements in two ways. The elements you are inserting either can be contained in the jQuery object on which you call a method or can be in the method argument. jQuery provides different methods so you can select which elements are contained in the jQuery object for method chaining. In my example, I used the appendTo method, which means I can arrange things so that the jQuery object contains the element parsed from the HTML fragment, allowing me to chain the call to the addClass method and have the class applied to the a element.

The append method reverses the relationship between the parent and child elements, like this:

```
$('#buttonDiv').append('<a href=#>Submit Order</a>').addClass("button");
```

In this statement, I select the parent element and provide the HTML fragment as the method argument. The append method returns a jQuery object that contains the buttonDiv element, so the addClass takes effect on the parent div element rather than the new a element.

To recap, I have hidden the original input element, added an a element, and, finally, assigned the a element to the button class. You can see the result in Figure 2-1.

Figure 2-1. Replacing the standard form submit button

With four lines of code (only two of which manipulate the DOM), I have upgraded the standard submit button to something consistent with the rest of the web app. As I said at the start of this chapter, a little code can lead to significant enhancements.

Responding to Events

I am not quite done with the new a element. The browser knows that an input element whose type attribute is submit should submit the HTML form to the server, and it performs this action automatically when the button is clicked.

The a element that I added to the DOM looks like a button, but the browser doesn't know what the element is for and so doesn't apply the same automatic action. I have to add some JavaScript code that will complete the effect and make the a element behave like a button and not just look like one.

You do this by responding to *events*. An event is a message that is sent by the browser when the state of an element changes, for example, when the user clicks the element or moves the mouse over it. You tell the browser which events you are interesting in and provide JavaScript callback functions that are executed when event occurs. An event is said to have been *triggered* when it is sent by the browser, and the callback functions are responsible for *handling* the event. In the following sections, I'll show you how to handle events to complete the functionality of the substitute button.

Handling the Click Event

The most important for this example is click, which is triggered when the user presses and releases the mouse button (in other words, when the user clicks) an element. For this example, I want to handle the click event by submitting the HTML form to the server. The DOM API provides support for dealing with events, but jQuery provides a more elegant alternative, which you can see in Listing 2-7.

Listing 2-7. Handling the click Event

```
<!DOCTYPE html>
<html>
<head>
    <title>CheeseLux</title>
    <link rel="stylesheet" type="text/css" href="styles.css"/>
    <script src="jquery-1.7.1.js" type="text/javascript"></script>
<script>
    $(document).ready(function() {
        $('#buttonDiv input:submit').hide();
        $('<a href=#>Submit Order</a>').appendTo("#buttonDiv")
            .addClass("button").click(function() {
                $('form').submit();
            })
    })
</script>
</head>
<body>
    <div id="logobar">
        <img src="cheeselux.png">
            <span id="tagline">Gourmet European Cheese</span>
    </div>

    <form action="/basket" method="post">

        <div class="cheesegroup">
            <div class="grouptitle">French Cheese</div>

            <div class="groupcontent">
                <label for="camembert" class="cheesename">Camembert ($18)</label>
                <input name="camembert" value="0"/>
            </div>

            <div class="groupcontent">
                <label for="tomme" class="cheesename">Tomme de Savoie ($19)</label>
                <input name="tomme" value="0"/>
            </div>

            <div class="groupcontent">
                <label for="morbier" class="cheesename">Morbier ($9)</label>
                <input name="morbier" value="0"/>
            </div>
        </div>
```

```
<div id="buttonDiv">
    <input type="submit" />
</div>
    </form>
</body>
</html>
```

jQuery provides some helpful methods that make handling common events simple. These events are named after the event; so, the click method registers the callback function passed as the method argument as a handler for the click event. I have chained the call to the click event to the other methods that create and format the a element. To submit the form, I select the form element by type and call the submit method. That's all there is to it. I now have the basic functionality of the button in place. Not only does it have the same visual style as the rest of the web app, but clicking the button will submit the form to the server, just as the original button did.

Handling Mouse Hover Events

There are two other events that I want to handle to complete the button functionality; they are mouseenter and mouseleave. The mouseenter event is triggered when the mouse pointer is moved over the element, and the mouseleave event is triggered the mouse leaves the element.

I want to handle these events to give the user a visual cue that the button can be clicked, and I do this by changing the style of the button when the mouse is over the element. The easiest way to handle these events is to use the jQuery hover method, as shown in Listing 2-8.

Listing 2-8. Using the jQuery hover Method

```
...
<script>
    $(document).ready(function() {
        $('#buttonDiv input:submit').hide();
        $('<a href=#>Submit Order</a>').appendTo("#buttonDiv")
            .addClass("button").click(function() {
                $('form').submit();
            })
            .hover(
                function(){
                    $('#buttonDiv a').addClass("buttonHover");
                }, function() {
                    $('#buttonDiv a').removeClass("buttonHover");
                })
    })
</script>
...
```

The hover method takes two functions as arguments. The first function is executed when the mouseenter event is triggered, and the second function is triggered in response to the mouseleave event. In this example, I have used these functions to add and remove the buttonHover class from the a element. This class changes the value of the CSS background-color property to highlight the button when the mouse is positioned above the element. You can see the effect in Figure 2-2.

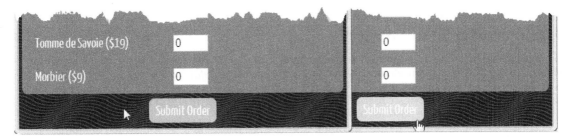

Figure 2-2. Using events to apply a class to an element

Using the Event Object

The two functions that I passed as arguments to the hover method in the previous example are largely the same. I can collapse these two functions into a single handler that can process both events, as shown in Listing 2-9.

Listing 2-9. Handling Multiple Events in a Single Handler Function

```
...
<script>
    $(document).ready(function() {
        $('#buttonDiv input:submit').hide();
        $('<a href=#>Submit Order</a>').appendTo("#buttonDiv")
            .addClass("button").click(function() {
                $('form').submit();
            }).hover(function(e){
                var elem = $('#buttonDiv a')
                if (e.type == "mouseenter") {
                    elem.addClass("buttonHover");
                } else {
                    elem.removeClass("buttonHover");
                }
            })
    })
</script>
...
```

The callback function in this example takes an argument, e. This argument is an Event object provided by the browser to give you information about the event you are handling. I have used the Event.type property to differentiate between the types of events that my function expects. The type property returns a string that contains the event name. If the event name is mouseenter, then I call the addClass method. If not, I call the removeClass method that has the effect of removing the specified class from the class attribute of the elements in the jQuery object, the opposite effect of the addClass method.

Dealing with Default Actions

To make life easier for the programmer, the browser performs some actions automatically when certain events are triggered for specific element types. These are known as *default actions,* and they mean you don't have to create event handlers for every single event and element in an HTML document. For example, the browser will navigate to the URL specified by the href attribute of an a element in response to the click event. This is the basis for navigation in a web page.

I cheated a little by setting the href attribute to #. This is a common technique when defining elements whose actions are going to be managed by JavaScript because the browser won't navigate away from the current document when the default action is performed. In other words, I don't have to worry about the default action because it doesn't really do anything that the user will notice.

Default actions can be more important when you need to change the behavior of the element and you can't do little tricks like using # as a URL. Listing 2-10 provides a demonstration, where I have changed the href attribute for the a element to a real web page. I have used the attr method to set the href attribute of the a element to http://apress.com. With this modification, clicking the element doesn't submit the form anymore; it navigates to the Apress website.

Listing 2-10. Managing Default Actions

```
...
<script>
    $(document).ready(function() {
        $('#buttonDiv input:submit').hide();
        $('<a href=#>Submit Order</a>')
            .appendTo("#buttonDiv")
            .attr("href", "http://apress.com")
            .addClass("button").click(function() {
                $('form').submit();
            }).hover(function(e){
                var elem = $('#buttonDiv a')
                if (e.type == "mouseenter") {
                    elem.addClass("buttonHover");
                } else {
                    elem.removeClass("buttonHover");
                }
            })
    })
</script>
...
```

To fix this, a call to the preventDefault method on the Event object passed to the event handler function is required. This disables the default action for the event, meaning that only the code in the event handler function will be used. You can see the use of this method in Listing 2-11.

Listing 2-11. Preventing the Default Action

```
...
<script>
    $(document).ready(function() {
        $('#buttonDiv input:submit').hide();
        $('<a href=#>Submit Order</a>')
            .appendTo("#buttonDiv")
            .attr("href", "http://apress.com")
            .addClass("button").click(function(e) {
                $('form').submit();
                e.preventDefault();
            }).hover(function(e){
                var elem = $('#buttonDiv a')
                if (e.type == "mouseenter") {
                    elem.addClass("buttonHover");
                } else {
                    elem.removeClass("buttonHover");
                }
            })
    })
</script>
...
```

There is no default action for the mouseenter and mouseleave events on an a element, so in this listing, I need only to call the preventDefault method when handling the click event. When I click the element now, the form is submitted, and the href attribute value doesn't have any effect.

Adding Dynamic Basket Data

You have seen how you can improve a web application simply by adding and modifying elements and handling events. In this section, I go one step further to demonstrate how you can use these simple techniques to create a more responsive version of the cheese shop by incorporating the information displayed in the basket phase alongside the product selection. I have called this a *dynamic* basket because I will be updating the information shown to users when they change the quantities of individual cheese products, rather than the *static* basket, which is shown when users submit their selections using the unenhanced version of this web app.

Adding the Basket Elements

The first step is to add the additional elements I need to the document. I could add the elements using HTML fragments and the appendTo method, but for variety I am going to use another technique, known as *latent content*. Latent content refers to HTML elements that are in the document but are hidden using CSS and are revealed and managed using JavaScript. Those users who don't have JavaScript enabled won't see the elements and will get the basic functionality, but once I reveal the elements and set up my event handling, those users with JavaScript will get a richer and more polished experience. Listing 2-12 shows the addition of the latent content to the HTML document.

Listing 2-12. Adding Hidden Elements to the HTML Document

```
<!DOCTYPE html>
<html>
<head>
    <title>CheeseLux</title>
    <link rel="stylesheet" type="text/css" href="styles.css"/>
    <script src="jquery-1.7.1.js" type="text/javascript"></script>
    <script>
    $(document).ready(function() {
        $('#buttonDiv input:submit').hide();
        $('<a href=#>Submit Order</a>')
            .appendTo("#buttonDiv").addClass("button").click(function(e) {
                $('form').submit();
                e.preventDefault();
            }).hover(function(e){
                var elem = $('#buttonDiv a')
                if (e.type == "mouseenter") {
                    elem.addClass("buttonHover");
                } else {
                    elem.removeClass("buttonHover");
                }
            })
    })
    </script>
</head>
<body>
    <div id="logobar">
        <img src="cheeselux.png">
            <span id="tagline">Gourmet European Cheese</span>
    </div>

    <form action="/basket" method="post">

        <div class="cheesegroup">
            <div class="grouptitle">French Cheese</div>

            <div class="groupcontent">
                <label for="camembert" class="cheesename">Camembert ($18)</label>
                <input name="camembert" value="0"/>
                <span class="subtotal latent">($<span>0</span>)</span>
            </div>

            <div class="groupcontent">
                <label for="tomme" class="cheesename">Tomme de Savoie ($19)</label>
                <input name="tomme" value="0"/>
                <span class="subtotal latent">($<span>0</span>)</span>
            </div>

            <div class="groupcontent">
                <label for="morbier" class="cheesename">Morbier ($9)</label>
```

```
                    <input name="morbier" value="0"/>
                    <span class="subtotal latent">($<span>0</span>)</span>
                </div>

                <div class="sumline latent"></div>
                <div class="groupcontent latent">
                    <label class="cheesename">Total:</label>
                    <input class="placeholder" name="spacer" value="0"/>
                    <span class="subtotal latent" id="total">$0</span>
                </div>
            </div>

            <div id="buttonDiv">
                <input type="submit" />
            </div>
        </form>
    </body>
</html>
```

I have highlighted the additional elements in the listing. They are all assigned to the `latent` class, which has the following definition in the `styles.css` file:

```
...
.latent {
    display: none;
}
...
```

I showed you earlier in the chapter that the jQuery `hide` method sets the CSS `display` property to `none` to hide elements from the user, and I have followed the same approach when setting up this class. The elements are in the document but not visible to the user.

Showing the Latent Content

Now that the latent elements are in place, I can work with them using jQuery. The first step is to reveal them to the user. Since I am manipulating the elements using JavaScript, they will be revealed only to users who have JavaScript enabled. Listing 2-13 shows the addition to the `script` element.

Listing 2-13. Revealing the Latent Content

```
...
<script>
    $(document).ready(function() {
        $('#buttonDiv input:submit').hide();
        $('<a href=#>Submit Order</a>')
            .appendTo("#buttonDiv").addClass("button").click(function(e) {
                $('form').submit();
                e.preventDefault();
            }).hover(function(e){
                var elem = $('#buttonDiv a')
                if (e.type == "mouseenter") {
                    elem.addClass("buttonHover");
```

31

```
            } else {
                elem.removeClass("buttonHover");
            }
        });

    $('.latent').show();
    })

</script>
...
```

The highlighted statement selects all of the elements that are members of the latent class and then calls the show method. The show method adds a style attribute to each selected element that sets the display property to inline, which has the effect of revealing the elements. The elements are still members of the latent class, but values defined in a style *attribute* override those that are defined in a style *element*, and so the elements become visible.

Responding to User Input

To create a dynamic basket, I want to be able to display subtotals for each item and an overall total whenever the user changes a quantity for a product. I am going to handle two events to get the effect I want. The first event is change, which is triggered when the user enters a new value and then moves the focus to another element. The second event is keyup, which is triggered when the user releases a key, having previously pressed it. The combination of these two events means I can be confident that I will be able to respond smoothly to new values. jQuery defines change and keyup methods that I could use in the same way I used the click method earlier, but since I want to handle both events in the same way, I am going to use the bind method instead, as shown in Listing 2-14.

Listing 2-14. Binding to the change and keyup Events

```
...
<script>

    var priceData = {
        camembert: 18,
        tomme: 19,
        morbier: 9
    }

    $(document).ready(function() {
        $('#buttonDiv input:submit').hide();
        $('<a href=#>Submit Order</a>')
            .appendTo("#buttonDiv").addClass("button").click(function(e) {
                $('form').submit();
                e.preventDefault();
            }).hover(function(e){
                var elem = $('#buttonDiv a')
                if (e.type == "mouseenter") {
                    elem.addClass("buttonHover");
                } else {
                    elem.removeClass("buttonHover");
```

```
            }
        })

    $('.latent').show();

    $('input').bind("change keyup", function() {
        var subtotal = $(this).val() * priceData[this.name];
        $(this).siblings("span").children("span").text(subtotal)
    })
})
```

```
</script>
...
```

The advantage of the bind method is that it lets me handle multiple events using the same anonymous JavaScript function. To do this, I have selected the input elements in the document to get a jQuery object and called the bind method on it. The first argument to the bind method is a string containing the names of the events to handle, where event names are separated by the space character. The second argument is the function that will handle the events when they are triggered. There are only two statements in the event handler function, but they are worth unpacking because they contain an interesting mix of jQuery, the DOM API, and pure JavaScript.

■ **Tip** Handling two events like this means that my callback function may end up being invoked when it doesn't really need to be. For example, if the user presses the Tab key, the focus will change to the next element, and both the change and keyup events will be triggered, even though the value in the input element hasn't changed. I tend toward accepting this duplication as the cost of ensuring a fluid user experience. I'd rather my function was executed more often than really needed and not miss any user interaction.

Calculating the Subtotal

The first statement in the function is responsible for calculating the subtotal for the cheese product whose input value has changed. Here is the statement:

```
var subtotal = $(this).val() * priceData[this.name];
```

When handling an event with jQuery, you can use the variable called this to refer to the element that triggered the event. The this variable is an HTMLElement object, which is what the DOM API uses to represent elements in the document. There are a core set of properties defined by the HTMLElement, the most important of which are described in Table 2-3.

Table 2-3. Basic HTMLElement Properties

Property	Description
className	Gets or sets the list of classes that the element belongs to
id	Gets or sets the value of the id attribute
tagName	Returns the tag name (indicating the element type)

The core properties are supplemented to accommodate the unique characteristics of different element types. An example of this is the name property, which returns the value of the name attribute on those elements that support it, including the input element. I have used this property on the this variable to get the name of the input element so that I can, in turn, use it to get a value from the priceData object that I added to the script:

```
var subtotal = $(this).val() * priceData[this.name];
```

The priceData object is a simple JavaScript object that has one property corresponding to each kind of cheese and where the value of each property is the price for the cheese.

The this variable can also be used to create jQuery objects, like this:

```
var subtotal = $(this).val() * priceData[this.name];
```

By passing an HTMLElement object as the argument to the jQuery $ function, I have created a jQuery object that acts just as though I had selected the element using a CSS selector. This allows me to easily apply jQuery methods to objects from the DOM API. In this statement, I call the val method, which returns the value of the value attribute of the first element in the jQuery object.

■ **Tip** There is only one element in my jQuery object, but jQuery methods are designed to work with multiple elements. When you use a method like val to read some value from the element, you get the value from the first element in the selection, but when you use the same method to set the value (by passing the value as an argument), all of the selected elements are modified.

Using the this variable, I have been able to get the value of the input element that triggered the event and the price for the product associated with it. I then multiply the price and the quantity together to determine the subtotal, which I assign to a local variable called, simply enough, subtotal.

Displaying the Subtotal

The second statement in the handler function is responsible for displaying the subtotal to the user. This statement also operates in two parts. The first part selects the element that will be used to display the value:

```
$(this).siblings("span").children("span").text(subtotal)
```

Once again, I create a jQuery object using the `this` variable. I make a call to the `siblings` method, which returns a jQuery object that contains any sibling to the elements in the original jQuery object that matches the specified CSS selector. This method returns a jQuery object that contains the latent `span` element next to the `input` element that triggered the event.

I chain a call to the `children` method, which returns a jQuery object that contains any children of the element in the previous jQuery object that match the specified selector. I end up with a jQuery object that contains the nested `span` element. I could have simplified the selectors in this example, but I wanted to demonstrate how jQuery supports navigation through the elements in a document and how the contents of the jQuery object in a chain of method calls changes. These changes are described in Table 2-4.

Table 2-4. Basic HTMLElement Properties

Method Call	Contents of jQuery Object
`$(this)`	The input element that triggered the event
`.siblings("span")`	The span element that is a sibling to the input element that triggered the event
`.children("span")`	The span element that is a child of the span element that is a sibling to the input element that triggered the event

By combining method calls like this, I am able to navigate through the element hierarchy to create a jQuery object that contains precisely the element or elements I want to work with, in this case, the child of a sibling to whichever element triggered an event.

The second part of the statement is a call to the `text` method, which sets the text content of the elements in a jQuery object. In this case, the text is the value of the `subtotal` variable:

`$(this).siblings("span").children("span").text(subtotal)`

The net result is that the subtotal for a cheese is updated as soon as a user changes the quantity required.

Calculating the Overall Total

To complete the basket, I need to generate an overall total each time a subtotal changes. I have defined a new function in the `script` element and added a call to it in the event handler function for the `input` elements. Listing 2-15 shows the additions.

Listing 2-15. Calculating the Overall Total

```
...
<script>

    var priceData = {
        camembert: 18,
        tomme: 19,
        morbier: 9
    }

    $(document).ready(function() {
        $('#buttonDiv input:submit').hide();
        $('<a href=#>Submit Order</a>')
            .appendTo("#buttonDiv").addClass("button").click(function(e) {
                $('form').submit();
                e.preventDefault();
            }).hover(function(e){
                var elem = $('#buttonDiv a')
                if (e.type == "mouseenter") {
                    elem.addClass("buttonHover");
                } else {
                    elem.removeClass("buttonHover");
                }
            })

        $('.latent').show();

        $('input').bind("change keyup", function() {
            var subtotal = $(this).val() * priceData[this.name];
            $(this).siblings("span").children("span").text(subtotal)
            calculateTotal();
        })
    })

    function calculateTotal() {
        var total = 0;
        $('span.subtotal span').not('#total').each(function(index, elem) {
            total += Number($(elem).text());
        })
        $('#total').text("$" + total);
    }

</script>
...
```

The first statement in the calculateTotal function defines a local variable and initializes to zero. I use this variable to sum the individual subtotals. The next statement is the most interesting one in this function. The first part of the statement selects a set of elements:

```
...
$('span.subtotal span').not('#total').each(function(index, elem) {
...
```

I start by selecting all span elements that are descendants of span elements that are part of the subtotal class. This is another way of selecting the subtotal elements. I then use the not method to remove elements from the selection. In this case, I remove the element whose id is total. I do this because I defined the subtotal and total elements using the same classes and styles, and I don't want the current total to be included when calculating a new total.

Having selected the items, I then use the each method. This method calls a function once for each element in a jQuery object. The arguments to the function are the index of the current element in the selection and the HTMLElement object that represents the element in the DOM.

I get the content of each subtotal element using the text method. I create a jQuery object by passing the HTMLElement object as an argument to the $ function, just as I did with the this variable earlier in this chapter.

The text method returns a string, so I use the JavaScript Number function to create a numeric value that I can add to the running total:

```
total += Number($(elem).text());
```

Finally, I select the total element and use the text method to display the overall total:

```
$('#total').text("$" + total);
```

The effect of adding this function is that a change in the quantity for a cheese is immediately reflected in the total, as well as in the individual subtotals.

Changing the Form Target

By adding a dynamic basket, I have pulled the functionality of the basket web page into the main page of the application. It doesn't make sense to send JavaScript-enabled users to the basket web page when they submit the form, because it just duplicated information they have already seen. I am going to change the target of the form element so that submitting the form goes straight to the shipping page, skipping over the basket page entirely. Listing 2-16 shows the statement that changes the target.

Listing 2-16. Changing the Target for the form Element

```
...
<script>
    var priceData = {
        camembert: 18,
        tomme: 19,
        morbier: 9
    }

    $(document).ready(function() {
        $('#buttonDiv input:submit').hide();
        $('<a href=#>Submit Order</a>')
            .appendTo("#buttonDiv").addClass("button").click(function(e) {
                $('form').submit();
                e.preventDefault();
```

```
        }).hover(function(e){
            var elem = $('#buttonDiv a')
            if (e.type == "mouseenter") {
                elem.addClass("buttonHover");
            } else {
                elem.removeClass("buttonHover");
            }
        })

    $('.latent').show();

    $('input').bind("change keyup", function() {
        var subtotal = $(this).val() * priceData[this.name];
        $(this).siblings("span").children("span").text(subtotal)
        calculateTotal();
    })

    $('form').attr("action", "/shipping");
})

function calculateTotal() {
    var total = 0;
    $('span.subtotal span').not('#total').each(function(index, elem) {
        total += Number($(elem).text());
    })
    $('#total').text("$" + total);
}
</script>
...
```

By this point, it should be obvious how the new statement works. I select the form element by type (since there is only one such element in the document) and call the attr method to set a new value for the action attribute. The user is taken to the shipping details page when the form is submitted, skipping the basket page entirely. You can see the effect in Figure 2-3.

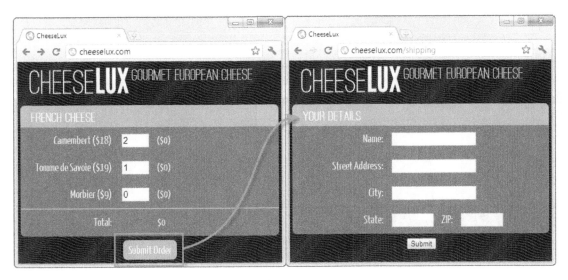

Figure 2-3. Changing the flow of the application

As this example demonstrates, you can change the flow of a web application as well as the appearance and interactivity of individual pages. Of course, the back-end services need to understand the various paths that different kinds of user can follow through a web app, but this is easy to achieve with a little forethought and planning.

Understanding Progressive Enhancement

The techniques I have demonstrated in this chapter are basic but very effective. By using JavaScript to manage the elements in the DOM and respond to events, I have been able to make the example web app more responsive for the user, provide useful and timely information about the cost of the user's product selections, and streamline the flow of the app itself.

But—and this is important—because these changes are done through JavaScript, the basic nature and structure of the web app remain unchanged for non-JavaScript users. Figure 2-4 shows the main web app page when JavaScript is enabled and disabled.

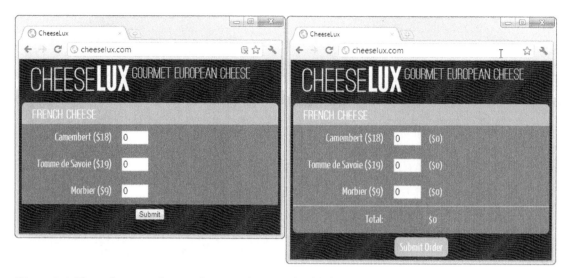

Figure 2-4. The web app as shown when JavaScript is disabled and enabled

The version that non-JavaScript users experience remains fully functional but is clunkier to use and requires more steps to place an order.

Creating a base level of functionality and then selectively enriching it is an example of *progressive enhancement*. Progressive enhancement isn't just about the availability of JavaScript; it encompasses selective enrichment based on any factor, such as the amount of bandwidth, the type of browser, or even the level of experience of the user. However, when creating web apps, the most common form of progressive enhancement is driven by whether the user has JavaScript enabled.

■ **Tip** A similar term to *progressive enhancement* is *graceful degradation*. For my purposes in this book, progressive enhancement and graceful degradation are the same—the notion that the core content and features of a web application are available to all users, irrespective of the capabilities of a user's browser.

If you don't want to support non-JavaScript browsers, then you should make it obvious to non-JavaScript visitors that there is a problem. The easiest way to do this is by using the noscript and meta elements to redirect the browser to a page that explains the situation, as shown in Listing 2-17.

Listing 2-17. Dealing with Non-JavaScript Users

```
...
<head>
    <title>CheeseLux</title>
    <link rel="stylesheet" type="text/css" href="styles.css"/>
    <script src="jquery-1.7.1.js" type="text/javascript"></script>
    <script>
        ... JavaScript code goes here...
```

```
    </script>
    <noscript>
        <meta http-equiv="refresh" content="0; noscript.html"/>
    </noscript>
</head>
...
```

This combination of elements redirects the user to a page called noscript.html, which is an HTML document that tells the user that I require JavaScript (and, obviously, doesn't rely on JavaScript itself). You can find this page in the source code download that accompanies this book and see the result in Figure 2-5.

Figure 2-5. Enforcing a JavaScript-only policy in a web app

It is tempting to require JavaScript, but I recommend caution; you might be surprised by how many users don't enable JavaScript or simply can't. This is especially true for users in large corporations, where computers are usually locked down and where features that are common in the general population are disabled in the name of security, including, sadly, JavaScript in browsers. Some web apps just don't make sense without JavaScript, but give careful thought to the potential users/customers you will be excluding before deciding that you are building one of them.

■ **Note** This is a book about building web apps with JavaScript, so I am not going to maintain progressive enhancement in the chapters that follow. Don't take that as an endorsement of a JavaScript-only policy. In my own projects, I try to support non-JavaScript users whenever possible, even when it requires a lot of additional effort.

Revisiting the Button: Using a UI Toolkit

I want to finish this chapter by showing you a different approach to obtaining one of the results in this chapter: creating a visually consistent button. The techniques I used previously demonstrated how you can manipulate the DOM and respond to events to tailor the appearance and behavior of elements, which is the main premise in this chapter.

That said, for professional development, it a good principle to never write what you can obtain from a good JavaScript library, and when I want to create visually rich elements, I use a UI toolkit. In this section, I'll show you how easy it is to create a custom button with jQuery UI, which is produced by the jQuery team and is one of the most widely used JavaScript UI toolkits available.

Setting Up jQuery UI

Setting up jQuery UI is a multistage process. The first stage is to create a *theme*, which defines the CSS styles that are used by the jQuery UI *widgets* (which is the name given to the styled elements that a UI toolkit creates). To create a theme, go to http://jqueryui.com, click the Themes button, expand each section on the left side of the screen, and specify the styles you want. As you make changes, the sample widgets on the right side of the screen will update to reflect the new settings. It took me about five minutes (and a bit of trial and error) to create a theme that matches the appearance of the example web app. I have included the theme I created in the source code download for this book if you don't want to create your own.

■ **Tip** If you don't want to create a custom theme, you can select a predefined style from the gallery. This can be useful if you are not trying to match an existing app design, although the colors used in some of gallery styles are quite alarming.

When you are done, click the Download Theme button. You will see a screen that allows you to select which components of jQuery UI are included in the download. You can create a smaller download if you get into the detail of jQuery UI, but for this book ensure that all of the components are selected and click the Download button. Your browser will download a `.zip` file that contains the jQuery UI library, the CSS theme you created, and some supporting images.

The second part of the setup is to copy the following files from the `.zip` file into the content directory of the Node.js server:

- The `development-bundle\ui\jquery-ui-1.8.16.custom.js` file
- The `development-bundle\themes\custom-theme\jquery-ui-1.8.16.custom.css` file
- The `development-bundle\themes\custom-theme\images` folder

The names of the files include the jQuery UI version numbers. As I write this, the current version is 1.8.16, but you will probably have a later version by the time this book goes into print.

Tip Once again, I am using the uncompressed versions of the JavaScript file to make debugging easier. You will find the minimized version in the `js` folder of the `.zip` file.

Creating a jQuery UI Button

Now that jQuery UI is set up, I can use it in my HTML document to create a button widget and simplify my code. Listing 2-18 shows the additions required to import jQuery UI into the document and to create a button.

Importing jQuery UI is simply a matter of adding a `script` element to import the JavaScript file and a `link` element to import the CSS file. You don't need to explicitly reference the `images` directory.

Tip Notice that the `script` element that imports the jQuery UI JavaScript file comes *after* the one that imports jQuery. This ordering is important since jQuery UI depends on jQuery.

Listing 2-18. Using jQuery UI to Create a Button

```html
<!DOCTYPE html>
<html>
<head>
    <title>CheeseLux</title>
    <link rel="stylesheet" type="text/css" href="styles.css"/>
    <script src="jquery-1.7.1.js" type="text/javascript"></script>
    <script src="jquery-ui-1.8.16.custom.js" type="text/javascript"></script>
    <link rel="stylesheet" type="text/css" href="jquery-ui-1.8.16.custom.css"/>
<script>

    var priceData = {
        camembert: 18,
        tomme: 19,
        morbier: 9
    }

    $(document).ready(function() {

        $('#buttonDiv input:submit').button().css("font-family", "Yanone, sans-serif");

        $('.latent').show();

        $('input').bind("change keyup", function() {
            var subtotal = $(this).val() * priceData[this.name];
            $(this).siblings("span").children("span").text(subtotal)
            calculateTotal();
        })
```

```
        $('form').attr("action", "/shipping");
    })

    function calculateTotal() {
        var total = 0;
        $('span.subtotal span').not('#total').each(function(index, elem) {
            total += Number($(elem).text());
        })
        $('#total').text("$" + total);
    }
</script>
<noscript>
    <meta http-equiv="refresh" content="0; noscript.html"/>
</noscript>
</head>
...
```

When using jQuery UI, I don't have to hide the input element and insert a substitute. Instead, I use jQuery to select the element I want to modify and call the button method, as follows:

```
$('#buttonDiv input:submit').button()
```

With a single method call, jQuery UI changes the appearance of the labels and handles the highlighting when the mouse hovers over the button. I don't need to worry about handling the click event in this case, because the default action for a submit input element is to submit the form, which is exactly what I want to happen.

I have made one additional method call, using the css method. This method applies a CSS property directly to the selected elements using the style attribute, and I have used it to set the font-family property on the input element. The jQuery UI theme system doesn't have much support for dealing with fonts and generates its widgets using a single font family. I have set up web fonts from the Google Fonts (www.google.com/webfonts and the excellent League of Movable Type (www.theleagueofmoveabletype.com), so I must override the jQuery UI CSS styles to apply my preferred font to the button element. You can see the result of using jQuery UI to create a button in Figure 2-6. The result is, as you can see, consistent with the rest of the web app but much simpler to create in JavaScript.

Figure 2-6. Creating a button with jQuery UI

Toolkits like jQuery UI are just a convenient wrapper around the same DOM, CSS, and event techniques I described earlier. It is important to understand what's happening under the covers, but I recommend using jQuery UI or another good UI library. These libraries are comprehensively tested, and they save you from having to write and debug custom code, allowing you to spend more time on the features that set your web app apart from the competition.

Summary

As I mentioned at the start of this chapter, the techniques I used in these examples are simple, reliable, and entirely suited to small web apps. There is nothing intrinsically wrong with using these approaches if the app is so small that there can never be any issue about maintaining it because every aspect of its behavior is immediately obvious to a programmer.

However, if you are reading this book, you want to go further and create web apps that are large, are complex, and have many moving parts. And when applied to such web apps, these techniques create some fundamental problems. The underlying issue is that the different aspects of the web app are all mixed together. The application data (the products and the basket), the presentation of that data (the HTML elements), and the interactions between them (the JavaScript events and handler functions) are distributed throughout the document. This makes it hard to add additional data, extend the functionality, or fix bugs without introducing errors.

In the chapters that follow, I show you how to apply heavy-duty techniques from the world of server-side development to the web app. Client-side development has been the poor cousin of server-side work for many years, but as browsers become more capable (and as web app programmers become more ambitious), we can no longer pretend that the client side is anything other than a full-fledged platform in its own right. It is time to take web app development seriously, and in the chapters that follow, I show you how to create a solid, robust, and scalable foundation for your web app.

CHAPTER 3

Adding a View Model

If you have done any serious desktop or server-side development, you will have encountered either the *Model-View-Controller* (MVC) design pattern or its derivative *Model-View-View-Model* (MVVM). I am not going to describe either pattern in any detail, other than to say that the core concept in both is separating the data, operations, and presentation of an application into separate components.

There is a lot of benefit in applying the same basic principles to a web application. I am not going to get bogged down in the design patterns and terminology. Instead, I am going to focus on demonstrating the process for structuring a web app and explaining the benefits that are gained from doing so.

Resetting the Example

The best way to understand how to apply a view model and the benefits that doing so confers is to simply do it. The first thing to do is cut everything but the basics out of the application so that I have a clean slate to start from. As you can see in Listing 3-1, I have removed everything but the basic structure of the document.

Listing 3-1. Wiping the Slate

```
<!DOCTYPE html>
<html>
<head>
    <title>CheeseLux</title>
    <link rel="stylesheet" type="text/css" href="styles.css"/>
    <script src="jquery-1.7.1.js" type="text/javascript"></script>
    <script src="jquery-ui-1.8.16.custom.js" type="text/javascript"></script>
    <link rel="stylesheet" type="text/css" href="jquery-ui-1.8.16.custom.css"/>
    <noscript>
        <meta http-equiv="refresh" content="0; noscript.html"/>
    </noscript>
    <script>
        $(document).ready(function() {
            $('#buttonDiv input:submit').button().css("font-family", "Yanone");
        })
    </script>
</head>
<body>
    <div id="logobar">
        <img src="cheeselux.png">
            <span id="tagline">Gourmet European Cheese</span>
```

```
        </div>
        <form action="/shipping" method="post">

            <div id="buttonDiv">
                <input type="submit" />
            </div>
        </form>
    </body>
</html>
```

Creating a View Model

The next step is to define some data, which will be the foundation of the view model. To get started, I have added an object that describes the products in the cheese shop, as shown in Listing 3-2.

Listing 3-2. Adding Data to the Document

```
<script>

    var cheeseModel = {
        category: "French Cheese",
        items: [ {id: "camembert", name: "Camembert", price: 18},
                 {id: "tomme", name: "Tomme de Savoie", price: 19},
                 {id: "morbier", name: "Morbier", price: 9}]
    };

    $(document).ready(function() {
        $('#buttonDiv input:submit').button().css("font-family", "Yanone");

    });
</script>
```

I have created an object that contains details of the cheese products and assigned it to a variable called cheeseModel. The object describes the same products that I used Chapter 2 and is the foundation of my view model, which I will build throughout the chapter; it is a simple data object now, but I'll be doing a lot more with it soon.

■ **Tip** If you find yourself staring at the blinking cursor with no real idea how to define your application data, then my advice is simple: just start typing. One of the biggest benefits of embracing a view model is that it makes changes easier, and that includes changes to the structure of the underlying data. Don't worry if you don't get it right, because you can always correct it later.

Adopting a View Model Library

Following the principle of not writing what is available in a good JavaScript library, I will introduce a view model into the web app using a view model library. The one I'll be using is called Knockout (KO). I like the KO approach to application structure, and the main programmer for KO is Steve Sanderson, who is my coauthor for the *Pro ASP.NET MVC* book from Apress and an all-around nice guy. To get KO, go to http://knockoutjs.com and click the Download link. Select the most recent version (which is 2.0.0 as I write this) from the list of files and copy it to the Node.js content directory.

■ **Tip** Don't worry if you don't get on with KO. Other structure libraries are available. The main competition comes from Backbone (http://documentcloud.github.com/backbone) and AngularJS (http://angularjs.org). The implementation details in these alternative libraries may differ, but the underlying principles remain the same.

In the sections that follow, I will bring my view model and the view model library together to decouple parts of the example application.

Generating Content from the View Model

To begin, I am going to use the data to generate elements in the document so that I can display the products to the user. This is a simple use of the view model, but it reproduces the basic functionality of the implementation in Chapter 2 and gives me a good foundation for the rest of the chapter. Listing 3-3 shows the addition of the KO library to the document and the generation of the elements from the data.

Listing 3-3. Generating Elements from the View Model

```
<!DOCTYPE html>
<html>
<head>
    <title>CheeseLux</title>
    <link rel="stylesheet" type="text/css" href="styles.css"/>
    <script src="jquery-1.7.1.js" type="text/javascript"></script>
    <script src="jquery-ui-1.8.16.custom.js" type="text/javascript"></script>
    <script src='knockout-2.0.0.js' type='text/javascript'></script>
    <link rel="stylesheet" type="text/css" href="jquery-ui-1.8.16.custom.css"/>
    <noscript>
        <meta http-equiv="refresh" content="0; noscript.html"/>
    </noscript>
    <script>
        var cheeseModel = {
            category: "French Cheese",
            items: [ {id: "camembert", name: "Camembert", price: 18},
                     {id: "tomme", name: "Tomme de Savoie", price: 19},
                     {id: "morbier", name: "Morbier", price: 9}]
        };

        $(document).ready(function() {
```

```
            $('#buttonDiv input:submit').button().css("font-family", "Yanone");

            ko.applyBindings(cheeseModel);
        });
    </script>
</head>
<body>
    <div id="logobar">
        <img src="cheeselux.png">
            <span id="tagline">Gourmet European Cheese</span>
    </div>
    <form action="/shipping" method="post">
        <div class="cheesegroup">
            <div class="grouptitle" data-bind="text: category"></div>

            <div data-bind="foreach: items">
                <div class="groupcontent">
                    <label data-bind="attr: {for: id}" class="cheesename">
                        <span data-bind="text: name">
                        </span> $(<span data-bind="text:price"></span>)</label>
                    <input data-bind="attr: {name: id}" value="0"/>
                </div>
            </div>
        </div>
        <div id="buttonDiv">
            <input type="submit" />
        </div>
    </form>
</body>
</html>
```

There are three sets of additions in this listing. The first is importing the KO JavaScript library into the document with a `script` element. The second addition tells KO to use my view model object:

```
ko.applyBindings(cheeseModel);
```

The ko object is the gateway to the KO library functionality, and the `applyBindings` method takes the view model object as an argument and uses it, as the name suggests, to fulfill the *bindings* defined in the document; these are the third set of additions. You can see the result of these bindings in Figure 3-1, and I explain how they work in the sections that follow.

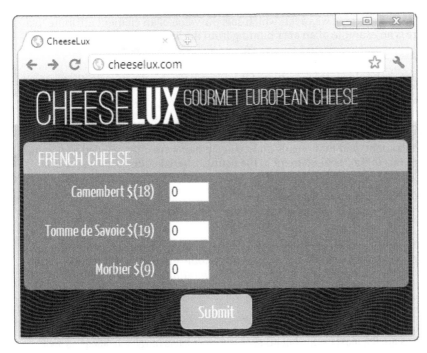

Figure 3-1. Creating content from the view model

Understanding Value Bindings

A *value binding* is a relationship between a property in the view model and an HTML element. This is the simplest kind of binding available. Here is an example of an HTML element that has a value binding:

```
<div class="grouptitle" data-bind="text: category"></div>
```

All KO bindings are defined using the data-bind attribute. This is an example of a text binding, which has the effect of setting the text content of the HTML element to the value of the specified view model property, in this case, the category property.

When the applyBindings method is called, KO searches for bindings and inserts the appropriate data value into the document, transforming the element like this:

```
<div class="grouptitle" data-bind="text: category">French Cheese</div>
```

■ **Tip** I like having the KO data bindings defined in the elements where they will be applied, but some people don't like this approach. There is a simple library available that supports *unobtrusive* KO data bindings, meaning that the bindings are set up using jQuery in the script element. You can get the code and see an example at https://gist.github.com/1006808.

51

The other binding I used in this example was `attr`, which sets the value of an element attribute to a property from the model. Here is an example of an `attr` binding from the listing:

```
<input data-bind="attr: {name: id}" value="0"/>
```

This binding specifies that KO should insert the value of the `id` property for the `name` attribute, which produces the following result when the bindings are applied:

```
<input data-bind="attr: {name: id}" value="0" name="camembert">
```

KO value bindings don't support any formatting or combining of values. In fact, value bindings *just* insert a single value into the document, and that means that extra elements are often needed as targets for value bindings. You can see this in the `label` element in the listing, where I added a couple of span elements:

```
<label data-bind="attr: {for: id}" class="cheesename">
    <span data-bind="text: name"></span> $(<span data-bind="text:price"></span>)
</label>
```

I wanted to insert two data values as the content for the `label` element with some surrounding characters to indicate currency. The way to get the desired effect is simple enough, albeit it adds some complexity to the HTML structure. An alternative is to create *custom bindings*, which I explain in Chapter 4.

■ **Tip** The `text` and `attr` bindings are the most useful, but KO supports other kinds of value bindings as well: `visible`, `html`, `css`, and `style`. I use the `visible` binding later in the chapter and the `css` binding in Chapter 4, but you should consult the KO documentation at `knockoutjs.com` for details of the others.

Understanding Flow Control Bindings

Flow control bindings provide the means to use the view model to control which elements are included in the document. In the listing, I used the `foreach` binding to enumerate the `items` view model property. The `foreach` binding is used on view model properties that are arrays and duplicates the set of child elements for each item in the array:

```
<div data-bind="foreach: items">
    ...
</div>
```

Value bindings on the child elements can refer to the properties of the individual array items, which is how I am able to specify the `id` property for the `attr` binding on the `input` element: KO knows which array item is being processed and inserts the appropriate value from that item.

■ **Tip** In addition to the foreach binding, KO also supports the if, ifnot, and with bindings, which allow content to be selectively included in or excluded from a document. I describe the if and ifnot bindings later in this chapter, but you should consult the KO documentation at knockoutjs.com for full details.

Taking Advantage of the View Model

Now that I have the basic structure of the application in place, I can use the view model and KO to do more. I will start with some basic feature and then step things up to show you some more advanced techniques.

Adding More Products to the View Model

The first benefit that a view model brings is the ability to make changes more quickly and with fewer errors than would otherwise be possible. The simplest demonstration of this is to add more products to the cheese shop catalog. Listing 3-4 shows the changes required to add cheeses from other countries.

Listing 3-4. Adding to the View Model

```
<!DOCTYPE html>
<html>
<head>
    <title>CheeseLux</title>
    <link rel="stylesheet" type="text/css" href="styles.css"/>
    <script src="jquery-1.7.1.js" type="text/javascript"></script>
    <script src="jquery-ui-1.8.16.custom.js" type="text/javascript"></script>
    <script src='knockout-2.0.0.js' type='text/javascript'></script>
    <link rel="stylesheet" type="text/css" href="jquery-ui-1.8.16.custom.css"/>
    <noscript>
        <meta http-equiv="refresh" content="0; noscript.html"/>
    </noscript>
    <script>
        var cheeseModel = {
            products: [
                {category: "British Cheese", items : [
                    {id: "stilton", name: "Stilton", price: 9},
                    {id: "stinkingbishop", name: "Stinking Bishop", price: 17},
                    {id: "cheddar", name: "Cheddar", price: 17}]},

                {category: "French Cheese", items: [
                    {id: "camembert", name: "Camembert", price: 18},
                    {id: "tomme", name: "Tomme de Savoie", price: 19},
                    {id: "morbier", name: "Morbier", price: 9}]},

                {category: "Italian Cheese", items: [
                    {id: "gorgonzola", name: "Gorgonzola", price: 8},
                    {id: "fontina", name: "Fontina", price: 11},
```

```
                    {id: "parmesan", name: "Parmesan", price: 16}]}]
        };

        $(document).ready(function() {
            $('#buttonDiv input:submit').button().css("font-family", "Yanone");

            ko.applyBindings(cheeseModel);
        });
    </script>
</head>
<body>
    <div id="logobar">
        <img src="cheeselux.png">
            <span id="tagline">Gourmet European Cheese</span>
    </div>
    <form action="/shipping" method="post">

        <div data-bind="foreach: products">
            <div class="cheesegroup">
                <div class="grouptitle" data-bind="text: category"></div>

                <div data-bind="foreach: items">
                    <div class="groupcontent">
                        <label data-bind="attr: {for: id}" class="cheesename">
                            <span data-bind="text: name">
                            </span> $(<span data-bind="text:price"></span>)</label>
                        <input data-bind="attr: {name: id}" value="0"/>
                    </div>
                </div>
            </div>
        </div>

        <div id="buttonDiv">
            <input type="submit" />
        </div>
    </form>
</body>
</html>
```

The biggest change was to the view model itself. I changed the structure of the data object so that each category of products is an element in an array assigned to the products property (and, of course, I added two new categories). In terms of the HTML content, I just had to add a foreach flow control binding so that the elements contained within are duplicated for each category.

■ **Tip** The result of these additions is a long, thin HTML document. This is not an ideal way of displaying data, but as I said in Chapter 1, this is a book about advanced programming and not a book about design. There are lots of ways to present this data more usefully, and I suggest starting by looking at the tabs widgets offered by UI toolkits such as jQuery UI or jQuery Tools.

Creating Observable Data Items

In the previous example, I used KO like a simple template engine; I took the values from the view model and used them to generate a set of elements. I like using template engines because they simplify markup and reduce errors. But a bigger benefit of view models comes when you create *observable data items*. Put simply, an observable data item is a property in the view model that, when updated, causes all of the HTML elements that have value bindings to that property to update as well. Listing 3-5 shows how to create and use an observable data item.

Listing 3-5. Creating Observable Data Items

```
<!DOCTYPE html>
<html>
<head>
    <title>CheeseLux</title>
    <link rel="stylesheet" type="text/css" href="styles.css"/>
    <script src="jquery-1.7.1.js" type="text/javascript"></script>
    <script src="jquery-ui-1.8.16.custom.js" type="text/javascript"></script>
    <script src='knockout-2.0.0.js' type='text/javascript'></script>
    <link rel="stylesheet" type="text/css" href="jquery-ui-1.8.16.custom.css"/>
    <noscript>
        <meta http-equiv="refresh" content="0; noscript.html"/>
    </noscript>
    <script>
        var cheeseModel = {
            products: [
                {category: "British Cheese", items : [
                    {id: "stilton", name: "Stilton", price: 9},
                    {id: "stinkingbishop", name: "Stinking Bishop", price: 17},
                    {id: "cheddar", name: "Cheddar", price: 17}]},
                {category: "French Cheese", items: [
                    {id: "camembert", name: "Camembert", price: 18},
                    {id: "tomme", name: "Tomme de Savoie", price: 19},
                    {id: "morbier", name: "Morbier", price: 9}]},
                {category: "Italian Cheese", items: [
                    {id: "gorgonzola", name: "Gorgonzola", price: 8},
                    {id: "fontina", name: "Fontina", price: 11},
                    {id: "parmesan", name: "Parmesan", price: 16}]}]
        };
```

```
        function mapProducts(func) {
            $.each(cheeseModel.products, function(catIndex, outerItem) {
                $.each(outerItem.items, function(itemIndex, innerItem) {
                    func(innerItem);
                });
            });
        }

        $(document).ready(function() {
            $('#buttonDiv input').button().css("font-family", "Yanone");


            mapProducts(function(item) {
                item.price = ko.observable(item.price);
            });

            ko.applyBindings(cheeseModel);

            $('#discount').click(function() {
                mapProducts(function(item) {
                    item.price(item.price() - 2);
                });
            });
        });
    </script>
</head>
<body>
    <div id="logobar">
        <img src="cheeselux.png">
            <span id="tagline">Gourmet European Cheese</span>
    </div>
    <form action="/shipping" method="post">
        <div id="buttonDiv">
            <input id="discount" type="button" value="Apply Discount" />
        </div>

        <div data-bind="foreach: products">
            <div class="cheesegroup">
                <div class="grouptitle" data-bind="text: category"></div>

                <div data-bind="foreach: items">
                    <div class="groupcontent">
                        <label data-bind="attr: {for: id}" class="cheesename">
                            <span data-bind="text: name">
                            </span> $(<span data-bind="text:price"></span>)</label>
                        <input data-bind="attr: {name: id}" value="0"/>
                    </div>
                </div>
            </div>
        </div>
```

```
        <div id="buttonDiv">
            <input type="submit" />
        </div>
    </form>
</body>
</html>
```

The mapProducts function is a simple utility that allows me to apply a function to each individual cheese product. This function uses the jQuery each method, which executes a function for every item in an array. By using the each function twice, I can reach the inner array of cheese products in each category.

In this example, I have transformed the price property for each cheese product into an observable data item, as follows:

```
mapProducts(function(item) {
    item.price = ko.observable(item.price);
});
```

The ko.observable method takes the initial value for the data item as its argument and sets up the plumbing that is required to disseminate updates to the bindings in the document. I don't have to make any changes to the bindings themselves; KO takes care of all the details for me.

All that remains is to set up a situation that will cause a change to occur. I have done this by adding a new button to the document and defining a handler for the click event as follows:

```
$('#discount').click(function() {
    mapProducts(function(item) {
        item.price(item.price() - 2);
    });
});
```

When the button is clicked, I use the mapProducts function to change the value of the price property for each cheese object in the view model. Since this is an observable data item, the new value will be pushed out to the value bindings and cause the document to be updated.

Notice the slightly odd syntax I use when altering the value. The original price property was a JavaScript Number, which meant I could change the value like this:

```
item.price -= 2;
```

But the ko.observable method transforms the property into a JavaScript function in order to work with some older versions of Internet Explorer. This means you read the value of an observable data item by calling the function (in other words, by calling item.price()) and update the value by passing an argument to the function (in other words, by calling item.price(newValue)). This can take a little while to get used to, and I still forget to do this.

Figure 3-2 shows the effect of the observable data item. When the Apply Discount button is clicked, all of the prices displayed to the user are updated, as Figure 3-2 shows.

Figure 3-2. Using an observable data item

The power and flexibility of an observable data item is significant; it creates an application where changes from the view mode, irrespective of how they arise, cause the data bindings in the document to be updated immediately. As you'll see in the rest of the chapter, I make a lot of use of observable data items as I add more complex features to the example web app.

Creating Bidirectional Bindings

A *bidirectional binding* is a two-way relationship between a form element and an observable data item. When the view model is updated, so is the value shown in the element, just as for a regular observable. In addition, changing the element value causes an update to go in the *other* direction: the property in the view model is updated. So, for example, if I use a bidirectional binding for an input element, KO ensures that the model is updated when the user enters a new value. By using bidirectional relationships between multiple elements and the same model property, you can easily keep a complex web app synchronized and consistent.

To demonstrate a bidirectional binding, I will add a Special Offers section to the cheese shop. This allows me to pick some products from the full section, apply a discount, and, ideally, draw the customer's attention to a product that they might not otherwise consider.

Listing 3-6 contains the changes to the web app to support the special offers. To set up a bidirectional binding, I am going to do two other interesting things: extend the view model and use KO *templates* to generate elements. I'll explain all three changes in the sections that follow the listing.

Listing 3-6. Using Live Bindings to Create Special Offers

```html
<!DOCTYPE html>
<html>
<head>
    <title>CheeseLux</title>
    <link rel="stylesheet" type="text/css" href="styles.css"/>
    <script src="jquery-1.7.1.js" type="text/javascript"></script>
    <script src="jquery-ui-1.8.16.custom.js" type="text/javascript"></script>
    <script src='knockout-2.0.0.js' type='text/javascript'></script>
    <link rel="stylesheet" type="text/css" href="jquery-ui-1.8.16.custom.css"/>
    <noscript>
        <meta http-equiv="refresh" content="0; noscript.html"/>
    </noscript>
    <script>
        var cheeseModel = {
            products: [
                {category: "British Cheese", items : [
                    {id: "stilton", name: "Stilton", price: 9},
                    {id: "stinkingbishop", name: "Stinking Bishop", price: 17},
                    {id: "cheddar", name: "Cheddar", price: 17}]},
                {category: "French Cheese", items: [
                    {id: "camembert", name: "Camembert", price: 18},
                    {id: "tomme", name: "Tomme de Savoie", price: 19},
                    {id: "morbier", name: "Morbier", price: 9}]},
                {category: "Italian Cheese", items: [
                    {id: "gorgonzola", name: "Gorgonzola", price: 8},
                    {id: "fontina", name: "Fontina", price: 11},
                    {id: "parmesan", name: "Parmesan", price: 16}]}]
        };

        function mapProducts(func) {
            $.each(cheeseModel.products, function(catIndex, outerItem) {
                $.each(outerItem.items, function(itemIndex, innerItem) {
                    func(innerItem);
                });
            });
        }

        $(document).ready(function() {
            $('#buttonDiv input:submit').button().css("font-family", "Yanone");

            cheeseModel.specials = {
                category: "Special Offers",
                discount: 3,
                ids: ["stilton", "tomme"],
                items: []
            };

            mapProducts(function(item) {
                if ($.inArray(item.id, cheeseModel.specials.ids) > -1) {
```

59

```
                    item.price -= cheeseModel.specials.discount;
                    cheeseModel.specials.items.push(item);
                }
                item.quantity = ko.observable(0);
            });

            ko.applyBindings(cheeseModel);
        });
    </script>
    <script id="categoryTmpl" type="text/html">
        <div class="cheesegroup">
            <div class="grouptitle" data-bind="text: category"></div>

            <div data-bind="foreach: items">
                <div class="groupcontent">
                    <label data-bind="attr: {for: id}" class="cheesename">
                        <span data-bind="text: name">
                        </span> $(<span data-bind="text:price"></span>)</label>
                    <input data-bind="attr: {name: id}, value: quantity"/>
                </div>
            </div>
        </div>
    </script>
</head>
<body>
    <div id="logobar">
        <img src="cheeselux.png">
            <span id="tagline">Gourmet European Cheese</span>
    </div>

    <div data-bind="template: {name: 'categoryTmpl', data: specials}"></div>
    <form action="/shipping" method="post">
        <div data-bind="template: {name: 'categoryTmpl', foreach: products}"></div>
        <div id="buttonDiv">
            <input type="submit" />
        </div>
    </form>
</body>
</html>
```

Extending the View Model

JavaScript's loose typing and dynamic nature makes it ideal for creating flexible and adaptable view models. I like being able to take the initial data and reshape it to create something that is more closely tailored to the needs of the web app, in this case, to add support for special offers. To start with, I add a property called specials to the view model, defining it as an object that has category and items properties like the rest of the model but with some useful additions:

```
cheeseModel.specials = {
    category: "Special Offers",
    discount: 3,
    ids: ["stilton", "tomme"],
    items: []
};
```

The `discount` property specifies the dollar discount I want to apply to the special offers, and the `ids` property contains an array of the IDs of products that will be special offers.

The `specials.items` array is empty when I first define it. To populate the array, I enumerate the `products` array to find those products that are in the `specials.ids` array, like this:

```
mapProducts(function(item) {
    if ($.inArray(item.id, cheeseModel.specials.ids) > -1) {
        item.price -= cheeseModel.specials.discount;
        cheeseModel.specials.items.push(item);
    }
    item.quantity = ko.observable(0);
});
```

I use the `inArray` method to determine whether the current item in the iteration is one of those that will be included as a special offer. The `inArray` method is another jQuery utility, and it returns the index of an item if it is contained within an array and `-1` if it is not. This is a quick and easy way for me to check to see whether the current item is one that I am interested in as a special offer.

If an item *is* on the specials list, then I reduce the value of the `price` property by the `discount` amount and use the `push` method to insert the item into the `specials.items` array.

```
item.price -= cheeseModel.specials.discount;
cheeseModel.specials.items.push(item);
```

After I have iterated through the items in the view model, the `specials.item` array contains a complete set of the products that are to be discounted, and, along the way, I have reduced each of their prices.

In this example, I have made the `quantity` property into an observable data item:

```
item.quantity = ko.observable(0);
```

This is important because I am going to display multiple `input` elements for the special offers: one element in the original cheese category and another in a new Special Offers category that I explain in the next section. By using an observable data item and bidirectional bindings on the `input` elements, I can easily make sure that the quantities entered for a cheese are consistently displayed, irrespective of which `input` element is used.

Generating the Content

All that remains now is to generate the content from the view model. I want to generate the same set of elements for the special offers as for the regular categories, so I have used the KO *template* feature, which allows me to generate the same set of elements at multiple points in the document. Here is the template from the listing:

```
<script id="categoryTmpl" type="text/html">
    <div class="cheesegroup">
        <div class="grouptitle" data-bind="text: category"></div>
```

```
        <div data-bind="foreach: items">
            <div class="groupcontent">
                <label data-bind="attr: {for: id}" class="cheesename">
                    <span data-bind="text: name">
                    </span> $(<span data-bind="text:price"></span>)</label>
                <input data-bind="attr: {name: id}, value: quantity"/>
            </div>
        </div>
    </div>
</script>
```

The template is contained in a script element. The type attribute is set to text/html, which prevents the browser from executing the content as JavaScript. Most of the bindings in the template are the same text and attr bindings I used in the previous example. The important addition is to the input element, as follows:

```
<input data-bind="attr: {name: id}, value: quantity"/>
```

The data-bind attribute for this element defines two bindings, separated by a comma. The first is a regular attr binding, but the second is a value binding, which is one of the bidirectional bindings that KO defines. I don't have to take any action to make the value binding bidirectional; KO takes care of it automatically. In this listing, I create a two-way binding to the quantity observable data item.

I generate content from the template using the template binding. When using a template, KO duplicates the elements that it contains and inserts them as children of the element that has the template binding. There are two points in the document where I use the template, and they are slightly different:

```
<div data-bind="template: {name: 'categoryTmpl', data: specials}"></div>
<form action="/shipping" method="post">
    <div data-bind="template: {name: 'categoryTmpl', foreach: products}"></div>

    <div id="buttonDiv">
        <input type="submit" />
    </div>
</form>
```

When using the template binding, the name property specifies the id attribute value of the template element. If you want to generate only one set of elements, then you can use the data property to specify which view model property will be used. I used data to specify the specials property in the listing, which creates a section of content for my special-offer products.

■ **Tip** You must remember to enclose the id of the template element in quotes. If you don't, KO will fail quietly without generating elements from the template.

You can use the foreach property if you want to generate a set of elements for each item in an array. I have done this for the regular product categories by specifying the products array. In this way, I can apply the template to each element in an array to generate content consistently.

■ **Tip** Notice that the special-offer elements are inserted outside the `form` element. The `input` elements for the special-offer products will have the same `name` attribute value as the corresponding `input` element in the regular product category. By inserting the special-offer elements outside the `form`, I prevent duplicate entries from being sent to the server when the form is submitted.

Reviewing the Result

Now that I have explained each of the changes I made to set up the bidirectional bindings, it is time to look at the results, which you can see in Figure 3-3.

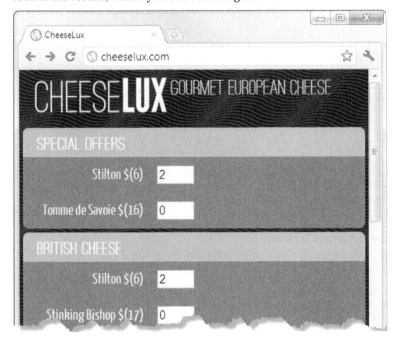

Figure 3-3. The result of extending the view model, creating a live binding, and using templates

This is good demonstration of how using a view model can save time and reduce errors. I have applied a $3 discount to the Special Offer products, which I did by altering the value of the `price` property in the view model. Even though the `price` property is not observable, the combination of the view model and the template ensures that the correct prices are displayed throughout the document when the elements are initially generated. (You can see that both `Stilton` listings are priced at $6, rather than the $9 originally specified by the view model.)

The bidirectional binding is the most interesting and useful feature in this example. All of the `input` elements have bidirectional bindings with their corresponding `quantity` property, and since there are two `input` elements in the document for each of the Special Offer cheeses, entering a value into one will immediately cause that value to be displayed in the other; you can see this has happened for the Stilton product in the figure (but it is an effect that is best experienced by loading the example in the browser).

So, with very little effort, I have been able to enhance the view model and use those enhancements to keep a form consistent and responsive, while adding new features to the application. In the next section, I'll build on these enhancements to create a dynamic basket, showing you some of the other benefits that can arise from a view model.

■ **Tip** If you submit this form to the server, the order summary will show the original, undiscounted price. This is, of course, because I applied the discount only in the browser. In a real application, the server would also need to know about the special offers, but I am going to skip over this, since this book focuses on client-side development.

Adding a Dynamic Basket

Now that I have explained and demonstrated how changes are detected and propagated with value and bidirectional bindings, I can complete the example so that all of the functionality present in Chapter 2 is available to the user. This means I need to implement a dynamic shopping basket, which I do in the sections that follow.

Adding Subtotals

With a view model, new features can be added quickly. The changes to add per-item subtotals are surprisingly simple, although I need to use some additional KO features. First, I need to enhance the view model. Listing 3-7 highlights the changes in the script element within the call to the mapProduct function.

Listing 3-7. Extending the View Model to Support Subtotals

```
...
mapProducts(function(item) {
    if ($.inArray(item.id, cheeseModel.specials.ids) > -1) {
        item.price -= cheeseModel.specials.discount;
        cheeseModel.specials.items.push(item);
    }
    item.quantity = ko.observable(0);
    item.subtotal = ko.computed(function() {
        return this.quantity() * this.price;
    }, item);
});
...
```

I have created what is known as a *computed observable data item* for the subtotal property. This is like a regular observable item, except that the value is produced by a function, which is passed as the first argument to the ko.computed method. The second method is used as the value of the this variable when the function is executed; I have set this to the item loop variable.

The nice thing about this feature is that KO manages all of the dependencies, such that when my computed observable function relies on a regular observable data item, a change to the regular item automatically triggers an update in the computed value. I'll use this behavior to manage the overall total later in this chapter.

Next, I need to add some elements with bindings to the template, as shown in Listing 3-8.

Listing 3-8. Adding Elements to the Template to Support Subtotals

```
<script id="categoryTmpl" type="text/html">
    <div class="cheesegroup">
        <div class="grouptitle" data-bind="text: category"></div>

        <div data-bind="foreach: items">
            <div class="groupcontent">
                <label data-bind="attr: {for: id}" class="cheesename">
                    <span data-bind="text: name">
                    </span> $(<span data-bind="text:price"></span>)</label>
                <input data-bind="attr: {name: id}, value: quantity"/>
                <span data-bind="visible: subtotal" class="subtotal">
                    ($<span data-bind="text: subtotal"></span>)
                </span>
            </div>
        </div>
    </div>
</script>
```

The inner span element uses a text data binding to display the value of the subtotal property I created a moment ago. To make things more interesting, the outer span element uses another KO binding; this one is visible. For this binding, the child elements are hidden when the specified property is *false-like* (zero, null, undefined, or false). For *truth-like* values (1, true, or a non-null object or array), the child elements are displayed. I have specified the subtotal value for the visible binding, and this little trick means that I will display a subtotal only when the user enters a nonzero value into the input element. You can see the result in Figure 3-4.

Figure 3-4. Selectively displaying subtotals

You can see how easy and quick it is to create new features once the basic structure has been added to the application. Some new markup and a little script go a long way. And, as a bonus, the subtotal feature works seamlessly with the special offers; since both operate on the view model, the discounts applied for the special offers are seamlessly (and effortlessly) incorporated into the subtotals.

Adding the Basket Line Items and Total

I don't want to use the inline basket approach that I took in Chapter 2 because some of the products are shown twice and the document is too long to make the user scroll down to see the total cost of their selection. Instead, I am going to create a separate set of basket elements that will be displayed alongside the products. You can what I have done in Figure 3-5.

Figure 3-5. Adding a separate basket

Listing 3-9 shows the changes required to support the basket.

Listing 3-9. Adding the Basket Elements and Line Items

```
<!DOCTYPE html>
<html>
<head>
    <title>CheeseLux</title>
    <link rel="stylesheet" type="text/css" href="styles.css"/>
    <script src="jquery-1.7.1.js" type="text/javascript"></script>
    <script src="jquery-ui-1.8.16.custom.js" type="text/javascript"></script>
    <script src='knockout-2.0.0.js' type='text/javascript'></script>
```

```
<link rel="stylesheet" type="text/css" href="jquery-ui-1.8.16.custom.css"/>
<noscript>
    <meta http-equiv="refresh" content="0; noscript.html"/>
</noscript>
<script>
    var cheeseModel = {
        products: [
            {category: "British Cheese", items : [
                {id: "stilton", name: "Stilton", price: 9},
                {id: "stinkingbishop", name: "Stinking Bishop", price: 17},
                {id: "cheddar", name: "Cheddar", price: 17}]},
            {category: "French Cheese", items: [
                {id: "camembert", name: "Camembert", price: 18},
                {id: "tomme", name: "Tomme de Savoie", price: 19},
                {id: "morbier", name: "Morbier", price: 9}]},
            {category: "Italian Cheese", items: [
                {id: "gorgonzola", name: "Gorgonzola", price: 8},
                {id: "fontina", name: "Fontina", price: 11},
                {id: "parmesan", name: "Parmesan", price: 16}]}]
    };

    function mapProducts(func) {
        $.each(cheeseModel.products, function(catIndex, outerItem) {
            $.each(outerItem.items, function(itemIndex, innerItem) {
                func(innerItem);
            });
        });
    }

    $(document).ready(function() {
        $('#buttonDiv input:submit').button().css("font-family", "Yanone");

        cheeseModel.specials = {
            category: "Special Offers",
            discount: 3,
            ids: ["stilton", "tomme"],
            items: []
        };

        mapProducts(function(item) {
            if ($.inArray(item.id, cheeseModel.specials.ids) > -1) {
                item.price -= cheeseModel.specials.discount;
                cheeseModel.specials.items.push(item);
            }
            item.quantity = ko.observable(0);
            item.subtotal = ko.computed(function() {
                return this.quantity() * this.price;
            }, item);
        });

        cheeseModel.total = ko.computed(function() {
            var total = 0;
```

```
                    mapProducts(function(elem) {
                        total += elem.subtotal();
                    });
                    return total;
                });

                ko.applyBindings(cheeseModel);

                $('div.cheesegroup').not("#basket").css("width", "50%");

                $('#basketTable a')
                    .button({icons: {primary: "ui-icon-closethick"}, text: false})
                    .click(function() {
                        var targetId = $(this).closest('tr').attr("data-prodId");
                        mapProducts(function(item) {
                            if (item.id == targetId) {
                                item.quantity(0);
                            }
                        });
                    })
            });
        </script>
        <script id="categoryTmpl" type="text/html">
            <div class="cheesegroup">
                <div class="grouptitle" data-bind="text: category"></div>

                <div data-bind="foreach: items">
                    <div class="groupcontent">
                        <label data-bind="attr: {for: id}" class="cheesename">
                            <span data-bind="text: name">
                            </span> $(<span data-bind="text:price"></span>)</label>
                        <input data-bind="attr: {name: id}, value: quantity"/>
                        <span data-bind="visible: subtotal" class="subtotal">
                            ($<span data-bind="text: subtotal"></span>)
                        </span>
                    </div>
                </div>
            </div>
        </script>
        <script id="basketRowTmpl" type="text/html">
            <tr data-bind="visible: quantity, attr: {'data-prodId': id}">
                <td data-bind="text: name"></td>
                <td>$<span data-bind="text: subtotal"></span></td>
                <td><a href="#"></a></td>
            </tr>
        </script>
    </head>
    <body>
        <div id="logobar">
            <img src="cheeselux.png">
            <span id="tagline">Gourmet European Cheese</span>
```

```
        </div>

        <div id="basket" class="cheesegroup basket">
            <div class="grouptitle">Basket</div>
            <div class="groupcontent">
                <table id="basketTable">
                    <thead><tr><th>Cheese</th><th>Subtotal</th><th></th></tr></thead>
                    <tbody data-bind="foreach: products">
                        <!-- ko template: {name: 'basketRowTmpl', foreach: items} -->
                        <!-- /ko -->
                    </tbody>
                    <tfoot>
                        <tr><td class="sumline" colspan=2></td></tr>
                        <tr>
                            <th>Total:</th><td>$<span data-bind="text: total"></span></td>
                        </tr>
                    </tfoot>
                </table>
            </div>
            <div class="cornerplaceholder"></div>

            <div id="buttonDiv">
                <input type="submit" value="Submit Order"/>
            </div>
        </div>

        <div data-bind="template: {name: 'categoryTmpl', data: specials}"></div>
        <form action="/shipping" method="post">
            <div data-bind="template: {name: 'categoryTmpl', foreach: products}"></div>
        </form>
</body>
</html>
```

I'll step through each category of change that I made and explain the effect it has. As I do this, please reflect on how little has to change to add this feature. Once again, a view model and some basic application structure create a foundation to which new features can be quickly and easily added.

Extending the View Model

The change to the view model in this listing is the addition of the total property, which is a computed observable that sums the individual subtotal values:

```
cheeseModel.total = ko.computed(function() {
    var total = 0;
    mapProducts(function(elem) {
        total += elem.subtotal();
    });
    return total;
});
```

As I mentioned previously, KO tracks dependencies between observable data items automatically. Any change to a subtotal value will cause total to be recalculated and the new value to be displayed in elements that are bound to it.

Adding the Basket Structure and Template

The outer structure of the HTML elements I added to the document is just a duplicate of a cheese category to maintain visual consistency. The heart of the basket is the table element, which contains several data bindings:

```
<table id="basketTable">
    <thead><tr><th>Cheese</th><th>Subtotal</th><th></th></tr></thead>
    <tbody data-bind="foreach: products">
        <!-- ko template: {name: 'basketRowTmpl', foreach: items} -->
        <!-- /ko -->
    </tbody>
    <tfoot>
        <tr><td class="sumline" colspan=2></td></tr>
        <tr>
            <th>Total:</th><td>$<span data-bind="text: total"></span></td>
        </tr>
    </tfoot>
</table>
```

The most important addition here is the oddly formatted HTML comments. This is known as a *containerless binding*, and it allows me to apply the template binding without needing a container element for the content that will be duplicated. Adding rows to a table from a nested array is a perfect situation for this technique because adding an element just so I can apply the binding would cause layout problems. The containerless binding is contained within a regular foreach binding, but you can nest the binding comments much as you would regular elements.

The other binding is a simple text value binding, which displays the overall total for the basket, using the calculated total observable I created a moment ago. I don't have to take any action to make sure that the total is up-to-date; KO manages the chain of dependencies between the total, subtotal, and quantity properties in the view model.

The template that I added to produce the table rows has four data bindings:

```
<script id="basketRowTmpl" type="text/html">
    <tr data-bind="visible: quantity, attr: {'data-prodId': id}">
        <td data-bind="text: name"></td>
        <td>$<span data-bind="text: subtotal"></span></td>
        <td><a href="#"></a></td>
    </tr>
</script>
```

You have seen these types of binding previously. The visible binding on the tr element ensures that table rows are visible only for those cheeses for which the quantity isn't zero; this prevents the basket from being filled up with rows for products that the user isn't interested in.

Note the attr binding on the tr element. I have defined a custom attribute using the HTML5 data attribute feature that embeds the id value of the product that the row represents into the tr element. I'll explain why I did this shortly.

I also moved the submit button so that it is under the basket, making it easier for the user to submit their order. The style that I assigned to the basket elements uses the fixed value for the CSS position property, meaning that the basket will always be visible, even as the user scrolls down the page. To accommodate the basket, I used jQuery to apply a new value for the CSS width property directly to the cheese category elements (but not the basket itself):

```
$('div.cheesegroup').not("#basket").css("width", "50%");
```

Removing Items from the Basket

The last set of changes builds on the a elements that are added to each table row in the basketRowTmpl template:

```
$('#basketTable a')
    .button({icons: {primary: "ui-icon-closethick"}, text: false})
    .click(function() {
        var targetId = $(this).closest('tr').attr("data-prodId");
        mapProducts(function(item) {
            if (item.id == targetId) {
                item.quantity(0);
            }
        });
    })
```

I use jQuery to select all the a elements and use jQuery UI to create buttons from them. jQuery UI themes include a set of icons, and the object that I pass to the jQuery UI button method creates a button that uses one of these images and displays no text. This gives me a nice small button with a cross.

In the click function, I use jQuery to navigate from the a element that triggered the click event to the first ancestor tr element using the closest method. This selects the tr element that contains the custom data attribute I inserted in the template earlier and that I read using the attr method:

```
var targetId = $(this).closest('tr').attr("data-prodId");
```

This statement lets me determine the id of the product the user wants to remove from the basket. I then use the mapProducts function to find the matching cheese object and set the quantity to zero. Since quantity is an observable data item, KO disseminates the new value, which causes the subtotal value to be recalculated and the visible binding on the corresponding tr element to be reevaluated. Since the quantity is zero, the table row will be hidden automatically. And, since subtotal is observable, the total will also be recalculated, and the new value is displayed to the user. As you can see, it is useful to have a view model where the dependencies between data values are managed seamlessly. The net result is a dynamic basket that is always consistent with the values in the view model and so always presents the correct information to the user.

Finishing the Example

Before I finish this topic, I just want to tweak a couple of things. First, the basket looks pretty poor when no items have been selected by the user, as shown in Figure 3-6. To address this, I will display some placeholder text when the basket is empty.

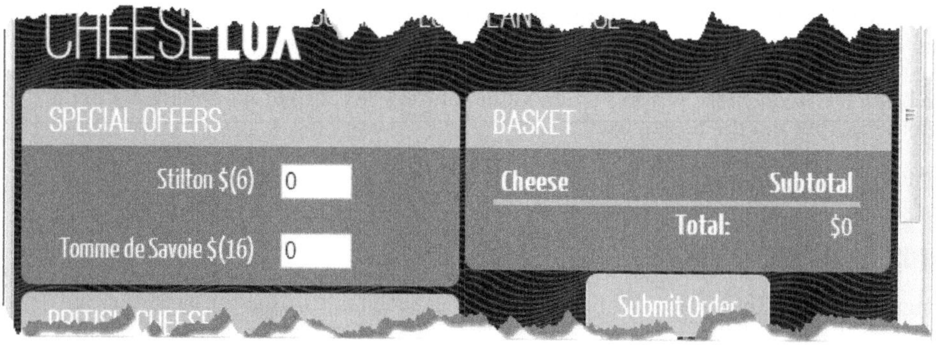

Figure 3-6. The empty basket

Second, the user has no way to clear the basket with a single action, so I will add a button that will reset the quantities of all of the products to zero. Finally, by moving the submit button outside the form element, I have lost the ability to rely on the default action. I must add an event handler so that the user can submit the form. Listing 3-10 shows the HTML elements that I have added to support these features.

Listing 3-10. Adding Elements to Finish the Example

```
...
<body>
    <div id="logobar">
        <img src="cheeselux.png">
        <span id="tagline">Gourmet European Cheese</span>
    </div>

    <div id="basket" class="cheesegroup basket">
        <div class="grouptitle">Basket</div>
        <div class="groupcontent">

            <div class="description" data-bind="ifnot: total">
                No products selected
            </div>

            <table id="basketTable" data-bind="visible: total">
                <thead>
                    <tr><th>Cheese</th><th>Subtotal</th><th></th></tr>
                </thead>
                <tbody data-bind="template: {name:'basketRowTmpl', foreach: items}">

                </tbody>
                <tfoot>
                    <tr><td class="sumline" colspan=2></td></tr>
                    <tr>
                        <th>Total:</th><td>$<span data-bind="text: total"></span></td>
                    </tr>
                </tfoot>
            </table>
```

```
        </div>
        <div class="cornerplaceholder"></div>

        <div id="buttonDiv">
            <input type="submit" value="Submit Order"/>
            <input type="reset" value="Reset"/>
        </div>
    </div>

    <div data-bind="template: {name: 'categoryTmpl', data: specials}"></div>
    <form action="/shipping" method="post">
        <div data-bind="template: {name: 'categoryTmpl', foreach: products}"></div>
    </form>
</body>
...
```

I have used the ifnot binding on the div element that contains the placeholder text. KO defines a pair of bindings, if and ifnot, that are similar to the visible binding but that add and remove elements to the DOM, rather than simply hiding them from view. The if binding shows its elements when the specified view model property is true-like and hides them if it is false-like. The ifnot binding is inverted; it shows its elements when the property is true-like.

By specifying the ifnot binding with the total property, I ensure that my placeholder element is shown only when total is zero, which happens when all of the subtotal values are zero, which happens when all of the quantity values are zero. Once again, I am relying on KO's ability to manage the dependencies between observable data items to get the effect I require.

I want the table element to be invisible when the placeholder is showing, so I have used the visible binding.

I could have used the if binding, but doing so would have caused a problem. The binding to the total property means that the table will not be shown initially, and with the if binding, the element would have been removed from the DOM. This means that the a elements would also not be present when I try to select them to set up the remove buttons. The visible binding leaves the elements in the document for jQuery to find but hides them from the user.

You might wonder why I don't move the jQuery selection so that it is performed before the call to ko.applyBindings. The reason is that the a elements I want to select with jQuery are contained in the KO template, which isn't used to create elements until the applyBindings method is called. There is no good way around this, and so the visible binding is required.

The only other change to the HTML elements is the addition of an input element whose type is reset. This element is outside of the form element, so I will have to handle the click event to remove items from the basket. Listing 3-11 shows the corresponding changes to the script element.

Listing 3-11. Enhancing the Script to Finish the Example

```
...
<script>

    // ...code removed for brevity... //

    $(document).ready(function() {

        $('#buttonDiv input').button().css("font-family", "Yanone")
            .click(function() {
```

```
            if (this.type == "submit") {
                $('form').submit();
            } else if (this.type == "reset") {
                mapProducts(function(item) {
                    item.quantity(0);
                })
            }
        });

        // ...code removed for brevity... //

    });
</script>
```

I have shown only part of the script in the listing because the changes are quite minor. Notice how I am able to use jQuery and plain JavaScript to manipulate the view model. I don't need to add any code for the basket placeholder, since it will be managed by KO. In fact, all I need do is widen the jQuery selection so that I create jQuery UI button widgets for both the submit and reset input elements and add a click handler function. In the function I submit the form or change the quantity values to zero depending on which button the user clicks. You can see the placeholder for the basket in Figure 3-7.

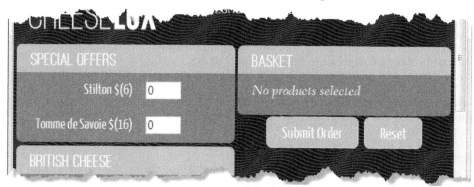

Figure 3-7. Using a placeholder when the basket is empty

You will have to load the examples in a browser if you want to see how the buttons work. The easiest way to do this is to use the source code download that accompanies this book and that is available without charge at Apress.com.

Summary

In this chapter, I showed you how to embrace the kind of design philosophy that you may have previously used in desktop or server-side development, or at least as much of that philosophy as makes sense for your project.

By adding a view model to my web app, I was able to create a much more dynamic version of the example application; it's one that is more scalable, easier to test and maintain, and makes changes and enhancement a breeze.

You may have noticed that the shape of a structured web application changes so that there is a lot more code relative to the amount of HTML markup. This is a good thing, because it puts the complexity of the application where you can better understand, test, and modify it. The HTML becomes a series of views or templates for your data, driven from the view model via the structure library. I cannot emphasize the benefits of embracing this approach enough; it really does set the foundation for professional-level web apps and will make creating, enhancing, and maintaining your projects simpler, easier, and more enjoyable.

## CHAPTER 4

Using URL Routing

In this chapter, I will show you how to add another server-side concept to your web app: URL routing. The idea behind URL routing is very simple: we associate JavaScript functions with *internal* URLs. An internal URL is one that is relative to the current document and contains a hash fragment. In fact, they are usually expressed as just the hash fragment on its own, such as #summary.

Under normal circumstances, when the user clicks a link that points to an internal URL, the browser will see whether there is an element in the document that has an id attribute value that matches the fragment and, if there is, scroll to make that element visible.

When we use URL routing, we respond to these navigation changes by executing JavaScript functions. These functions can show and hide elements, change the view model, or perform other tasks you might need in your application. Using this approach, we can provide the user with a mechanism to navigate through our application.

We could, of course, use events. The problem is, once again, scale. Handling events triggered by elements is a perfectly workable and acceptable approach for small and simple web applications. For larger and more complex apps, we need something better, and URL routing provides a nice approach that is simple, is elegant, and scales well. Adding new functional areas to the web app, and providing users with the means to use them, becomes incredibly simple and robust when we use URLs as the navigation mechanism.

Building a Simple Routed Web Application

The best way to explain URL routing is with a simple example. Listing 4-1 shows a basic web application that relies on routing.

Listing 4-1. A Simple Routed Web Application

```
<!DOCTYPE html>
<html>
<head>
    <title>Routing Example</title>
    <link rel="stylesheet" type="text/css" href="jquery-ui-1.8.16.custom.css"/>
    <link rel="stylesheet" type="text/css" href="styles.css"/>
    <script src="jquery-1.7.1.js" type="text/javascript"></script>
    <script src="jquery-ui-1.8.16.custom.js" type="text/javascript"></script>
    <script src='knockout-2.0.0.js' type='text/javascript'></script>
    <script src='utils.js' type='text/javascript'></script>
    <script src='signals.js' type='text/javascript'></script>
    <script src='crossroads.js' type='text/javascript'></script>
    <script src='hasher.js' type='text/javascript'></script>
```

```
<script>
    var viewModel = {
        items: ["Apple", "Orange", "Banana"],
        selectedItem: ko.observable("Apple")
    };

    $(document).ready(function() {
        ko.applyBindings(viewModel);

        $('div.catSelectors').buttonset();

        hasher.initialized.add(crossroads.parse, crossroads);
        hasher.changed.add(crossroads.parse, crossroads);
        hasher.init();

        crossroads.addRoute("select/Apple", function() {
            viewModel.selectedItem("Apple");
        });
        crossroads.addRoute("select/Orange", function() {
            viewModel.selectedItem("Orange");
        });
        crossroads.addRoute("select/Banana", function() {
            viewModel.selectedItem("Banana");
        });
    });
</script>
</head>
<body>
    <div class="catSelectors" data-bind="foreach: items">
        <a data-bind="formatAttr: {attr: 'href', prefix: '#select/', value: $data},
            css: {selectedItem: ($data == viewModel.selectedItem())}">
            <span data-bind="text: $data"></span>
        </a>
    </div>
    <div data-bind="foreach: items">
        <div class="item" data-bind="fadeVisible: $data == viewModel.selectedItem()">
            The selected item is: <span data-bind="text: $data"></span>
        </div>
    </div>
</body>
</html>
```

This is a relatively short listing, but there is a lot going on, so I'll break things down and explain the moving parts in the sections that follow.

Adding the Routing Library

Once again, I am going to use a publically available library to get the effect I require. There are a few URL routing libraries around, but the one that I like is called Crossroads. It is simple, reliable, and easy to use. It has one drawback, which is that it depends on two other libraries by the same author. I like to see dependencies rolled into a single library, but this is not a universally held preference, and it just means that we have to download a couple of extra files. Table 4-1 lists the projects and the JavaScript files that we require from the download archives, which should be copied into the Node.js server content directory. (All three files are part of the source code download for this book if you don't want to download these files individually. The download is freely available at Apress.com.)

Table 4-1. Crossroads JavaScript Libraries

Library Name	URL	Required File
Crossroads	http://millermedeiros.github.com/crossroads.js/	crossroads.js
Signals	http://millermedeiros.github.com/js-signals/	signals.js
Hasher	https://github.com/millermedeiros/hasher/	hasher.js

I added Crossroads, its supporting libraries, and my new cheeseutils.js file into the HTML document using script elements:

```
...
<script src="jquery-1.7.1.js" type="text/javascript"></script>
<script src="jquery-ui-1.8.16.custom.js" type="text/javascript"></script>
<script src='knockout-2.0.0.js' type='text/javascript'></script>
<script src='utils.js' type='text/javascript'></script>
<script src='signals.js' type='text/javascript'></script>
<script src='crossroads.js' type='text/javascript'></script>
<script src='hasher.js' type='text/javascript'></script>
<script>
...
```

Adding the View Model and Content Markup

URL routing works extremely well when combined with a view model in a web application. For this initial application, I have created a very simple view model, as follows:

```
var viewModel = {
    items: ["Apple", "Orange", "Banana"],
    selectedItem: ko.observable("Apple")
};
```

There are two properties in the view model. The items property refers to an array of three strings. The selectedItem property is an observable data item that keeps track of which item is presently selected. I use these values with data bindings to generate the content in the document, like this:

```
...
<div data-bind="foreach: items">
    <div class="item" data-bind="fadeVisible: $data == viewModel.selectedItem()">
        The selected item is: <span data-bind="text: $data"></span>
    </div>
</div>
...
```

The bindings that KO supports by default are pretty basic, but it is easy to create custom ones, which is exactly what I have done for the fadeVisible binding referred to in the listing. Listing 4-2 shows the definition of this binding, which I have placed in a file called utils.js (which you can see imported in a script element in Listing 4-1). There is no requirement to use an external file; I have used one because I intend to employ this binding again when I add routing to the CheeseLux example later in the chapter.

Listing 4-2. Defining a Custom Binding

```
ko.bindingHandlers.fadeVisible = {

    init: function(element, accessor) {
        $(element)[accessor() ? "show" : "hide"]();
    },

    update: function(element, accessor) {
        if (accessor() && $(element).is(":hidden")) {
            var siblings = $(element).siblings(":visible");
            if (siblings.length) {
                siblings.fadeOut("fast", function() {
                    $(element).fadeIn("fast");
                })
            } else {
                $(element).fadeIn("fast");
            }
        }
    }
}
```

Creating a custom binding is as simple as adding a new property to the ko.bindinghandlers object; the name of the property will be the name of the new binding. The value of the property is an object with two methods: init and update. The init method is called when ko.applyBindings is called, and the update method is called when observable data items that the binding depends on change.

The arguments to both methods are the element to which the binding has been applied to and an *accessor* object that provides access to the binding argument. The binding argument is whatever follows the binding name:

```
data-bind="fadeVisible: $data == viewModel.selectedItem()"
```

I have used $data in my binding argument. When using a foreach binding, $data refers to the current item in the array. I check this value against the selectedItem observable data item in the view model. I have to refer to the observable through the global variable because it is not within the context of the foreach binding, and this means I need to treat the observable like a function to get the value. When KO calls the init or update method of my custom binding, the expression in the binding argument is resolved, and the result of calling accessor() is true.

In my custom binding, the init method uses jQuery to show or hide the element to which the binding has been applied based on the accessor value. This means that only the elements that correspond to the selectedItem observable are displayed.

The update method works differently. I use jQuery effects to animate the transition from one set of elements to another. If the update method is being called for the elements that should be displayed, I select the elements that are presently visible and call the fadeOut method. This causes the elements to gradually become transparent and then invisible; once this has happened, I then use fadeIn to make the required elements visible. The result is a smooth transition from one set of elements to another.

Adding the Navigation Markup

I generate a set of a elements to provide the user with the means to select different items; in my simple application, these form the navigation markup. Here is the markup:

```
<div class="catSelectors" data-bind="foreach: items">
    <a data-bind="formatAttr: {attr: 'href', prefix: '#select/', value: $data},
        css: {selectedItem: ($data == viewModel.selectedItem())}">
            <span data-bind="text: $data">
    </a>
</div>
```

As I mentioned in Chapter 3, the built-in KO bindings simply insert values into the markup. Most of the time, this can be worked around by adding span or div elements to provide structure to which bindings can be attached. This approach doesn't work when it comes to attribute values, which is a problem when using URL routing. What I want is a series of a elements whose href attribute contains a value from the view model, like this:

```
<a href="#/select/Apple">Apple</a>
```

I can't get the result I want from the standard attr binding, so I have created another custom one. Listing 4-3 shows the definition of the formatAttr binding. I'll be using this binding later, so I have defined it in the util.js file, alongside the fadeVisible binding.

Listing 4-3. Defining the formatAttr Custom Binding

```
function composeString(bindingConfig ) {
    var result = bindingConfig.value;
    if (bindingConfig.prefix) { result = bindingConfig.prefix + result; }
    if (bindingConfig.suffix) { result += bindingConfig.suffix;}
    return result;
}

ko.bindingHandlers.formatAttr = {
    init: function(element, accessor) {
        $(element).attr(accessor().attr, composeString(accessor()));
    },
    update: function(element, accessor) {
        $(element).attr(accessor().attr, composeString(accessor()));
    }
}
```

The functionality of this binding comes through the accessor. The binding argument I have used on the element is a JavaScript object, which becomes obvious with some judicious reformatting:

```
formatAttr:
    {attr: 'href',
     prefix: '#select/',
     value: $data
    },
css: {selectedItem: ($data == viewModel.selectedItem())}
```

KO resolves the data values before passing this object to my init or update methods, giving me something like this:

81

```
{attr: 'href',
 prefix: '#select/',
 value: Apple}
```

I use the properties of this object to create the formatted string (using the composeString function I defined alongside the custom binding) to combine the content of value property with the value of the prefix and suffix properties if they are defined.

There are two other bindings. The css binding applies and removes a CSS class; I use this binding to apply the selectedItem class. This creates a simple toggle button, showing the user which button is clicked. The text binding is applied to a child span element. This is to work around a problem where jQuery UI and KO both assume control over the contents of the a element; applying the text attribute to a nested element avoids this conflict. I need this workaround because I use jQuery UI to create button widgets from the navigation elements, like this:

```
<script>
    var viewModel = {
        items: ["Apple", "Orange", "Banana"],
        selectedItem: ko.observable("Apple")
    };

    $(document).ready(function() {
        ko.applyBindings(viewModel);

        $('div.catSelectors').buttonset();

        ... other statements removed for brevity...
    });
</script>
```

By applying the buttonset method to a container element, I am able to create a set of buttons from the child a elements. I have used buttonset, rather than button, so that jQuery UI will style the elements in a contiguous block. You can see the effect that this creates in Figure 4-1.

Figure 4-1. The basic application to which routing is applied

There is no space between buttons created by the buttonset method, and the outer edges of the set are nicely rounded. You can also see one of the content elements in the figure. The idea is that clicking one of the buttons will allow the user to display the corresponding content item.

Applying URL Routing

I have almost everything in place: a set of navigational controls and a set of content elements. I now need to tie them together, which I do by applying the URL routing:

```
<script>
    var viewModel = {
        items: ["Apple", "Orange", "Banana"],
        selectedItem: ko.observable("Apple")
    };

    $(document).ready(function() {
        ko.applyBindings(viewModel);

        $('div.catSelectors').buttonset();

        hasher.initialized.add(crossroads.parse, crossroads);
        hasher.changed.add(crossroads.parse, crossroads);
        hasher.init();

        crossroads.addRoute("select/Apple", function() {
            viewModel.selectedItem("Apple");
        });
        crossroads.addRoute("select/Orange", function() {
            viewModel.selectedItem("Orange");
        });
        crossroads.addRoute("select/Banana", function() {
            viewModel.selectedItem("Banana");
        });
    });
</script>
```

The first three of the highlighted statements set up the Hasher library so that it works with Crossroads. Hasher responds to the internal URL change through the location.hash browser object and notifies Crossroads when there is a change.

Crossroads examines the new URL and compares it to each of the routes it has been given. Routes are defined using the addRoute method. The first argument to this method is the URL we are interested in, and the second argument is a function to execute if the user has navigated to that URL. So, for example, if the user navigates to #select/Apple, then the function that sets the selectedItem observable in the view model to Apple will be executed.

■ **Tip** We don't have to specify the # character when using the addRoute method because Hasher removes it before notifying Crossroads of a change.

In the example, I have defined three routes, each of which corresponds to one of the URLs that I created using the formatAttr binding on the a elements.

This is at the heart of URL routing. You create a set of URL routes that drive the behavior of the web app and then create elements in the document that navigate to those URLs. Figure 4-2 shows the effect of such navigation in the example.

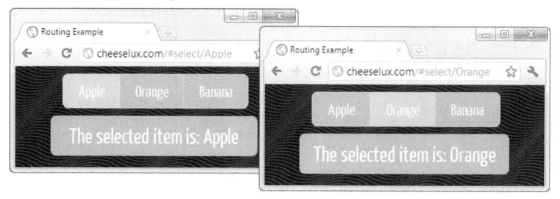

Figure 4-2. Navigating through the example web app

When the user clicks a button, the browser navigates to the URL specified by the href attribute of the underlying a element. This navigation change is detected by the routing system, which triggers the function that corresponds to the URL. The function changes the value of an observable item in the view model, and that causes the elements that represent the selected item to be displayed by the user.

The important point to understand is that we are working with the browser's navigation mechanism. When the user clicks one of the navigation elements, the browser moves to the target URL; although the URL is within the same document, the browser's history and URL bar are updated, as you can see in the figure.

This confers two benefits on a web application. The first is that the Back button works the way that most users expect it to work. The second is that the user can enter a URL manually and navigate to a specific part of the application. To see both of these behaviors in action, follow these steps:

1. Load the listing in the browser.

2. Click the Orange button.

3. Enter cheeselux.com/#select/Banana into the browser's URL bar.

4. Click the browser's Back button.

When you clicked the Orange button, the Orange item was selected, and the button was highlighted. Something similar happens for the Banana item when you entered the URL. This is because the navigation mechanism for the application is now mediated by the browser, and this is how we are able to use URL routing to decouple another aspect of the application.

The first benefit is, to my mind, the most useful. When the user clicks the Back button, the browser navigates back to the last visited URL. This is a navigation change, and if the previous URL is within our document, the new URL is matched against the set of routes defined by the application. This is an opportunity to unwind the application state to the previous step, which in the case of the sample application displays the Orange button. This is a much more natural way of working for a user, especially compared to using regular events, where clicking the Back button tends to navigate to the site the user visited *before* our application.

Consolidating Routes

In the previous example, I defined each route and the function it executed separately. If this were the only way to define routes, a complex web app would end up with a morass of routes and functions, and there would be no advantage over regular event handling. Fortunately, URLs routing is very flexible, and we can consolidate our routes with ease. I describe the techniques available for this in the sections that follow.

Using Variable Segments

Listing 4-4 shows how easy it is to consolidate the three routes from the earlier demonstration into a single route.

Listing 4-4. Consolidating Routes

```
<script>
    var viewModel = {
        items: ["Apple", "Orange", "Banana"],
        selectedItem: ko.observable("Apple")
    };

    $(document).ready(function() {
        ko.applyBindings(viewModel);

        $('div.catSelectors').buttonset();

        hasher.initialized.add(crossroads.parse, crossroads);
        hasher.changed.add(crossroads.parse, crossroads);
        hasher.init();

        crossroads.addRoute("select/{item}", function(item) {
            viewModel.selectedItem(item);
        });
    });
</script>
```

The path section of a URL is made up of segments. For example, the URL path select/Apple has two segments, which are select and Apple. When I specify a route, like this:

```
/select/Apple
```

the route will match a URL only if both segments match exactly. In the listing, I have been able to consolidate my routes by adding a *variable segment*. A variable segment allows a route to match a URL that has any value for the corresponding segment. So, to be clear, all of the navigation URLs in the simple web app will match my new route:

```
select/Apple
select/Orange
select/Banana
```

The first segment is still *static*, meaning that only URLs whose first segment is select will match, but I have essentially added a wildcard for the second segment.

So that I can respond appropriately to the URL, the content of the variable segment is passed to my function as an argument. I use this argument to change the value of the selectedItem observable in the view model, meaning that a URL of /select/Apple results in a call like this:

```
viewModel.selectedItem('Apple');
```

and a URL of select/Cherry will result in a call like this:

```
viewModel.selectedItem('Cherry');
```

Dealing with Unexpected Segment Values

That last URL is a problem. There isn't an item called Cherry in my web app, and setting the view model observable to this value will create an odd effect for the user, as shown in Figure 4-3.

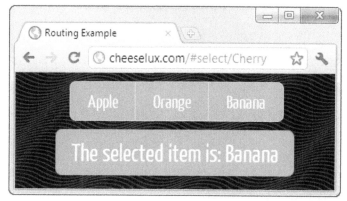

Figure 4-3. The result of an unexpected variable segment value

The flexibility that comes with URL routing can also be a problem. Being able to navigate to a specific part of the application is a useful tool for the user, but, as with all opportunities for the user to provide input, we have to guard against unexpected values. For my example application, the simplest way to validate variable segment values is to check the contents of the array in the view model, as shown in Listing 4-5.

Listing 4-5. Ignoring Unexpected Segment Values

```
...
crossroads.addRoute("select/{item}", function(item) {
    if (viewModel.items.indexOf(item) > -1) {
        viewModel.selectedItem(item);
    }
});
...
```

In this listing, I have taken the path of least resistance, which is to simply ignore unexpected values. There are lots of alternative approaches. I could have displayed an error message or, as Listing 4-6 shows, embraced the unexpected value and added it to the view model.

Listing 4-6. Dealing with Unexpected Values by Adding Them to the View Model

```
<script>
    var viewModel = {
        items: ko.observableArray(["Apple", "Orange", "Banana"]),
        selectedItem: ko.observable("Apple")
    };

    $(document).ready(function() {
        ko.applyBindings(viewModel);

        $('div.catSelectors').buttonset();

        hasher.initialized.add(crossroads.parse, crossroads);
        hasher.changed.add(crossroads.parse, crossroads);
        hasher.init();

        crossroads.addRoute("select/{item}", function(item) {
            if (viewModel.items.indexOf(item)== -1) {
                viewModel.items.push(item);
                $('div.catSelectors').buttonset();
            }
            viewModel.selectedItem(item);
        });
    });
</script>
```

If the value of the variable segment isn't one of the values in the items array in the view model, then I use the push method to add the new value. I changed the view model so that the items array is an observable item using the ko.observableArray method. An observable array is like a regular observable data item, except that bindings such as foreach are updated when the content of the array changes. Using an observable array means that adding an item causes Knockout to generate content and navigation elements in the document.

The last step in this process is to call the jQuery UI buttonset method again. KO has no knowledge of the jQuery UI styles that are applied to an a element to create a button, and this method has to be reapplied to get the right effect. You can see the result of navigating to #select/Cherry in Figure 4-4.

Figure 4-4. Incorporating unexpected segment values into the application state

Using Optional Segments

The limitation of variable segments is that the URL must contain a segment value to match a route. For example, the route select/{item} will match any two-segment URL where the first segment is select, but it won't match select/Apple/Red (because there are too many segments) or select (because there are too few segments).

We can use optional segments to increase the flexibility of our routes. Listing 4-7 shows the application on an optional segment to the example.

Listing 4-7. Using an Optional Segment in a Route

```
...
crossroads.addRoute("select/:item:", function(item) {
    if (!item) {
        item = "Apple";
    } else  if (viewModel.items.indexOf(item)== -1) {
        viewModel.items.push(item);
        $('div.catSelectors').buttonset();
    }
    viewModel.selectedItem(item);
});
...
```

To create an optional segment, I simply replace the brace characters with colons so that {item} becomes :item:. With this change, the route will match URLs that have one or two segments and where the first segment is select. If there is no second segment, then the argument passed to the function will be null. In my listing, I default to the Apple value if this is the case. A route can contain as many static, variable, and optional segments as you require. I will keep my routes simple in this example, but you can create pretty much any combination you require.

Adding a Default Route

With the introduction of the optional segment, my route will match one- and two-segment URLs. The final route I want to add is a *default route*, which is one that will be invoked when there are no segments in the URL at all. This is required to complete the support for the Back button. To see the problem I am solving, load the listing into the browser, click one of the navigation elements, and then hit the Back button. You can see the effect—or, rather, the lack of an effect—in Figure 4-5.

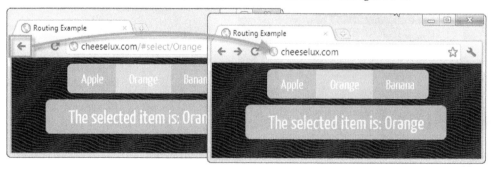

Figure 4-5. Navigating back to the application starting point

The application doesn't reset to its original state when the Back button is clicked. This happens only when clicking the Back button takes the browser back to the base URL for the web app (which is http://cheeselux.com in my case). Nothing happens because the base URL doesn't match the routes that the application defines. Listing 4-8 shows the addition of a new route to fix this problem.

Listing 4-8. Adding a Route for the Base URL

```
...
<script>
    var viewModel = {
        items: ko.observableArray(["Apple", "Orange", "Banana"]),
        selectedItem: ko.observable("Apple")
    };

    $(document).ready(function() {
        ko.applyBindings(viewModel);

        $('div.catSelectors').buttonset();

        hasher.initialized.add(crossroads.parse, crossroads);
        hasher.changed.add(crossroads.parse, crossroads);
        hasher.init();

        crossroads.addRoute("select/:item:", function(item) {
            if (!item) {
                item = "Apple";
            } else  if (viewModel.items.indexOf(item)== -1) {
                viewModel.items.push(item);
                $('div.catSelectors').buttonset();
            }
            viewModel.selectedItem(item);
        });

        crossroads.addRoute("", function() {
            viewModel.selectedItem("Apple");
        })

    });
</script>
...
```

This route contains no segments of any kind and will match only the base URL. Clicking the Back button until the base URL is reached now causes the application to return to its initial state. (Well, it returns sort of back to its original state; later in this chapter I'll explain a wrinkle in this approach and show you how to improve upon it.)

Adapting Event-Driven Controls to Navigation

It is not always possible to limit the elements in a document so that all navigation can be handled through a elements. When adding JavaScript events to a routed application, I follow a simple pattern that bridges between URL routing and conventional events and that gives me a lot of the benefits of routing and lets me use other kinds of elements as well. Listing 4-9 shows this pattern applied to some other element types.

Listing 4-9. Bridging Between URL Routing and JavaScript Events

```
...
<script>
    var viewModel = {
        items: ko.observableArray(["Apple", "Orange", "Banana"]),
        selectedItem: ko.observable("Apple")
    };

    $(document).ready(function() {
        ko.applyBindings(viewModel);

        $('div.catSelectors').buttonset();

        hasher.initialized.add(crossroads.parse, crossroads);
        hasher.changed.add(crossroads.parse, crossroads);
        hasher.init();

        crossroads.addRoute("select/:item:", function(item) {
            if (!item) {
                item = "Apple";
            } else  if (viewModel.items.indexOf(item)== -1) {
                viewModel.items.push(item);
                $('div.catSelectors').buttonset();
            }
            if (viewModel.selectedItem() != item) {
                viewModel.selectedItem(item);
            }
        });

        crossroads.addRoute("", function() {
            viewModel.selectedItem("Apple");
        })

        $('[data-url]').live("change click", function(e) {
            var target = $(e.target).attr("data-url");
            if (e.target.tagName == 'SELECT') {
                target += $(e.target).children("[selected]").val();
            }
            if (location.hash != target) {
                location.replace(target);
            }
        })
    });
</script>
...
```

The technique here is to add a data-url attribute to the elements whose events should result in a navigation change. I use jQuery to handle the change and click events for elements that have the data-url attribute. Handling both events allows me to cater for the different kinds of input elements. I use the live method, which is a neat jQuery feature that relies on event propagation to ensure that events are handled for elements that are added to the document after the script has executed; this is essential when the set of elements in the document can be altered in response to view model changes. This approach allows me to use elements like this:

```
...
<div class="eventElemContainer" data-bind="foreach: items">
    <label data-bind="attr: {for: $data}">
        <span data-bind="text: $data"></span>
        <input type="radio" name="item" data-bind="attr: {id: $data},
            formatAttr: {attr: 'data-url', prefix: '#select/', value: $data}">
    </label>
</div>
...
```

This markup generates a set of radio buttons for each element in the view model items array. I create the value for the data-url attribute with my custom formatAttr data binding, which I described earlier. The select element requires some special handling because while the select element triggers the change event, the information about which value has been selected is derived from the child option elements. Here is some markup that creates a select element that works with this pattern:

```
...
<div class="eventElemContainer">
    <select name="eventItemSelect" data-bind="foreach: items,
            attr: {'data-url': '#select/'}">
        <option data-bind="value: $data, text: $data,
            selected: $data == viewModel.selectedItem()">
        </option>
    </select>
</div>
...
```

Part of the target URL is in the data-url attribute of the select element, and the rest is taken from the value attribute of the option elements. Some elements, including select, trigger both the click and change events, so I check to see that the target URL differs from the current URL before using location.replace to trigger a navigation change. Listing 4-10 shows how this technique can be applied to select elements, buttons, radio buttons, and check boxes.

Listing 4-10. Bridging Between Events and Routing for Different Kinds of Elements

```
<!DOCTYPE html>
<html>
<head>
    <title>Routing Example</title>
    <link rel="stylesheet" type="text/css" href="jquery-ui-1.8.16.custom.css"/>
    <link rel="stylesheet" type="text/css" href="styles.css"/>
    <script src="jquery-1.7.1.js" type="text/javascript"></script>
    <script src="jquery-ui-1.8.16.custom.js" type="text/javascript"></script>
    <script src='knockout-2.0.0.js' type='text/javascript'></script>
    <script src='utils.js' type='text/javascript'></script>
    <script src='signals.js' type='text/javascript'></script>
    <script src='crossroads.js' type='text/javascript'></script>
```

```
<script src='hasher.js' type='text/javascript'></script>
<script>
    var viewModel = {
        items: ko.observableArray(["Apple", "Orange", "Banana"]),
        selectedItem: ko.observable("Apple")
    };

    $(document).ready(function() {
        ko.applyBindings(viewModel);

        $('div.catSelectors').buttonset();

        hasher.initialized.add(crossroads.parse, crossroads);
        hasher.changed.add(crossroads.parse, crossroads);
        hasher.init();

        crossroads.addRoute("select/:item:", function(item) {
            if (!item) {
                item = "Apple";
            } else  if (viewModel.items.indexOf(item)== -1) {
                viewModel.items.push(item);
                $('div.catSelectors').buttonset();
            }
            if (viewModel.selectedItem() != item) {
                viewModel.selectedItem(item);
            }
        });

        crossroads.addRoute("", function() {
            viewModel.selectedItem("Apple");
        })

        $('[data-url]').live("change click", function(e) {
            var target = $(e.target).attr("data-url");
            if (e.target.tagName == 'SELECT') {
                target += $(e.target).children("[selected]").val();
            }
            if (location.hash != target) {
                location.replace(target);
            }
        })
    });
</script>
</head>
<body>
    <div class="catSelectors" data-bind="foreach: items">
        <a data-bind="formatAttr: {attr: 'href', prefix: '#select/', value: $data},
            css: {selectedItem: ($data == viewModel.selectedItem())}">
            <span data-bind="text: $data"></span>
        </a>
    </div>
    <div data-bind="foreach: items">
```

```
        <div class="item" data-bind="fadeVisible: $data == viewModel.selectedItem()">
            The selected item is: <span data-bind="text: $data"></span>
        </div>
    </div>

    <div class="eventElemContainer">
        <select name="eventItemSelect" data-bind="foreach: items,
                attr: {'data-url': '#select/'}">
            <option data-bind="value: $data, text: $data,
                selected: $data == viewModel.selectedItem()">
            </option>
        </select>
    </div>

    <div class="eventElemContainer" data-bind="foreach: items">
        <input type="button" data-bind="value: $data,
            formatAttr: {attr: 'data-url', prefix: '#select/', value: $data}" />
    </div>

    <div class="eventElemContainer" data-bind="foreach: items">
        <label data-bind="attr: {for: $data}">
            <span data-bind="text: $data"></span>
            <input type="checkbox" data-bind="attr: {id: $data},
                formatAttr: {attr: 'data-url', prefix: '#select/', value: $data}">
        </label>
    </div>

    <div class="eventElemContainer" data-bind="foreach: items">
        <label data-bind="attr: {for: $data}">
            <span data-bind="text: $data"></span>
            <input type="radio" name="item" data-bind="attr: {id: $data},
                formatAttr: {attr: 'data-url', prefix: '#select/', value: $data}">
        </label>
    </div>
</body>
</html>
```

I have defined another custom binding to correctly set the selected attribute on the appropriate option element. I called this binding selected (obviously enough), and it is defined, as shown in Listing 4-11, in the utils.js file.

Listing 4-11. The Selected Data Binding

```
ko.bindingHandlers.selected = {
    init: function(element, accessor) {
        if (accessor()) {
            $(element).siblings("[selected]").removeAttr("selected");
            $(element).attr("selected", "selected");
        }
    },
    update: function(element, accessor) {
```

```
        if (accessor()) {
            $(element).siblings("[selected]").removeAttr("selected");
            $(element).attr("selected", "selected");
        }
    }
}
```

You might be tempted to simply handle events and trigger the application changes directly. This works, but you will have just added to the complexity of your application by taking on the overhead or creating and managing routes *and* keeping track of which events from which elements trigger difference state changes. My recommendation is to focus on URL routing and use bridging, as described here, to funnel events from elements into the routing system.

Using the HTML5 History API

The Crossroads library I have been using so far in this chapter depends on the Hasher library from the same author to receive notifications when the URL changes. The Hasher library monitors the URL and tells Crossroads when it changes, triggering the routing behavior.

There is a weakness in this approach, which is that the state of the application isn't preserved as part of the browser history. Here are some steps to demonstrate the issue:

1. Load the listing into the browser.

2. Click the Orange button.

3. Navigate directly to #select/Cherry.

4. Click the Banana button.

5. Click the Back button twice.

Everything starts off well enough. When you navigated to the #select/Cherry URL, the new item was added to the view model and selected properly. When you clicked the Back button the first time, the Cherry item was correctly selected again. The problem arises when you clicked the Back button for the second time. The selected item was correctly wound back to Orange, but the Cherry item remained on the list. The application is able to use the URL to select the correct item, but when the Orange item was selected originally, there was no Cherry item in the view model, and yet it is still displayed to the user.

For some web applications, this won't be a big deal, and it isn't for this simple example, either. After all, it doesn't really matter if the user can select an item that they explicitly added in the first place. But for other web apps, this is a critical issue, and making sure that the view model is correctly preserved in the browser history is essential. We can address this using the HTML5 History API, which gives us more access to the browser history than web programmers have previously enjoyed. We access the History API through the windows.history or global history object. There are two aspects of the History API that I am interested in for this situation.

◾ **Note** I am not going to cover the HTML5 API beyond what is needed to maintain application state. I provide full details in *The Definitive Guide to HTML5*, also published by Apress. You can read the W3C specification at http://dev.w3.org/html5/spec (the information on the History API is in section 5.4, but this may change since the HTML5 specification is still in draft).

The history.replaceState method lets you associate a state object with the entry in the browser's history for the current document. There are three arguments to this method; the first is the state object, the second argument is the title to use in the history, and the third is the URL for the document. The second argument isn't used by the current generation of browsers, but the URL argument allows you to effectively replace the URL in the history that is associated with the current document. The part I am interested in for this chapter is the first argument, which I will use to store the contents of the viewModel.items array in the history so that I can properly maintain the state when the user clicks the Back and Forward buttons.

◾ **Tip** You can also insert new items into the history using the history.pushState method. This method takes the same arguments as replaceState and can be useful for inserting additional state information.

The window browser object triggers a popstate event whenever the active history entry changes. If the entry has state information associated with it (because the replaceState or pushState method was used), then you can retrieve the state object through the history.state property.

Adding History State to the Example Application

Things aren't quite as simple as you might like when it comes to using the History API; it suffers from two problems that are common to most of the HTML5 APIs. The first problem is that not all browsers support the History API. Obviously, pre-HTML5 browsers don't know about the History API, but even some browser versions that support other HTML5 features do not implement the History API.

The second problem is that those browsers that *do* implement the HTML5 API introduce inconsistencies, which requires some careful testing. So, even as the History API helps us solve one problem, we are faced with others. Even so, the History API is worth using, as long as you accept that it isn't universally supported and that a fallback is required. Listing 4-12 shows the addition of the History API to the simple example web app.

Listing 4-12. Using the HTML5 History API to Preserve View Model State

```
<!DOCTYPE html>
<html>
<head>
    <title>Routing Example</title>
    <link rel="stylesheet" type="text/css" href="jquery-ui-1.8.16.custom.css"/>
```

```
<link rel="stylesheet" type="text/css" href="styles.css"/>
<script src="jquery-1.7.1.js" type="text/javascript"></script>
<script src="jquery-ui-1.8.16.custom.js" type="text/javascript"></script>
<script src="modernizr-2.0.6.js" type="text/javascript"></script>
<script src='knockout-2.0.0.js' type='text/javascript'></script>
<script src='utils.js' type='text/javascript'></script>
<script src='signals.js' type='text/javascript'></script>
<script src='crossroads.js' type='text/javascript'></script>
<script src='hasher.js' type='text/javascript'></script>
<script>
    var viewModel = {
        items: ko.observableArray(["Apple", "Orange", "Banana"]),
        selectedItem: ko.observable("Apple")
    };

    $(document).ready(function() {
        ko.applyBindings(viewModel);

        $('div.catSelectors').buttonset();

        crossroads.addRoute("select/:item:", function(item) {
            if (!item) {
                item = "Apple";
            } else  if (viewModel.items.indexOf(item)== -1) {
                viewModel.items.push(item);
            }

            if (viewModel.selectedItem() != item) {
                viewModel.selectedItem(item);
            }

            $('div.catSelectors').buttonset();
            if (Modernizr.history) {
                history.replaceState(viewModel.items(), document.title, location);
            }
        });

        crossroads.addRoute("", function() {
            viewModel.selectedItem("Apple");
        })

        if (Modernizr.history) {
            $(window).bind("popstate", function(event) {
                var state = history.state ? history.state
                    : event.originalEvent.state;
                if (state) {
                    viewModel.items.removeAll();
                    $.each(state, function(index, item) {
                        viewModel.items.push(item);
                    });
                }
```

```
                    crossroads.parse(location.hash.slice(1));
                });
            } else {
                hasher.initialized.add(crossroads.parse, crossroads);
                hasher.changed.add(crossroads.parse, crossroads);
                hasher.init();
            }

        });
    </script>
</head>
<body>
    <div class="catSelectors" data-bind="foreach: items">
        <a data-bind="formatAttr: {attr: 'href', prefix: '#select/', value: $data},
            css: {selectedItem: ($data == viewModel.selectedItem())}">
            <span data-bind="text: $data"></span>
        </a>
    </div>
    <div data-bind="foreach: items">
        <div class="item" data-bind="fadeVisible: $data == viewModel.selectedItem()">
            The selected item is: <span data-bind="text: $data"></span>
        </div>
    </div>
</body>
</html>
```

Storing the Application State

The first set of changes in the listing stores the application state when the main application route matches a URL. By responding to the URL change, I am able to preserve the state whenever the user clicks one of the navigation elements or enters a URL directly. Here is the code that stores the state:

```
...
<script src="modernizr-2.0.6.js" type="text/javascript"></script>
...
crossroads.addRoute("select/:item:", function(item) {
    if (!item) {
        item = "Apple";
    } else  if (viewModel.items.indexOf(item)== -1) {
        viewModel.items.push(item);
    }

    if (viewModel.selectedItem() != item) {
        viewModel.selectedItem(item);
    }

    $('div.catSelectors').buttonset();
    if (Modernizr.history) {
        history.replaceState(viewModel.items(), document.title, location);
    }
});
...
```

The new script element in the listing adds the Modernizr library to the web app. Modernizr is a *feature-detection library* that contains checks to determine whether numerous HTML5 and CSS3 features are supported by the browser. You can download Modernizr and get full details of the features it can detect at http://modernizr.com.

I don't want to call the methods of the History API unless I am sure that the browser implements it, so I check the value of the Modernizr.history property. A value of true means that the History API has been detected, and a value of false means the API isn't present.

You could write your own feature-detection tests if you prefer. As an example, here is the code behind the Modernizr.history test:

```
tests['history'] = function() {
    return !!(window.history && history.pushState);
};
```

Modernizr simply checks to see whether history.pushState is defined by the browser. I prefer to use a library like Modernizr because the tests it performs are well-validated and updated as needed and, further, because not all of the tests are quite so simple.

☰ **Tip** Feature-detection libraries such as Modernizr don't make any assessment of how well a feature has been implemented. The presence of the history.pushState method indicates that the History API is present, but it doesn't provide any insights into quirks or oddities that may have to be reckoned with. In short, a feature-detection library is no substitute for thoroughly testing your code on a range of browsers.

If the History API *is* present, then I call the replaceState method to associate the value of the view model items array with the current URL. I can perform no action if the History API isn't available because there isn't an alternative mechanism for storing state in the browser (although I could have used a *polyfill*; see the sidebar for details).

USING A HISTORY POLYFILL

A *polyfill* is a JavaScript library that provides support for an API for older browsers. Pollyfilla, from which the name originates, is the U.K. equivalent of the Spackle home-repair product, and the idea is that a polyfill library smoothes out the development landscape. Polyfill libraries can also work around differences between browser implementation features. The History API may seem like an ideal candidate for a polyfill, but the problem is that the browser doesn't provide any alternative means of storing state objects. The most common workaround is to express the state as part of the URL so that we might end up with something like this:

http://cheeselux.com/#select/Banana?items=Apple,Orange,Banana,Cherry

I don't like this approach because I don't like to see complex data types expressed in this way, and I think it produces confusing URLs. But you might feel differently, or a stateful history feature may be critical to your project. If that's the case, then the best History API polyfill that I have found is called History.js and is at http://github.com/balupton/history.js.

Restoring the Application State

Of course, storing the application state isn't enough. I also have to be able to restore it, and that means responding to the popstate event when it is triggered by a URL change. Here is the code:

```
...
crossroads.addRoute("select/:item:", function(item) {

    ...other statements removed for brevity...

    if (Modernizr.history) {
        $(window).bind("popstate", function(event) {
            var state = history.state ? history.state
                : event.originalEvent.state;
            if (state) {
                viewModel.items.removeAll();
                $.each(state, function(index, item) {
                    viewModel.items.push(item);
                });
            }
            crossroads.parse(location.hash.slice(1));
        });
    } else {
        hasher.initialized.add(crossroads.parse, crossroads);
        hasher.changed.add(crossroads.parse, crossroads);
        hasher.init();
    }
});
...
```

I have used Modernizr.history to check for the API before I use the bind method to register a handler function for the popstate event. This isn't strictly necessary since the event simply won't be triggered if the API isn't present, but I like to make it obvious that this block of code is related to the History API.

You can see an example of catering to a browser oddity in the function that handles the popstate event. The history.state property should return the state object associated with the current URL, but Google Chrome doesn't support this, and the value must be obtained from the state property of the Event object instead. jQuery normalizes Event objects, which means that I have to use the originalEvent property to get to the underlying event object that the browser generated, like this:

var state = history.state ? history.state: **event.originalEvent.state**;

With this approach I can get the state data from history.state if it is available and the event if it is not. Sadly, using the HTML5 APIs often requires this kind of workaround, although I expect the consistency of the various implementations will improve over time.

I can't rely on there being a state object every time the popstate event is triggered because not all entries in the browser history will have state associated with them.

When there *is* state data, I use the removeAll method to clear the items array in the view model and then populate it with the items obtained from the state data using the jQuery each function:

```
if (state) {
    viewModel.items.removeAll();
    $.each(state, function(index, item) {
        viewModel.items.push(item);
    });
}
```

Once the content of the view model has been set, I notify Crossroads that there has been a change in URL by calling the parse method. This was the function previously handled by the Hasher library, which removed the leading # character from URLs before passing them to Crossroads. I do the same to maintain compatibility with the routes I defined earlier:

```
crossroads.parse(location.hash.slice(1));
```

I want to preserve compatibility because I don't want to assume that the user has an HTML5 browser that supports the History API. To that end, if the Modernizr.history property is false, I fall back to using Hasher so that the basic functionality of the web app still works, even if I can't provide the state management feature:

```
if (Modernizr.history) {
    ...History API code...
} else {
    hasher.initialized.add(crossroads.parse, crossroads);
    hasher.changed.add(crossroads.parse, crossroads);
    hasher.init();
}
```

With these changes, I am able to use the History API when it is available to manage the state of the application and unwind it when the user uses the Back button. Figure 4-6 shows the key step from the sequence of tasks I had you perform at the start of this section. As the user moves back through the history, the Cherry item disappears.

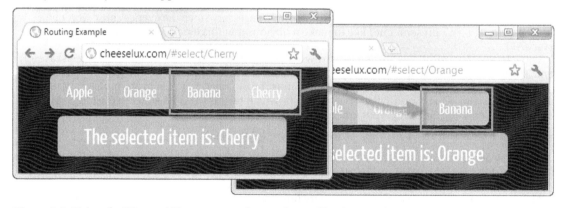

Figure 4-6. Using the History API to manage changes in application state

As an aside, I chose to store the application state every time the URL changed because it allows me to support the Forward button as well as the Back button. From the state shown in the figure, clicking the Forward button restores the Cherry item to the view model, demonstrating that the application state is properly preserved and restored in both directions.

Adding URL Routing to the CheeseLux Web App

I switched to a simple example in this chapter because I didn't want to overwhelm the routing code (which is pretty sparse) with the markup and data bindings (which can be verbose). But now that I have explained how URL routing works, it is time to introduce it to the CheeseLux demo, as shown in Listing 4-13.

Listing 4-13. Adding Routing to the CheeseLux Example

```
<!DOCTYPE html>
<html>
<head>
    <title>CheeseLux</title>
    <link rel="stylesheet" type="text/css" href="styles.css"/>
    <script src="jquery-1.7.1.js" type="text/javascript"></script>
    <script src="jquery-ui-1.8.16.custom.js" type="text/javascript"></script>
    <script src='knockout-2.0.0.js' type='text/javascript'></script>
    <script src='utils.js' type='text/javascript'></script>
    <script src='signals.js' type='text/javascript'></script>
    <script src='crossroads.js' type='text/javascript'></script>
    <link rel="stylesheet" type="text/css" href="jquery-ui-1.8.16.custom.css"/>
    <noscript>
        <meta http-equiv="refresh" content="0; noscript.html"/>
    </noscript>
    <script>
        var cheeseModel = {
            products: [
                {category: "British Cheese", items : [
                    {id: "stilton", name: "Stilton", price: 9},
                    {id: "stinkingbishop", name: "Stinking Bishop", price: 17},
                    {id: "cheddar", name: "Cheddar", price: 17}]},
                {category: "French Cheese", items: [
                    {id: "camembert", name: "Camembert", price: 18},
                    {id: "tomme", name: "Tomme de Savoie", price: 19},
                    {id: "morbier", name: "Morbier", price: 9}]},
                {category: "Italian Cheese", items: [
                    {id: "gorgonzola", name: "Gorgonzola", price: 8},
                    {id: "fontina", name: "Fontina", price: 11},
                    {id: "parmesan", name: "Parmesan", price: 16}]}]
        };

        $(document).ready(function() {
            $('#buttonDiv input:submit').button().css("font-family", "Yanone");

            cheeseModel.selectedCategory =
                ko.observable(cheeseModel.products[0].category);

            mapProducts(function(item) {
                item.quantity = ko.observable(0);
                item.subtotal = ko.computed(function() {
                    return this.quantity() * this.price;
```

101

```
        }, item);
        item.quantity.subscribe(function() {
            updateState();
        });
    }, cheeseModel.products, "items");

    cheeseModel.total = ko.computed(function() {
        var total = 0;
        mapProducts(function(elem) {
            total += elem.subtotal();
        }, cheeseModel.products, "items");
        return total;
    });

    $('div.cheesegroup').not("#basket").css("width", "50%");
    $('div.navSelectors').buttonset();

    ko.applyBindings(cheeseModel);

    $(window).bind("popstate", function(event) {
        var state = history.state ? history.state : event.originalEvent.state;
        restoreState(state);
        crossroads.parse(location.hash.slice(1));
    });

    crossroads.addRoute("category/:newCat:", function(newCat) {
        cheeseModel.selectedCategory(newCat ?
            newCat : cheeseModel.products[0].category);
        updateState();
    });

    crossroads.addRoute("remove/{id}", function(id) {
        mapProducts(function(item) {
            if (item.id == id) {
                item.quantity(0);
            }
        }, cheeseModel.products, "items");
    });

    $('#basketTable a')
        .button({icons: {primary: "ui-icon-closethick"},text: false});

    function updateState() {
        var state = {
            category: cheeseModel.selectedCategory()
        };
        mapProducts(function(item) {
            if (item.quantity() > 0) {
                state[item.id] = item.quantity();
            }
        }, cheeseModel.products, "items");
        history.replaceState(state, "",
```

```
                        "#select/" + cheeseModel.selectedCategory());
            }

            function restoreState(state) {
                if (state) {
                    mapProducts(function(item) {
                        item.quantity(state[item.id] ? state[item.id] : 0);
                    }, cheeseModel.products, "items");
                    cheeseModel.selectedCategory(state.category);
                }
            }
        });
    </script>
</head>
<body>
    <div id="logobar">
        <img src="cheeselux.png">
        <span id="tagline">Gourmet European Cheese</span>
    </div>

    <div class="cheesegroup">
        <div class="navSelectors" data-bind="foreach: products">
            <a data-bind="formatAttr: {attr: 'href', prefix: '#category/',
                value: category},
            css: {selectedItem: (category == cheeseModel.selectedCategory())}">
                <span data-bind="text: category">
            </a>
        </div>
    </div>

    <div id="basket" class="cheesegroup basket">
        <div class="grouptitle">Basket</div>
        <div class="groupcontent">

            <div class="description" data-bind="ifnot: total">
                No products selected
            </div>

            <table id="basketTable" data-bind="visible: total">
                <thead><tr><th>Cheese</th><th>Subtotal</th><th></th></tr></thead>
                <tbody data-bind="foreach: products">
                    <!-- ko foreach: items -->
                        <tr data-bind="visible: quantity, attr: {'data-prodId': id}">
                            <td data-bind="text: name"></td>
                            <td>$<span data-bind="text: subtotal"></span></td>
                            <td>
                                <a data-bind="formatAttr: {attr: 'href',
                                    prefix: '#remove/', value: id}"></a>
                            </td>
                        </tr>
                    <!-- /ko -->
                </tbody>
```

```
                    <tfoot>
                        <tr><td class="sumline" colspan=2></td></tr>
                        <tr>
                            <th>Total:</th><td>$<span data-bind="text: total"></span></td>
                        </tr>
                    </tfoot>
                </table>
            </div>
            <div class="cornerplaceholder"></div>

            <div id="buttonDiv">
                <input type="submit" value="Submit Order"/>
            </div>
        </div>

        <form action="/shipping" method="post">
            <!-- ko foreach: products -->
            <div class="cheesegroup"
                 data-bind="fadeVisible: category == cheeseModel.selectedCategory()">
                <div class="grouptitle" data-bind="text: category"></div>
                <div data-bind="foreach: items">
                    <div class="groupcontent">
                        <label data-bind="attr: {for: id}" class="cheesename">
                            <span data-bind="text: name">
                            </span> $(<span data-bind="text:price"></span>)</label>
                        <input data-bind="attr: {name: id}, value: quantity"/>
                        <span data-bind="visible: subtotal" class="subtotal">
                            ($<span data-bind="text: subtotal"></span>)
                        </span>
                    </div>
                </div>
            </div>
            <!-- /ko -->
        </form>
    </body>
</html>
```

I am not going to break this listing down line by line because much of functionality is similar to previous examples. There are, however, a couple of techniques that are worth learning and some changes that I need to explain, all of which I'll cover in the sections that follow. Figure 4-7 shows how the web app appears in the browser.

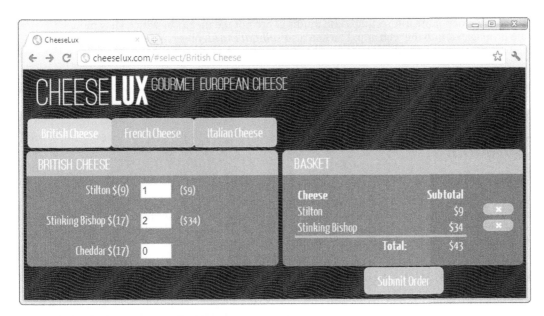

Figure 4-7. Adding routing to the CheeseLux example

Moving the mapProducts Function

The first change, and the most basic, is that I have moved the mapProducts function into the util.js file. In Chapter 9, I am going to show you how to package up this kind of function more usefully, and I don't want to keep recycling the same code in the listings. As I moved the function, I rewrote it so that it can work on any set of nested arrays. Listing 4-14 shows the new version of this function.

Listing 4-14. The Revised mapProducts Function

```
function mapProducts(func, data, indexer) {
    $.each(data, function(outerIndex, outerItem) {
        $.each(outerItem[indexer], function(itemIndex, innerItem) {
            func(innerItem, outerItem);
        });
    });
}
```

The two new arguments to the function are the outer nested array and the property name of the inner array. You can see how I have used this in the main listing so that the arguments are cheeseModel.products and items, respectively.

Enhancing the View Model

I made two changes to the view model. The first was to define an observable data item to capture the selected cheese category:

```
cheeseModel.selectedCategory = ko.observable(cheeseModel.products[0].category);
```

105

The second is much more interesting. Data bindings are not the means by which view model changes are propagated into the web app. You can also *subscribe* to an observable data item and specify a function that will be executed when the value changes. Here is the subscription I created:

```
mapProducts(function(item) {
    item.quantity = ko.observable(0);
    item.subtotal = ko.computed(function() {
        return this.quantity() * this.price;
    }, item);
    item.quantity.subscribe(function() {
        updateState();
    });
}, cheeseModel.products, "items");
```

I subscribed to the quantity observable on each cheese product. When the value changes, the updateState function will be executed. I'll describe this function shortly. Subscriptions are rather like events for the view model; they can be useful in any number of situations, and I often find myself using them when I want some task performed automatically.

Managing Application State

I want to preserve two kinds of state in this web app. The first is the selected product category, and the second is the contents of the basket. I store state information in the browser's history in the updateState function, which is executed whenever my quantity subscription is triggered or the selected category changes.

■ **Tip** The technique that I demonstrate here is a little odd when applied to a shopping basket, because web sites will usually go to great lengths to preserve your product selections. Ignore this, if you will, and focus on the state management technique, which is the real purpose of this section.

```
function updateState() {
    var state = {
        category: cheeseModel.selectedCategory()
    };
    mapProducts(function(item) {
        if (item.quantity() > 0) {
            state[item.id] = item.quantity();
        }
    }, cheeseModel.products, "items");
    history.replaceState(state, "", "#select/" + cheeseModel.selectedCategory());
}
```

■ **Tip** This listing requires the HTML5 History API, and unlike the earlier examples in this chapter, there is no fallback to the HTML4-compatible approach taken by the Hasher library.

I create an object that has a category property that contains the name of the selected category and one property for each individual cheese that has a nonzero quantity value. I write this to the browser history using the replaceState method, which I have highlighted in the listing.

Something clever is happening here. To explain what I am doing—and why—we have to start with the markup for the navigation elements that remove products from the basket. Here is the relevant HTML:

```
<a data-bind="formatAttr: {attr: 'href', prefix: '#remove/', value: id}"></a>
```

When the data bindings are applied, I end up with an element like this:

```
<a href="#/remove/stilton"></a>
```

In Chapter 3, I removed items from the basket by handling the click event from these elements. Now that I am using URL routing, I have to define a route, which I do like this:

```
crossroads.addRoute("remove/{id}", function(id) {
    mapProducts(function(item) {
        if (item.id == id) {
            item.quantity(0);
        }
    }, cheeseModel.products, "items");
});
```

My route matches any two-segment URL where the first segment is remove. I use the second segment to find the right item in the view model and change the value of the quantity property to zero.

At this point, I have a problem. I have navigated to a URL that I don't want the user to be able to navigate back to because it will match the route that just removes items from the basket, and that doesn't help me.

The solution is in the call to the history.replaceState method. When the quantity value is changed, my subscription causes the updateState function to be called, which in turn calls history.replaceState. The third argument is the important one:

```
history.replaceState(state, "", "#select/" + cheeseModel.selectedCategory());
```

The URL specified by this argument is used to replace the URL that the user navigated to. The browser doesn't navigate to the URL when it is changed, but when the user moves back through the browser history, it is the replacement URL that will be used by the browser. Irrespective of which route matches the URL, the history will always contain one that starts with #select/. In this way, I can use URL routing without exposing the inner workings of my web app to the user.

Summary

In this chapter, I have shown you how to add URL routing to your web applications. This is a powerful and flexible technique that separates application navigation from HTML elements, allowing for a more concise and expressive way of handling navigation and a more testable and maintainable code base. It can take a while to get used to using routing at the client, but it is well worth the investment of time and energy, especially for large and complex projects.

CHAPTER 5

Creating Offline Web Apps

The HTML5 specification includes support for the *Application Cache*, which is used to create web applications that are available to users even when no network connection is available. This is ideal if your users need to work offline or in environments where connectivity is constrained (such as on an airplane, for example).

As with all of the more complex HTML5 features, using the application cache isn't entirely smooth sailing. There are some differences in implementations between browsers and some oddities that you need to be aware of. In this chapter, I'll show you how to create an effective offline web application and how to avoid various pitfalls.

■ **Caution** The browser support for offline storage is at an early stage, and there are a lot of inconsistencies. I have tried to point out potential problems, but because each browser release tends to refine the implementation of HTML5 features, you should expect to see some variations when you run the examples in this chapter.

Resetting the Example

Once again, I am going to simplify the CheeseLux example so that I am not listing reams of code that relate to other chapters. Listing 5-1 shows the revised document.

Listing 5-1. The Reset CheeseLux Example

```
<!DOCTYPE html>
<html>
<head>
    <title>CheeseLux</title>
    <link rel="stylesheet" type="text/css" href="styles.css"/>
    <script src="jquery-1.7.1.js" type="text/javascript"></script>
    <script src="jquery-ui-1.8.16.custom.js" type="text/javascript"></script>
    <script src='knockout-2.0.0.js' type='text/javascript'></script>
    <script src='utils.js' type='text/javascript'></script>
    <script src='signals.js' type='text/javascript'></script>
    <script src='hasher.js' type='text/javascript'></script>
    <script src='crossroads.js' type='text/javascript'></script>
    <link rel="stylesheet" type="text/css" href="jquery-ui-1.8.16.custom.css"/>
```

```
<noscript>
    <meta http-equiv="refresh" content="0; noscript.html"/>
</noscript>
<script>
    var cheeseModel = {
        products: [
            {category: "British Cheese", items : [
                {id: "stilton", name: "Stilton", price: 9},
                {id: "stinkingbishop", name: "Stinking Bishop", price: 17},
                {id: "cheddar", name: "Cheddar", price: 17}]},
            {category: "French Cheese", items: [
                {id: "camembert", name: "Camembert", price: 18},
                {id: "tomme", name: "Tomme de Savoie", price: 19},
                {id: "morbier", name: "Morbier", price: 9}]},
            {category: "Italian Cheese", items: [
                {id: "gorgonzola", name: "Gorgonzola", price: 8},
                {id: "fontina", name: "Fontina", price: 11},
                {id: "parmesan", name: "Parmesan", price: 16}]}]
    };

    $(document).ready(function() {
        $('#buttonDiv input:submit').button();
        $('div.navSelectors').buttonset();

        enhanceViewModel();
        ko.applyBindings(cheeseModel);

        hasher.initialized.add(crossroads.parse, crossroads);
        hasher.changed.add(crossroads.parse, crossroads);
        hasher.init();

        crossroads.addRoute("category/:cat:", function(cat) {
            cheeseModel.selectedCategory(cat || cheeseModel.products[0].category);
        });

    });
</script>
</head>
<body>
    <div id="logobar">
        <img src="cheeselux.png">
        <span id="tagline">Gourmet European Cheese</span>
    </div>

    <div class="cheesegroup">
        <div class="navSelectors" data-bind="foreach: products">
            <a data-bind="formatAttr: {attr: 'href', prefix: '#category/',
                value: category},
            css: {selectedItem: (category == cheeseModel.selectedCategory())}">
                <span data-bind="text: category">
            </a>
        </div>
```

```
        </div>

        <form action="/shipping" method="post">
            <div data-bind="foreach: products">
                <div class="cheesegroup"
                     data-bind="fadeVisible: category == cheeseModel.selectedCategory()">
                    <div class="grouptitle" data-bind="text: category"></div>
                    <!-- ko foreach: items -->
                    <div class="groupcontent">
                        <label data-bind="attr: {for: id}" class="cheesename">
                            <span data-bind="text: name">
                            </span> $(<span data-bind="text:price"></span>)</label>
                        <input data-bind="attr: {name: id}, value: quantity"/>
                        <span data-bind="visible: subtotal" class="subtotal">
                            ($<span data-bind="text: subtotal"></span>)
                        </span>
                    </div>
                    <!-- /ko -->
                    <div class="groupcontent">
                        <label class="cheesename">Total:</label>
                        <span class="subtotal" id="total">
                            $<span data-bind="text: cheeseModel.total()"></span>
                        </span>
                    </div>
                </div>
            </div>
            <div id="buttonDiv">
                <input type="submit" value="Submit Order"/>
            </div>
        </form>
    </body>
</html>
```

This example builds on the view model and routing concepts from previous chapters, but I have simplified some of the functionality. Instead of a basket, I have added a `total` display to the bottom of each category of cheese. I have moved the code that creates the observable view model items into a function called `enhanceViewModel` in the `utils.js` file. Everything else in this listing should be self-evident.

Using the HTML5 Application Cache

The starting point for using the application cache is to create a *manifest*. This tells the browser which files are required to run the application offline so that the browser can ensure that they are all present in the cache. Manifest files have the appcache file suffix, so I have called my manifest file `cheeselux.appcache`. You can see the contents of this file in Listing 5-2.

Listing 5-2. A Simple Manifest File

```
CACHE MANIFEST

# HTML document
example.html
offline.html

# script files
jquery-1.7.1.js
jquery-ui-1.8.16.custom.js
knockout-2.0.0.js
signals.js
crossroads.js
hasher.js
utils.js

# CSS files
styles.css
jquery-ui-1.8.16.custom.css

# images
#blackwave.png
cheeselux.png
images/ui-bg_flat_75_eb8f00_40x100.png
images/ui-bg_flat_75_fbbe03_40x100.png
images/ui-icons_ffffff_256x240.png
images/ui-bg_flat_75_595959_40x100.png
images/ui-bg_flat_65_fbbe03_40x100.png

# fonts
fonts/YanoneKaffeesatz-Regular.ttf
fonts/fanwood_italic-webfont.ttf
fonts/ostrich-rounded-webfont.woff
```

A basic manifest file starts with the CACHE MANIFEST header and then lists all the files that the application requires, including the HTML file whose html element contains the manifest attribute (discussed in a moment). In the listing, I have broken the files down by type and used comments (which are lines starting with the # character) to make it easier to figure out what's happening.

■ **Tip** You will notice that I have commented out the entry for the blackwave.png file. I use this file to demonstrate the behavior of a cached application in a moment.

The manifest is added to the HTML document through the manifest attribute of the html element, as Listing 5-3 shows.

Listing 5-3. Adding the Manifest to the HTML Document

```
<!DOCTYPE html>
<html manifest="cheeselux.appcache">
    <head>
        ...
    </head>
    <body>
        ...
    </body>
</html>
```

When the HTML document is loaded, the browser detects the manifest attribute, requests the specified appcache file from the web server, and begins loading and caching each file listed in the manifest file. The files that are downloaded when the browser processes the manifest are called the *offline content*. Some browsers will prompt the user for permission to store offline content.

■ **Caution** Be careful when you create the manifest. If any of the items listed cannot be obtained from the server, then the browser will not cache the application at all.

Understanding When Cached Content Is Used

The offline content isn't used when it is first loaded by the browser. It is cached for the *next time* that the user loads or reloads the page. The name *offline content* is misleading. Once the browser has offline content for a web app, it will be used whenever the user visits the web app's URL, even when there is a network connection available. The browser takes responsibility for ensuring that the latest version of the offline content is being used, but as you'll learn, this is a complicated process and requires some programmer intervention.

I commented out the blackwave.png file in the manifest to demonstrate how the browser handles offline content. I use blackwave.png as the background image for the CheeseLux web app, and this gives me a nice way to demonstrate the basic behavior of a cached web application.

To start with, add the manifest attribute to the example as shown in Listing 5-3, and load the document into your browser. Different browsers deal with cached applications in different ways. For example, Google Chrome will quietly process the manifest and start downloading the content it specified. Mozilla Firefox will usually prompt the user to allow offline content, as shown in Figure 5-1. If you are using Firefox, click the Allow button to start the browser processing the manifest.

Figure 5-1. Firefox prompting the user to allow the web app to store data locally

---

■ **Tip** All of the mainstream browsers allow the user to disable cached applications, which means you cannot rely on being able to store data even if the browser implements the feature. In such cases, the application manifest will simply be ignored. You may need to change the configuration of your browser to cache the example content.

You should see the CheeseLux web app with the black background. At this point, the browser has two copies of the web app. The first copy is in the regular browser cache, and this is the version that is currently running. The second copy is in the application cache and contains the items specified in the manifest. Simply reload the page to switch to the application cache version. When you do reload, the background will be white, as shown in Figure 5-2.

Figure 5-2. Switching to the application cache

The difference is caused by the fact that the blackwave.png file is commented out in the manifest. The browser keeps the application cache and the regular cache separate, which means that even though it has a blackwave.png file in the regular cache, it won't use it for a cached application.

■ **Tip** Notice that you have not done anything to the network connection. The browser is still online, but the application has been loaded using solely offline content. This is something that I'll return to soon.

Accepting Changes to the Manifest

The most significant change in behavior for a cached application is that refreshing the web page doesn't cause the application content to be cached. The idea is that updates to a cached application need to be managed to avoid inconsistent changes. Uncommenting the blackwave.png line in the manifest and reloading, for example, wouldn't change the background to black.

Listing 5-4 shows the minimum amount of code that is needed in a web app to support updates. I'll show you how to use more of the Application Cache API later in the chapter, but we need these changes before we can go any further.

Listing 5-4. Accepting Changes in the Manifest

```
...
<script>
    var cheeseModel = {
        products: [
            {category: "British Cheese", items : [
                {id: "stilton", name: "Stilton", price: 9},
                {id: "stinkingbishop", name: "Stinking Bishop", price: 17},
                {id: "cheddar", name: "Cheddar", price: 17}]},
            {category: "French Cheese", items: [
                {id: "camembert", name: "Camembert", price: 18},
                {id: "tomme", name: "Tomme de Savoie", price: 19},
                {id: "morbier", name: "Morbier", price: 9}]},
            {category: "Italian Cheese", items: [
                {id: "gorgonzola", name: "Gorgonzola", price: 8},
                {id: "fontina", name: "Fontina", price: 11},
                {id: "parmesan", name: "Parmesan", price: 16}]}]
    };

    $(document).ready(function() {
        $('#buttonDiv input:submit').button();
        $('div.navSelectors').buttonset();

        enhanceViewModel();
        ko.applyBindings(cheeseModel);

        hasher.initialized.add(crossroads.parse, crossroads);
        hasher.changed.add(crossroads.parse, crossroads);
        hasher.init();

        crossroads.addRoute("category/:cat:", function(cat) {
            cheeseModel.selectedCategory(cat || cheeseModel.products[0].category);
        });

        $(window.applicationCache).bind("updateready", function() {
            window.applicationCache.swapCache();
        });

    });
</script>
```

...

The HTML5 Application Cache API is expressed through the `window.applicationCache` browser object. This object triggers events to inform the web app of changes in the cache status. The most important for us at the moment is the `updateready` event, which means that there is updated cache data available. In addition to the events, the `applicationCache` object defines some useful methods and properties. Once again, I'll return to these later in the chapter, but the method I care about now is `swapCache`, which applies the updated manifest and its contents to the application cache.

I am now ready to demonstrate updating a cached web application. But before I do, I must remove the existing cached data. I have created a zombie web app by applying a manifest without adding the call to the `swapCache` method, and there is no way I can get updates to take effect. I need to clear the cache and start again. There is no way to clear the cache using JavaScript, and the browser has a different mechanism for manually clearing application cache data. For Google Chrome, you delete the regular browsing history. For Mozilla Firefox, you must select the Advanced ➤ Network options tab, select the web site from the list, and click the Remove button.

Once you have cleared the application cache, reload the listing to load the manifest and cache the data. Reload the page again to switch to the cached version of the application (which will have the white background).

Finally, you can uncomment the `blackwave.png` entry in the `cheeselux.appcache` file. At this point, you will need to reload the web page *twice*. The first time causes the browser to check for an updated manifest, find that there is a new version, and download the updated resources into the cache. At this point, the `updateready` event is triggered, and my script calls the `swapCache` method, applying the updates to the cache. Those changes don't take effect until the next time that the web app is loaded, which is why the second reload is required. This is an awkward approach, but I'll show you how to improve upon it shortly. At this point, the cache will have been updated with a manifest that does include the `blackwave.png` file, and the web app background will have turned black.

■ **Tip** The browser checks to see only if the manifest file has changed. Changes to individual resources, including HTML and script files, are ignored unless the manifest also changes. If the manifest has changed, then the browser will check to see whether the individual resources have been updated since they were last downloaded (and, of course, will download any resources that have been added to the manifest).

Taking Control of the Cache Update Process

I took you the long way around the updates because I wanted to emphasize the way in which the browser tries to isolate us from having to deal with an inconsistent cache. There is no standard way for a JavaScript web app to respond to a cache change while it is running, so the HTML5 Application Cache standard errs on the side of caution, and cache updates are applied only when the application is loaded.

■ **Caution** The current implementations of the application cache are fine for use by normal users, but they tend to struggle during the development phase when there are lots of changes to the manifest and lots of updates applied to the cache. There will come a point where you start getting odd behavior, and no changes you make to your manifest or your application will sort matters out. When this happens, the simplest thing to do is to clear the browser history and application cache contents and see whether the problems persist. Most of the time, I find that sudden changes in behavior are caused by the browser and that starting over fixes things (although this sometimes requires clearing the files directly from the disk using the file explorer, because the browser's ability to manage the application cache also goes awry).

We can use the applicationCache browser object to manage a cached application in a more elegant way. The first thing we can do is to monitor the status of the cache and present the user with some options. Listing 5-5 shows how this can be done.

Listing 5-5. Taking Active Control of the Application Cache

```html
<!DOCTYPE html>
<html manifest="cheeselux.appcache">
<head>
    <title>CheeseLux</title>
    <link rel="stylesheet" type="text/css" href="styles.css"/>
    <script src="jquery-1.7.1.js" type="text/javascript"></script>
    <script src="jquery-ui-1.8.16.custom.js" type="text/javascript"></script>
    <script src='knockout-2.0.0.js' type='text/javascript'></script>
    <script src='utils.js' type='text/javascript'></script>
    <script src='signals.js' type='text/javascript'></script>
    <script src='hasher.js' type='text/javascript'></script>
    <script src='crossroads.js' type='text/javascript'></script>
    <link rel="stylesheet" type="text/css" href="jquery-ui-1.8.16.custom.css"/>
    <noscript>
        <meta http-equiv="refresh" content="0; noscript.html"/>
    </noscript>
    <script>
        var cheeseModel = {
            products: [
                {category: "British Cheese", items : [
                    {id: "stilton", name: "Stilton", price: 9},
                    {id: "stinkingbishop", name: "Stinking Bishop", price: 17},
                    {id: "cheddar", name: "Cheddar", price: 17}]},
                {category: "French Cheese", items: [
                    {id: "camembert", name: "Camembert", price: 18},
                    {id: "tomme", name: "Tomme de Savoie", price: 19},
                    {id: "morbier", name: "Morbier", price: 9}]},
                {category: "Italian Cheese", items: [
                    {id: "gorgonzola", name: "Gorgonzola", price: 8},
```

```
                               {id: "fontina", name: "Fontina", price: 11},
                               {id: "parmesan", name: "Parmesan", price: 16}]}],
               cache: {
                   status: ko.observable(window.applicationCache.status)
               }
           };

           $(document).ready(function() {
               $('#buttonDiv input:submit').button();
               $('div.navSelectors').buttonset();

               enhanceViewModel();
               ko.applyBindings(cheeseModel);

               hasher.initialized.add(crossroads.parse, crossroads);
               hasher.changed.add(crossroads.parse, crossroads);
               hasher.init();

               crossroads.addRoute("category/:cat:", function(cat) {
                   cheeseModel.selectedCategory(cat || cheeseModel.products[0].category);
               });

               $(window.applicationCache).bind("checking noupdate downloading " +
                       "progress cached updateready", function(e) {
                           cheeseModel.cache.status(window.applicationCache.status);
               });

               $('div.tagcontainer a').button().click(function(e) {
                   e.preventDefault();
                   if ($(this).attr("data-action") == "update") {
                       window.applicationCache.update();
                   } else {
                       window.applicationCache.swapCache();
                       window.location.reload(false);
                   }
               });
           });
       </script>
   </head>
   <body>
       <div id="logobar">
           <img src="cheeselux.png">
           <div class="tagcontainer">
               <span id="tagline">Gourmet European Cheese</span>
               <div>
                   <a data-bind="visible: cheeseModel.cache.status() != 4"
                       data-action="update" class="cachelink">Check for Updates</a>
                   <a data-bind="visible: cheeseModel.cache.status() == 4"
                       data-action="swapCache" class="cachelink">Apply Update</a>
               </div>
           </div>
```

```
    </div>

    <div class="cheesegroup">
        <div class="navSelectors" data-bind="foreach: products">
            <a data-bind="formatAttr: {attr: 'href', prefix: '#category/',
               value: category},
            css: {selectedItem: (category == cheeseModel.selectedCategory())}">
                <span data-bind="text: category">
            </a>
        </div>
    </div>

    <form action="/shipping" method="post">
        <div data-bind="foreach: products">
            <div class="cheesegroup"
                data-bind="fadeVisible: category == cheeseModel.selectedCategory()">
                <div class="grouptitle" data-bind="text: category"></div>
                <!-- ko foreach: items -->
                <div class="groupcontent">
                    <label data-bind="attr: {for: id}" class="cheesename">
                        <span data-bind="text: name">
                        </span> $(<span data-bind="text:price"></span>)</label>
                    <input data-bind="attr: {name: id}, value: quantity"/>
                    <span data-bind="visible: subtotal" class="subtotal">
                        ($<span data-bind="text: subtotal"></span>)
                    </span>
                </div>
                <!-- /ko -->
                <div class="groupcontent">
                    <label class="cheesename">Total:</label>
                    <span class="subtotal" id="total">
                        $<span data-bind="text: cheeseModel.total()"></span>
                    </span>
                </div>
            </div>
        </div>
        <div id="buttonDiv">
            <input type="submit" value="Submit Order"/>
        </div>
    </form>
</body>
</html>
```

To start with, I have added a new observable data item to the view model, which represents the state of the application cache:

```
cache: {
    status: ko.observable(window.applicationCache.status)
}
```

I am using the view model because I want to disseminate the status into the HTML markup using data bindings. To keep the value up-to-date, I subscribe to a set of events triggered by the window.applicationCache object, like this:

```
$(window.applicationCache).bind("checking noupdate downloading " +
    "progress cached updateready", function(e) {
        cheeseModel.cache.status(window.applicationCache.status);
});
```

Seven cache events are available. I have listed them in Table 5-1. I have used the bind method to handle six of them, because the seventh, obsolete, arises only when the manifest file isn't available from the web server.

Table 5-1. *HTML5 Application Cache Events*

Event Name	Description
cached	The initial manifest and content for the application have been downloaded.
checking	The browser is checking for an update to the manifest file.
noupdate	The browser has finished checking the manifest, and there were no updates.
downloading	The browser is downloading updated offline content.
progress	Used by the browser to indicate download progress.
updateready	The content download is complete, and there is a cache update ready.
obsolete	The manifest is invalid.

I update the cache.status data item in the view model when I received an application cache event. The current status is available from the window.applicationCache.status property, and I have described the range of values that are returned in Table 5-2.

Table 5-2. *Values Returned by the applicationCache.status Property*

Value	Name	Description
0	UNCACHED	Returned for web apps that do not specify a manifest or when there is a manifest but the offline content has not been downloaded.
1	IDLE	The cache is not performing any action. This is the default value once the offline content has been downloaded and cached.
2	CHECKING	The browser is checking for an updated manifest.
3	DOWNLOADING	The browser is downloading updated offline content.
4	UPDATEREADY	There is updated offline content waiting to be applied to the cache.
5	OBSOLETE	The cached data is obsolete.

As you can see, the status values correspond with some of the application cache events. For this example, I care only about the UPDATEREADY status value, which I use to control the visibility of some a elements I added to the logo area of the page:

```
<div>
    <a data-bind="visible: cheeseModel.cache.status() != 4"
        data-action="update" class="cachelink">Check for Updates</a>
    <a data-bind="visible: cheeseModel.cache.status() == 4"
        data-action="swapCache" class="cachelink">Apply Update</a>
</div>
```

When the cache is idle, I display the element that prompts the user to check for an update, and when there is an update available, I prompt the user to install it. Figure 5-3 shows both of these buttons in situ.

Figure 5-3. Adding buttons to control the cache

As you can see in the figure, I have used jQuery UI to create buttons from the a elements. I have also used the jQuery click method to register a handler for the click event, as follows:

```
$('div.tagcontainer a').button().click(function(e) {
    e.preventDefault();
    if ($(this).attr("data-action") == "update") {
        window.applicationCache.update();
    } else {
        window.applicationCache.swapCache();
        window.location.reload(false);
    }
});
```

I have used regular JavaScript events to control the cache because I want the user to be able to check for updates repeatedly. Browsers ignore requests to navigate to the same internal URL that is being displayed. You can see this happening if you click one of the cheese category buttons. Clicking the same button repeatedly doesn't do anything, and the button is effectively disabled until another category is selected. If I had used URL routing to deal with the cache buttons, then the user would be able to check for an update once and then not be able to do so again until they navigated to another internal URL (which for this example would require selecting a cheese category). So, instead, I used JavaScript events that are triggered every time the button is clicked, irrespective of the rest of the application state.

When either cache button is clicked, I read the value of the data-action attribute. If the attribute value is update, then I call the cache update method. This causes the browser to check with the server to see whether the manifest has changed. If it has, then the status of the cache will change to UPDATEREADY, and the Apply Update button will be shown to the user.

When the Apply Update button is clicked, I call the swapCache method to push the updates into the application cache. These updates won't take effect until the application is reloaded, which I force by calling the window.location.reload method. This means the updates are applied to the cache and immediately used in response to a single action by the user. The simplest way to test these additions is to toggle the status of the blackwave.png image in the manifest and apply the resulting update. See the information on the cache control header if you want to test more substantial changes.

APPLICATION CACHE ENTRIES AND THE CACHE-CONTROL HEADER

Calling the applicationCache method doesn't always cause the browser to contact the server to see whether the manifest has changed. All of the mainstream browsers honor the HTTP Cache-Control header and will check for updates only when the life of the manifest has expired.

Further, even if the manifest *has* changed, the browser honors the Cache-Control value for individual manifest items. This can lead to a situation where an update to an HTML or script file is ignored if the manifest changes within the Cache-Control lifetime of the affected resource.

In production, this behavior is perfectly reasonable. But during development and testing, it's a huge pain since changes made to the contents of HTML and script files won't be immediately reflected in an update. To get around this, I have set a very short cache life on the content served by the Node.js server. You'll need to do something similar to your development servers to get the same effect.

Adding Network and Fallback Entries to the Manifest

Regular manifest entries tell the browser to proactively obtain and cache resources that the web app requires. In addition, the application cache supports two other manifest entry types: *network* and *fallback* entries. Network entries, also known as *whitelist entries*, specify a resource that the browser should not cache. Requests for these resources will always result in a request to the server while the browser is online. This is useful to ensure that the user always receives the latest version of a file, even though the rest of the application is cached.

The fallback entries tell the browser what to do when the browser is offline and the user requests a network entry. Fallback entries allow you to substitute an alternative file rather than displaying an error to the user. Listing 5-6 shows the use of both kinds of entry in the cheeselux.appcache file.

Listing 5-6. Using a Network Entry in the Application Manifest

```
CACHE MANIFEST

# HTML document
example.html

# script files
jquery-1.7.1.js
jquery-ui-1.8.16.custom.js
```

```
knockout-2.0.0.js
signals.js
crossroads.js
hasher.js
utils.js

# CSS files
styles.css
jquery-ui-1.8.16.custom.css

# images
blackwave.png
cheeselux.png
images/ui-bg_flat_75_eb8f00_40x100.png
images/ui-bg_flat_75_fbbe03_40x100.png
images/ui-icons_ffffff_256x240.png
images/ui-bg_flat_75_595959_40x100.png
images/ui-bg_flat_65_fbbe03_40x100.png

# fonts
fonts/YanoneKaffeesatz-Regular.ttf
fonts/fanwood_italic-webfont.ttf
fonts/ostrich-rounded-webfont.woff

NETWORK:
news.html
```

The network entries are prefixed with the word NETWORK and a colon (:). As with the regular entries, each resource occupies a single line. In this listing, I have created a network entry for the file news.html. I have created a button that links to this file in the example.html file, like this:

```
<div id="logobar">
    <img src="cheeselux.png">
    <div class="tagcontainer">
        <span id="tagline">Gourmet European Cheese</span>
        <div>
            <a data-bind="visible: cheeseModel.cache.status() != 4"
                data-action="update" class="cachelink">Check for Updates</a>
            <a data-bind="visible: cheeseModel.cache.status() == 4"
                data-action="swapCache" class="cachelink">Apply Update</a>
            <a class="cachelink" href="news.html">News</a>
        </div>
    </div>
</div>
```

When the browser is online, clicking this link displays the news.html file. You can see the effect in Figure 5-4.

Figure 5-4. Linking to the news.html page

Because it is in the NETWORK section, the news.html file is never added to the application cache. When I click the News button, the browser acts as it would for regular content. It contacts the server, gets the resources, and adds them to the regular (nonapplication) cache, before showing them to the user. I can make changes to the news.html file, and they will be displayed to the user even when the application cache hasn't been updated.

When the browser goes offline, there is no way to get hold of the content that is not in the application cache. This is where the FALLBACK entries come in. The format of these entries is different from the others.

■ **Caution** Browsers take different views about what being offline means. I explain more about this in the "Monitoring Offline Status" section later in this chapter.

The first part specifies a prefix for resources, and the second part specifies a file to use when a resource that matches the prefix is requested while the browser is offline. So, in Listing 5-7, I have set the manifest so that any request to any URL (represented by /) should be given the file offline.html instead.

Listing 5-7. Using a Fallback Entry in the Application Manifest

```
...
# fonts
fonts/YanoneKaffeesatz-Regular.ttf
fonts/fanwood_italic-webfont.ttf
fonts/ostrich-rounded-webfont.woff

FALLBACK:
/ offline.html
```

Tip Browsers handle fallback for resources in the network inconsistently. You should not rely on the fallback section to provide substitute content for URLs that are listed in the network section, only those that are in the main part of the manifest. Support for providing fallbacks for individual files is also inconsistent, which is why I have used the broadest possible fallback in the examples for this chapter. I expect the reliability and consistency of these features to improve as the HTML5 implementations stabilize.

When the browser is offline, clicking the News button triggers a request for a URL that the browser cannot service from the application cache, and the fallback entry is used instead. You can see the result in Figure 5-5. The URL in the browser address bar shows the URL that was requested, but the content that is shown is from the fallback resource.

Figure 5-5. Using the fallback entry

The HTML5 Application Cache specification provides support for more complex fallback entries, including per-URL fallbacks and the use of wildcards. However, as I write this, Google Chrome doesn't support these entries, and a general fallback, such as I have shown in the listing, is all that can be reliably used.

The specification for the HTML5 Application Cache feature is ambiguous about whether the browser should use the regular content cache to satisfy requests for network entry resources. And, of course, different approaches have been adopted. Google Chrome takes the most literal interpretation of the standard. When the browser is offline, network entry resources are not available to the web app. Mozilla Firefox and Opera take a more forgiving approach: if the resource is in the main browser cache when the browser goes offline, it will be available to the web app. Of course, the browsers are updated frequently, so there might be a different set of behaviors by the time you read this.

■ **Caution** The implementation of the network and fallback features can be inconsistent. There are some oddities in the implementations of the mainstream browsers, and as a consequence, I tend to avoid using these kinds of entries for cached applications. The regular cache entries work well, however, and can be relied upon in those browsers that support the application cache feature.

Monitoring Offline Status

HTML5 defines the ability to determine whether the browser is online. What being offline means depends on the platform and the browser. For mobile devices, being offline usually requires the user to switch to airplane mode or to explicitly switch off networking in some other way. Simply being out of coverage doesn't usually change the browser status.

Explicit user action is required for most desktop browsers as well. For example, Firefox and Opera both have menu items that toggle the browser between online and offline modes. The exception is Google Chrome, which monitors the underlying network connections and switches to offline if no network devices are enabled.

■ **Note** Chrome will go into offline mode only when there is no enabled network connection. To create the screenshot in this section, I had to disable my main (wireless) connection, manually disable an Ethernet port that was enabled but not plugged in to anything, *and* disable a connection created by a virtual machine package. Only then did Chrome decide it was time to go offline. Most users won't have this problem, but it is something to bear in mind, especially if you are not getting the offline behavior you expect.

Recent versions of the mainstream browsers implement an HTML5 feature that reports on whether the browser is online or offline. This is useful both in terms of presenting the user with a useful and contextual interface and in terms of managing the internal operations of the web app. To demonstrate this feature, I am going to change the example web app so that the cache control and News buttons are displayed only when the browser is online. Listing 5-8 shows the changes to the script element.

Listing 5-8. Detecting the State of the Network

```
<script>
    var cheeseModel = {
        products: [
            {category: "British Cheese", items : [
                {id: "stilton", name: "Stilton", price: 9},
                {id: "stinkingbishop", name: "Stinking Bishop", price: 17},
                {id: "cheddar", name: "Cheddar", price: 17}]},
            {category: "French Cheese", items: [
                {id: "camembert", name: "Camembert", price: 18},
                {id: "tomme", name: "Tomme de Savoie", price: 19},
                {id: "morbier", name: "Morbier", price: 9}]},
            {category: "Italian Cheese", items: [
                {id: "gorgonzola", name: "Gorgonzola", price: 8},
                {id: "fontina", name: "Fontina", price: 11},
                {id: "parmesan", name: "Parmesan", price: 16}]}],
        cache: {
            status: ko.observable(window.applicationCache.status),
            online: ko.observable(window.navigator.onLine)
        }
    };

    $(document).ready(function() {
        $('#buttonDiv input:submit').button();
        $('div.navSelectors').buttonset();

        enhanceViewModel();
        ko.applyBindings(cheeseModel);

        hasher.initialized.add(crossroads.parse, crossroads);
        hasher.changed.add(crossroads.parse, crossroads);
        hasher.init();

        crossroads.addRoute("category/:cat:", function(cat) {
            cheeseModel.selectedCategory(cat || cheeseModel.products[0].category);
        });

        $(window.applicationCache).bind("checking noupdate downloading " +
                "progress cached updateready", function(e) {
                    cheeseModel.cache.status(window.applicationCache.status);

        });

        $(window).bind("online offline", function() {
            cheeseModel.cache.online(window.navigator.onLine);
        });

        $('div.tagcontainer a').button().filter(':not([href])').click(function(e) {
            e.preventDefault();
            if ($(this).attr("data-action") == "update") {
```

```
                window.applicationCache.update();
            } else {
                window.applicationCache.swapCache();
                window.location.reload(false);
            }
        });
    });
</script>
```

The window browser object supports the online and offline events that are triggered when the browser status changes. You can get the current status through the window.navigator.onLine property, which returns true if the browser is online and false if it is offline. Note that the L in onLine is uppercase. I have added an online observable data item to the view model, which I update in response to the online and offline events. This is the same technique that I used for the application cache status, and it allows me to use the view model to propagate changes through to my markup. Listing 5-9 shows the changes to the HTML elements that display the News and application cache control buttons.

Listing 5-9. Adding Elements and Bindings to Respond to the Browser Online Status

```
<div id="logobar">
    <img src="cheeselux.png">
    <div class="tagcontainer">
        <span id="tagline">Gourmet European Cheese</span>
        <div>
            <span data-bind="visible: cheeseModel.cache.online()">
                <a data-bind="visible: cheeseModel.cache.status() != 4"
                    data-action="update" class="cachelink">Check for Updates</a>
                <a data-bind="visible: cheeseModel.cache.status() == 4"
                    data-action="swapCache" class="cachelink">Apply Update</a>
                <a class="cachelink" href="/news.html">News</a>
            </span>
            <span data-bind="visible: !cheeseModel.cache.online()">
                (Offline)
            </span>
        </div>
    </div>
</div>
```

When the browser is online, the cache control and the News buttons are displayed. When the browser is offline, I replace the buttons with a simple placeholder. You can see the effect in Figure 5-6.

■ **Tip** You need to ensure that you have the right version of the offline content before taking the browser offline. Before running this example, you should either change the manifest or clear the browser's history.

Figure 5-6. Responding to the browser online status

Understanding with Ajax and POST Requests

The application cache makes it difficult to work with Ajax and, more broadly, posting forms in general. And things get worse when the browser is offline, although perhaps not in the way you might expect. In this section, I'll show you the problems and the limited options that are available to deal with them. First, however, I need to update the CheeseLux web app so that it depends on an Ajax GET request to operate. Listing 5-10 shows the required changed to the `script` element (no changes are needed to the markup for this example).

Listing 5-10. Adding an Ajax GET RequestRequest

```
...
<script>
    var cheeseModel = {
        cache: {
            status: ko.observable(window.applicationCache.status),
            online: ko.observable(window.navigator.onLine)
        }
    };

    $.getJSON("products.json", function(data) {
        cheeseModel.products = data;
    }).success(function() {
        $(document).ready(function() {
            $('#buttonDiv input:submit').button();
            $('div.navSelectors').buttonset();

            enhanceViewModel();
            ko.applyBindings(cheeseModel);

            hasher.initialized.add(crossroads.parse, crossroads);
            hasher.changed.add(crossroads.parse, crossroads);
            hasher.init();

            crossroads.addRoute("category/:cat:", function(cat) {
                cheeseModel.selectedCategory(cat || cheeseModel.products[0].category);
            });

            $(window.applicationCache).bind("checking noupdate downloading " +
                    "progress cached updateready", function(e) {
                        cheeseModel.cache.status(window.applicationCache.status);
            });

            $(window).bind("online offline", function() {
                cheeseModel.cache.online(window.navigator.onLine);
            });

            $('div.tagcontainer a').button().filter(':not([href])').click(function(e) {
                e.preventDefault();
                if ($(this).attr("data-action") == "update") {
                    window.applicationCache.update();
                } else {
                    window.applicationCache.swapCache();
                    window.location.reload(false);
                }
            });
        });
    });
</script>
...
```

In this listing, I have used the jQuery getJSON method. This is a convenience method that makes an Ajax GET request for the JSON file specified by the first method argument, which is products.json in this case. When the Ajax requests has completed, jQuery parses the JSON data to create a JavaScript object, which is passed to the function specified by the second method argument. In my listing, the function simply takes the JavaScript object and assigns it to the products property of the view model. The products.json file contains a superset of the data I have been defining inline. The same categories, products, and prices are defined, along with an additional description of each cheese. Listing 5-11 shows an extract from products.json.

Listing 5-11. An Extract from the products.json File

```
...
{"id": "stilton", "name": "Stilton", "price": 9,
 "description": "A semi-soft blue cow's milk cheese produced in the Nottinghamshire region. A
strong cheese with a distinctive smell and taste and crumbly texture."},
...
```

In the listing I chain the getJSON method with a call to success. The success method is part of the jQuery support for JavaScript *Promises*, which make it easy to use and manage asynchronous operations like Ajax requests. The function passed to the success method won't be executed until the getJSON method has completed, ensuring that my view model is complete before the rest of my script is run.

This approach to getting core data from JSON is a common one, especially where the data is sourced from a different set of systems to the rest of the web app. And, if used carefully, it can ensure that the user has the most recent data but still has the benefit of a cached application.

Understanding the Default Ajax GET Behavior

The browser treats an Ajax GET request in a very simple way. The request will fail if the Ajax request is for a resource that is not in the manifest, even when the browser is online.

For my example application, this means that data is returned from the request and it dies a horrible death. The function I passed as an argument to the getJSON method is executed only if the Ajax request succeeds, and the same is true for the function passed to the success method. Because neither function is executed, the main part of my script code isn't performed, and I leave the user stranded. Worse, since the application cache control buttons are never set up, I don't give the user a means to update the application to fix the problem.

I have shown this scenario because it is very commonly encountered when programmers first start using the application cache. I'll show you how to make the Ajax connection work shortly, but first, there are a couple of important changes to be made.

Restructuring the Application

The first change is to structure the application so that the core behavior that will get the user back out of trouble will always be executed. My initial listing is just too optimistic, and I need to separate those parts of the code that should always be run. There are lots of different techniques for doing this, but I find the simplest is just to create another function that is contingent on the jQuery ready event. Listing 5-12 shows the changes I require to the script element.

Listing 5-12. Restructuring the script Element

```
...
<script>
    var cheeseModel = {
        cache: {
            status: ko.observable(window.applicationCache.status),
            online: ko.observable(window.navigator.onLine)
        }
    };

    $.getJSON("products.json", function(data) {
        cheeseModel.products = data;
    }).success(function() {
        $(document).ready(function() {
            enhanceViewModel();
            ko.applyBindings(cheeseModel);

            hasher.initialized.add(crossroads.parse, crossroads);
            hasher.changed.add(crossroads.parse, crossroads);
            hasher.init();

            crossroads.addRoute("category/:cat:", function(cat) {
                cheeseModel.selectedCategory(cat || cheeseModel.products[0].category);
            });
        });
    }).complete(function() {
        $(document).ready(function() {
            $('#buttonDiv input:submit').button();
            $('div.navSelectors').buttonset();
            $(window).bind("online offline", function() {
                cheeseModel.cache.online(window.navigator.onLine);
            });

            $(window.applicationCache).bind("checking noupdate downloading " +
                "progress cached updateready", function(e) {
                    cheeseModel.cache.status(window.applicationCache.status);
            });

            $('div.tagcontainer a').button().filter(':not([href])').click(function(e) {
                e.preventDefault();
                if ($(this).attr("data-action") == "update") {
                    window.applicationCache.update();
                } else {
                    window.applicationCache.swapCache();
                    window.location.reload(false);
                }
            });
        });
    });
```

```
</script>
...
```

I have pulled all of the code that isn't contingent on a successful Ajax request together and placed it in a function passed to the complete method, which I add to the chain of method calls. This function will be executed when the Ajax request finishes, irrespective of whether it succeeded or failed.

Now, even when the Ajax request fails, the controls for updating the cache and applying changes are always available. Given that Ajax problems are the most likely reason for errors at the client, giving the user a way to apply an update is essential. Otherwise, you are going to have to provide per-browser instructions for clearing the cache. It is not a perfect solution, because I am unable to apply my data bindings, so elements that I would rather were hidden are visible. I could use the CSS display property to hide some of these items, but I think just giving the user the ability to download and apply an update is what is essential. You can see the effect before and after the restructuring in Figure 5-7.

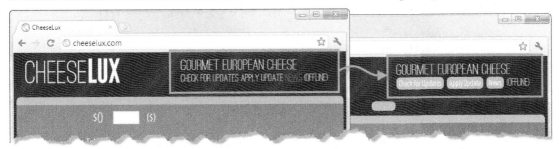

Figure 5-7. The effect of restructuring the application

Handling the Ajax Error

The other change I need to make is to add some kind of error handler for when the Ajax request fails. This may seem like a basic technique, but many web applications are coded only for success, and when the connection fails, everything falls apart. There are lots of ways of handling Ajax errors, but the one shown in Listing 5-13 uses some jQuery features.

Listing 5-13. Adding Support for Handling Ajax Errors

```
<script>
    var cheeseModel = {
        cache: {
            status: ko.observable(window.applicationCache.status),
            online: ko.observable(window.navigator.onLine)
        }
    };

    $.getJSON("products.json", function(data) {
        cheeseModel.products = data;
    }).success(function() {
        $(document).ready(function() {
            enhanceViewModel();
            ko.applyBindings(cheeseModel);
```

```
            hasher.initialized.add(crossroads.parse, crossroads);
            hasher.changed.add(crossroads.parse, crossroads);
            hasher.init();

            crossroads.addRoute("category/:cat:", function(cat) {
                cheeseModel.selectedCategory(cat || cheeseModel.products[0].category);
            });
        });
    }).error(function() {
        var dialogHTML = '<div>Try again later</div>';
        $(dialogHTML).dialog({
            modal: true,
            title: "Ajax Error",
            buttons: [{text: "OK", click: function() {$(this).dialog("close")}}]
        });
    }).complete(function() {
        $(document).ready(function() {
            $('#buttonDiv input:submit').button();
            $('div.navSelectors').buttonset();
            $(window).bind("online offline", function() {
                cheeseModel.cache.online(window.navigator.onLine);
            });

            $(window.applicationCache).bind("checking noupdate downloading " +
                "progress cached updateready", function(e) {
                    cheeseModel.cache.status(window.applicationCache.status);
            });

            $('div.tagcontainer a').button().filter(':not([href])').click(function(e) {
                e.preventDefault();
                if ($(this).attr("data-action") == "update") {
                    window.applicationCache.update();
                } else {
                    window.applicationCache.swapCache();
                    window.location.reload(false);
                }
            });
        });
    });
});
</script>
```

jQuery makes it easy to handle errors with the error method. This is another part of the Promises feature, and the function passed to the error method will be executed if there is a problem with the request. In this example, I created a simple jQuery UI dialog box that tells the user that there is a problem.

Adding the Ajax URL to the Main Manifest or FALLBACK Sections

The worst thing you can do at this point is add the Ajax URL to the main section of the manifest. The browser will treat the URL like any other resource, downloading and caching the content when the manifest is processed. When the client makes the Ajax request, the browser will return the content from the application cache, and the data won't be updated until a manifest change triggers a cache update. The result of this is that your users will be working with stale data, which is generally contrary to the reasoning behind making the Ajax request in the first place.

You get pretty much the same result if you add the URL to the FALLBACK section. Every request, even when the browser is online, will be satisfied by whatever you set as the fallback, and no request will ever be made to the server.

Adding the Ajax URL to the Manifest NETWORK Section

The best approach (albeit far from ideal) is to add the Ajax URL to the NETWORK section of the manifest. When the browser is online, the Ajax requests will be passed to the server, and the latest data will be presented to the user.

The problems start when the browser is offline. There are two different approaches to handling Ajax requests in an offline browser. The first approach, which you can see in Google Chrome, is that the Ajax request will fail. Your Ajax error handler will be invoked, and there is a clean failure.

The other approach can be seen in Firefox. When the browser is offline, Ajax requests will be serviced using the main browser cache if possible. This creates the odd situation where the user will get stale data if a request for the same URL was made before the browser went offline and will get an error if this is the first time that the URL has been asked for.

Understanding the POST Request Behavior

The way that POST requests are handled is a lot more consistent than for GET requests. If the browser is online, then the POST request will be made to the server. If the browser is offline, then the request will fail. This is true for POST requests that are made using regular HTML and for POST requests made using Ajax.

This leads to annoyed users because POSTing a form usually comes after some period of activity on their part. In the case of the CheeseLux example, the user will have paged through the categories and entered the amounts of each product they require. When they come to submit their order, the browser will show an error page. You can't even use the FALLBACK section of the manifest to nominate a page to be shown instead of the error.

The only sensible thing to do is to intercept the form submission and use the navigator.onLine property and events to monitor the browser status and prevent the user from trying to post content when the browser is offline. In Chapter 6, I'll show you some techniques for preserving the result of the user's effort, ready for when the browser comes back online.

Summary

In this chapter, I showed you how to use the HTML5 Application Cache to create offline applications. By using the application cache, you can create applications that are available even when the user doesn't have a network connection. Although the core of the application cache is well-supported, there are some anomalies, and careful design and testing are required to get a result that is reliable and robust. In the next chapter, I'll show you how to use some related functionality that helps smooth out some of the rough edges of offline apps and that can be used to create a better experience for the user.

## CHAPTER 6

Storing Data in the Browser

A natural complement to offline applications is client-side data storage. HTML5 defines some useful JavaScript APIs for storing data in the browser, ranging from simple name/value pairs to using a JavaScript object database. In this chapter, I show you how to build applications that rely on persistently stored data, including details of how to use such data in an offline web application.

■ **Caution** The browser support for data storage is mixed. You should run the examples in this chapter using Google Chrome, with the exception of those in the IndexedDB section, which will run only in Mozilla Firefox.

Using Local Storage

The simplest way to store data in the browser is to use the HTML5 *local storage* feature. This allows you to store simple name/value pairs and retrieve or modify them later. The data is stored persistently but is not guaranteed to be stored forever. The browser is free to delete your data if it needs the space (or if the data hasn't been accessed for a long time), and, of course, the user can clear the data store at any time, even when your web app is running. The result is data that is broadly, but not indefinitely, persistent. Using local storage is very similar to using a regular JavaScript array, as Listing 6-1 demonstrates.

Listing 6-1. Using Local Storage

```
<!DOCTYPE html>
<html>
<head>
    <title>Local Storage Example</title>
    <link rel="stylesheet" type="text/css" href="jquery-ui-1.8.16.custom.css"/>
    <link rel="stylesheet" type="text/css" href="styles.css"/>
    <script src="jquery-1.7.1.js" type="text/javascript"></script>
    <script src="jquery-ui-1.8.16.custom.js" type="text/javascript"></script>
    <script src='knockout-2.0.0.js' type='text/javascript'></script>
    <script src='utils.js' type='text/javascript'></script>
    <script src='signals.js' type='text/javascript'></script>
    <script src='crossroads.js' type='text/javascript'></script>
    <script src='hasher.js' type='text/javascript'></script>
    <script>
        var viewModel = {
```

```
            items: ["Apple", "Orange", "Banana"],
            selectedItem: ko.observable("Apple")
        };

        $(document).ready(function() {
            ko.applyBindings(viewModel);

            $('div.catSelectors').buttonset();

            hasher.initialized.add(crossroads.parse, crossroads);
            hasher.changed.add(crossroads.parse, crossroads);
            hasher.init();

            crossroads.addRoute("select/{item}", function(item) {
                viewModel.selectedItem(item);
                localStorage["selection"] = item;
            });

            viewModel.selectedItem(localStorage["selection"] || viewModel.items[0]);
        });
    </script>
</head>
<body>
    <div class="catSelectors" data-bind="foreach: items">
        <a data-bind="formatAttr: {attr: 'href', prefix: '#select/', value: $data},
            css: {selectedItem: ($data == viewModel.selectedItem())}">
            <span data-bind="text: $data"></span>
        </a>
    </div>
    <div data-bind="foreach: items">
        <div class="item" data-bind="fadeVisible: $data == viewModel.selectedItem()">
            The selected item is: <span data-bind="text: $data"></span>
        </div>
    </div>
</body>
</html>
```

To demonstrate local storage, I have used the simple example from Chapter 4, which allows me to focus on the storage techniques without the features from other chapters getting in the way. As the listing shows, getting started with local storage is pretty simple. The global localStorage object acts like an array. When the user makes a selection in this simple web app, I store the selected item using array-style notation, like this:

localStorage["selection"] = item;

▪ **Tip** Keys are case-sensitive (so that selection and Selection would represent different data items), and assigning a value to a key that already exists overwrites the previously defined value.

This statement creates a new local storage *item*, which I can read back using the same array-style notation, like this:

```
viewModel.selectedItem(localStorage["selection"] || viewModel.items[0]);
```

The effect of adding these two statements to the example is to create simple persistence for the user's selection. When the web app is loaded, I check to see whether there is data stored under the selection key and, if there is, set the corresponding data item in the view model, which restores the user's selection from an earlier session.

■ **Tip** It is important not to use local storage for sensitive information or to trust the integrity of data retrieved from local storage for critical functions in your web app. Users can see and edit the contents of local storage, which means that nothing you store is secret and everything can be changed. Don't store anything you don't want publically disseminated, and don't rely on local storage to give privileged access to your web app.

From that point on, I update the value associated with the selection key each time my route is matched by a URL change. I included a fallback to a default selection to cope with the possibility that the local storage data has been deleted (or this is the first time that the user has loaded the web app). To test this feature, load the example web app, select one of the options, and then reload the web page. The browser will reload the document, execute the JavaScript code afresh, and restore your selection.

Storing JSON Data

The specification for local storage requires that keys and values are strings, just like in the previous example. Being able to store a list of name/value pairs isn't always that useful, but we can build on the support for strings to use local storage for JSON data, as shown in Listing 6-2.

Listing 6-2. Using Local Storage for JSON Data

```
...
<script>
    var viewModel = {
        selectedItem: ko.observable()
    };

    function loadViewModelData() {
        var storedData = localStorage["viewModelData"];
        if (storedData) {
            var storedDataObject = JSON.parse(storedData);
            viewModel.items = storedDataObject.items;
            viewModel.selectedItem(storedDataObject.selectedItem);
        } else {
            viewModel.items = ["Apple", "Orange", "Banana"];
            viewModel.selectedItem("Apple");
        }
    }
```

```
function storeViewModelData() {
    var viewModelData = {
        items: viewModel.items,
        selectedItem: viewModel.selectedItem()
    };
    localStorage["viewModelData"] = JSON.stringify(viewModelData);
}

$(document).ready(function() {
    loadViewModelData();

    ko.applyBindings(viewModel);

    $('div.catSelectors').buttonset();

    hasher.initialized.add(crossroads.parse, crossroads);
    hasher.changed.add(crossroads.parse, crossroads);
    hasher.init();

    crossroads.addRoute("select/{item}", function(item) {
        viewModel.selectedItem(item);
        storeViewModelData();
    });
});
</script>
...
```

I have defined two new functions in the script element to support storing JSON. The storeViewModelData function is called whenever the user makes a selection. JSON is only able to store data values and not JavaScript functions, so I extract the data values from the view model and use them to create a new object. I pass this object to the JSON.stringify method, which returns a JSON string, like this:

```
{"items":["Apple","Orange","Banana"],
 "selectedItem":"Banana"}
```

I store this string by associating it with the viewModelData key in local storage. The corresponding function is loadViewModelData. I call this function when the jQuery ready event is fired and use it to complete the view model.

■ **Tip** The persistent nature of local storage means that if you reuse a key to store a different kind of data, you run the risk of encountering the old format that was stored in a previous session. The simplest way to handle this in development is to clear the browser's cache. In production, you must be able to detect the old data and either process it or, at the very least, be able to discard it without generating any errors.

I load the JSON string and use the JSON.parse method to create a JavaScript object if there is local storage data associated with the viewModelData key. I can then read the properties of the object to populate the view model. Of course, I cannot rely on there being data available, so I fall back to some sensible default values if needed.

STORING OBJECT DATA

It wasn't hard to separate the data from the object that contained it in my simple example, but it can be significantly more difficult in a complex web application. You might be tempted to shortcut this process by storing objects directly, rather than mapping data to strings. Don't do this; it will only cause you problems. Here is a code snippet that shows local storage being used with objects:

```
...
<script>
    var viewModel = {};

    function loadViewModelData() {
        var storedData = localStorage["viewModelData"];
        if (storedData) {
            viewModel = storedData;
        } else {
            viewModel.items = ["Apple", "Orange", "Banana"];
            viewModel.selectedItem = ko.observable("Apple");
        }
    }

    function storeViewModelData() {
        localStorage["viewModelData"] = viewModel;
    }

    $(document).ready(function() {
        loadViewModelData();

        ko.applyBindings(viewModel);

        $('div.catSelectors').buttonset();

        hasher.initialized.add(crossroads.parse, crossroads);
        hasher.changed.add(crossroads.parse, crossroads);
        hasher.init();

        crossroads.addRoute("select/{item}", function(item) {
            viewModel.selectedItem(item);
            storeViewModelData();
        });
    });
</script>
...
```

This technique doesn't work. The browser won't complain when you store objects, and if you read the value back within the same session, everything looks fine. But the browser serializes the object in order to store it for future sessions. For most JavaScript objects, the stored value will be [object Object], which is the result you get if you call the toString method. When the user revisits the web app, the value in local storage isn't a valid JavaScript object and can't be parsed. This is the kind of problem that should be detected during testing, but I see this issue a lot, not least because even projects that take testing seriously don't generally revisit the application for multiple sessions.

Storing Form Data

Local storage is ideally suited for making form data persistent. The key/value mapping suits the nature of form elements very well, and with very little effort, you can create forms that are persistent between sessions, as Listing 6-3 shows.

Listing 6-3. Using Local Storage to Create Persistent Forms

```html
<!DOCTYPE html>
<html>
<head>
    <title>Local Storage Example</title>
    <link rel="stylesheet" type="text/css" href="jquery-ui-1.8.16.custom.css"/>
    <link rel="stylesheet" type="text/css" href="styles.css"/>
    <script src="jquery-1.7.1.js" type="text/javascript"></script>
    <script src="jquery-ui-1.8.16.custom.js" type="text/javascript"></script>
    <script src='knockout-2.0.0.js' type='text/javascript'></script>
    <script>
        var viewModel = {
            personalDetails: [
                {name: "name", label: "Name", value: ko.observable()},
                {name: "city", label: "City", value: ko.observable()},
                {name: "country", label: "Country", value: ko.observable()}
            ]
        };

        $(document).ready(function() {
            $.each(viewModel.personalDetails, function(index, item) {
                item.value(localStorage[item.name] || "");
                item.value.subscribe(function(newValue) {
                    localStorage[item.name] = newValue;
                });
            });

            ko.applyBindings(viewModel);

            $('#buttonDiv input').button().click(function(e) {
                localStorage.clear();
            });
        });
    </script>
</head>
```

```
<body>
    <form action="/formecho" method="POST">
        <div class="cheesegroup">
            <div class="grouptitle">Your Details</div>
            <div class="groupcontent centered">
                <div data-bind="foreach: personalDetails">
                    <span data-bind="text: label"></span>:
                    <input class="stwin" data-bind="attr: {name: name}, value: value">
                </div>
            </div>
        </div>
        <div id="buttonDiv">
            <input type="submit" value="Submit">
            <input type="reset" value="Reset">
        </div>
    </form>
</body>
</html>
```

I have defined a simple three-field form element in this example, which you can see in Figure 6-1. The form captures the user's name, city, and country and is posted to the /formecho URL at the server, which simply responds with details of the data that was submitted.

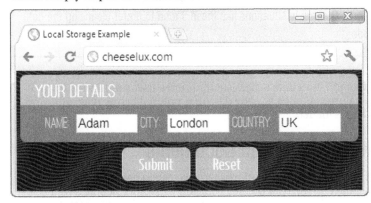

Figure 6-1. Using local storage with form elements

I have used a view model as an intermediary between the input elements and local storage. When the user enters a value into one of the input elements, the value data binding updates the corresponding observable data item in the view model. I use the subscribe function to receive notifications of these changes and write the update to local storage, like this:

```
$.each(viewModel.personalDetails, function(index, item) {
    item.value(localStorage[item.name] || "");
    item.value.subscribe(function(newValue) {
        localStorage[item.name] = newValue;
    });
});
```

I set up the subscription by enumerating through the items in the view model. I use this opportunity to set the initial values in the view model from local storage if there is data available, like this:

```
item.value(localStorage[item.name] || "");
```

When I set the initial value, the values from local storage are propagated through the view model to the input elements, keeping everything up-to-date.

It doesn't make sense to continue to store the form data once the form has been submitted or when the user clicks the Reset button. When either the Submit or Reset button is clicked, I remove the data from local storage, like this:

```
$('#buttonDiv input').button().click(function(e) {
    localStorage.clear();
});
```

The clear method removes all of the data in local storage for the web app (but not for other web apps; only the user or the browser itself can affect storage across web apps). I did not prevent the default action for either button, which means that the form will be submitted by the submit button, and the form will be reset by the reset button.

Tip Strictly speaking, I need not have handled the click event for the reset button since the view model would have led to empty values being written to local storage. In situations like these, I tend to prefer cleansing the data twice in order to get simpler JavaScript code.

The effect of this little web app is that the form data is persistent until the user submits the form. If the user navigates away from the form before submitting it, the data they entered before navigating away will be restored the next time the web app is loaded.

Synchronizing View Model Data Between Documents

The data in local storage is stored on a per-origin basis, meaning that each origin has its own separate local storage area. This means you don't have to worry about key collision with other people's web applications. It also means that we can use web storage to synchronize view models between different documents within the same domain.

When using local storage in this way, I want to be notified when another document modifies a stored data value. I can receive such notifications by handling the storage event, which is emitted by the window browser object. To make this event easier to use, I have created a new kind of observable data item that automatically persists itself to local storage and that loads changed values in response to the storage event. I added this new functionality to the utils.js file, as shown in Listing 6-4.

Listing 6-4. Creating a Persistent Observable Data Item

```
...
ko.persistentObservable = function(keyName, initialValue) {
    var obItem = ko.observable(localStorage[keyName] || initialValue);

    $(window).bind("storage", function(e) {
```

```
            if (e.originalEvent.key == keyName) {
                obItem(e.originalEvent.newValue);
            }
    });
    obItem.subscribe(function(newValue) {
        localStorage[keyName] = newValue;
    });
    return obItem;
}
...
```

This code is a wrapper around the standard observable data item, the local storage data array, and the storage event. The function is called with a key name that refers to a data item in local storage. When the function is called, I use the key to check whether there is already data in local storage for the specified key and, if there is, set the initial value of the observable. If there isn't a default value, I use the initialValue function argument:

```
var obItem = ko.observable(localStorage[keyName] || initialValue);
```

I use jQuery to bind to the storage event on the window object. jQuery normalizes events, wrapping the event objects emitted by elements with a jQuery-specific substitute. I need to get to the underlying event object because it contains information about the change in local storage; I do this through the originalEvent property. When handling the storage event, the originalEvent property returns a StorageEvent object, the most useful properties of which are described in Table 6-1.

Table 6-1. Properties of the StorageEvent Object

Property	Description
key	Returns the key for the item that has been modified
oldValue	Returns the old value for the item that has been modified
newValue	Returns the new value for the item that has been modified
url	Returns the URL of the document that made the change

In the example, I use the key property to determine whether this is an event for the data item that I am monitoring and, if it is, the newValue property to update the regular observable data item:

```
$(window).bind("storage", function(e) {
    if (e.originalEvent.key == keyName) {
        obItem(e.originalEvent.newValue);
    }
});
```

Finally, I use the KO subscribe method so that I can update the local storage value in response to changes in the view model:

```
obItem.subscribe(function(newValue) {
    localStorage[keyName] = newValue;
});
```

With just a few lines of code, I have been able to create a persistent observable data item for my view model.

I have not had to take any special precautions to prevent an infinite loop of event-update-subscription-event occurring. There are two reasons for this. First, the KO observable data item that my code wraps around is smart enough to issue updates only when an updated value is different from the existing value.

Second, the browser triggers the storage event only in *other* documents in the same origin and *not* the document in which the change was made. I have always thought this was slightly odd, but it does mean that my code is simpler than it would otherwise have been.

To demonstrate my newly persistent data items, I have defined a new document called embedded.html, the content of which is shown in Listing 6-5.

Listing 6-5. A New Document That Uses Persistent Observable Data Items

```
<!DOCTYPE html>
<html>
<head>
    <title>Embedded Storage Example</title>
    <link rel="stylesheet" type="text/css" href="jquery-ui-1.8.16.custom.css"/>
    <link rel="stylesheet" type="text/css" href="styles.css"/>
    <script src="jquery-1.7.1.js" type="text/javascript"></script>
    <script src="jquery-ui-1.8.16.custom.js" type="text/javascript"></script>
    <script src='knockout-2.0.0.js' type='text/javascript'></script>
    <script src='utils.js' type='text/javascript'></script>
    <script>
        var viewModel = {
            personalDetails: [
                {name: "name", label: "Name", value: ko.persistentObservable("name")},
                {name: "city", label: "City", value: ko.persistentObservable("city")},
                {name: "country", label: "Country",
                    value: ko.persistentObservable("country")}
            ]
        };

        $(document).ready(function() {
            ko.applyBindings(viewModel);
        });
    </script>
</head>
<body>
    <div class="cheesegroup">
        <div class="grouptitle">Embedded Document</div>
        <div class="groupcontent centered">
            <div data-bind="foreach: personalDetails">
                <span data-bind="text: label"></span>:
                <input class="stwin" data-bind="attr: {name: name}, value: value">
            </div>
        </div>
    </div>
</body>
</html>
```

This document duplicates the input elements from the main example, but without the form and button elements. It does, however, have a view model that uses the persistentObservable data item, meaning that changes to the input element values in this document will be reflected in local storage and, equally, that changes in local storage will be reflected in the input elements. I have not supplied default values for the persistent observable items; if there is no local storage value, then I want the initial value to default to null, which I achieve by not supplying a second argument to the persistentObservable function.

All that remains is to modify the main document. For simplicity, I am embedding one document inside another, but local storage is shared across any documents from the same origin, meaning that this technique will work when those documents are within different browser tabs or windows. Listing 6-6 shows the modifications to example.html, including embedding the embedded.html document.

Listing 6-6. Modifying the Main Example Document

```
<!DOCTYPE html>
<html>
<head>
    <title>Local Storage Example</title>
    <link rel="stylesheet" type="text/css" href="jquery-ui-1.8.16.custom.css"/>
    <link rel="stylesheet" type="text/css" href="styles.css"/>
    <script src="jquery-1.7.1.js" type="text/javascript"></script>
    <script src="jquery-ui-1.8.16.custom.js" type="text/javascript"></script>
    <script src='knockout-2.0.0.js' type='text/javascript'></script>
    <script src='utils.js' type='text/javascript'></script>
    <script>
        var viewModel = {
            personalDetails: [
                {name: "name", label: "Name", value: ko.persistentObservable("name")},
                {name: "city", label: "City", value: ko.persistentObservable("city")},
                {name: "country", label: "Country",
                    value: ko.persistentObservable("country")}
            ]
        };

        $(document).ready(function() {

            ko.applyBindings(viewModel);

            $('#buttonDiv input').button().click(function(e) {
                localStorage.clear();
            });
        });
    </script>
</head>
<body>
    <form action="/formecho" method="POST">
        <div class="cheesegroup">
            <div class="grouptitle">Your Details</div>
            <div class="groupcontent centered">
                <div data-bind="foreach: personalDetails">
                    <span data-bind="text: label"></span>:
```

```
                    <input class="stwin" data-bind="attr: {name: name}, value: value">
                </div>
            </div>
        </div>

        <iframe src="embedded.html"></iframe>

        <div id="buttonDiv">
            <input type="submit" value="Submit">
            <input type="reset" value="Reset">
        </div>
    </form>
</body>
</html>
```

I have used the same keys for the persistentObservable function when defining the view model and added an iframe element that embeds the other HTML document. Since both are loaded from the same origin, the browser shares the same local storage between them. Changing the value of an input element in one document will trigger a corresponding change in the other document, via local storage and the two view models.

■ **Caution** The browsers don't provide any guarantees about the integrity of a data item if updates are written to local storage from two documents simultaneously. It is hard to cater for this eventuality (and I have never seen it happen), but it is prudent to assume that data corruption can occur if you are sharing local storage.

Using Session Storage

The complement to local storage is *session storage*, which is accessed through the sessionStorage object. The sessionStorage and localStorage objects are used in the same way and emit the same storage event. The difference is that the data is deleted when the document is closed in the browser (more specifically, the data is deleted when the top-level browsing context is destroyed, but that's usually the same thing).

The most common use for session storage is to preserve data when a document is reloaded. This is a useful technique, although I have to admit that I tend to use local storage to achieve the same effect instead. The main benefit of session storage is performance, since the data is usually held in memory and doesn't need to be written to disk. That said, if you care about the marginal performance gains that this offers, then you may need to consider whether the browser is the best environment for your app. Listing 6-7 shows how I have added support for session persistence to my observable data item in utils.js.

Listing 6-7. Defining a Semi-persistent Observable Data Item Using Session Storage

```
ko.persistentObservable = function(keyName, initialValue, useSession) {
    var storageObject = useSession ? sessionStorage : localStorage
    var obItem = ko.observable(storageObject[keyName] || initialValue);
```

```
    $(window).bind("storage", function(e) {
        if (e.originalEvent.key == keyName) {
            obItem(e.originalEvent.newValue);
        }
    });
    obItem.subscribe(function(newValue) {
        storageObject[keyName] = newValue;
    });
    return obItem;
}
```

Since the `sessionStorage` and `localStorage` objects expose the same features and use the same event, I am able to easily modify my local storage observable item to add support for session storage. I have added an argument to the function that, if true, switches to session storage. I use local storage if the argument is not provided or is `false`. Listing 6-8 shows how I have applied session storage to two of the observable data items in the example view model.

Listing 6-8. Using Session Storage

```
...
var viewModel = {
    personalDetails: [
        {name: "name", label: "Name", value: ko.persistentObservable("name")},
        {name: "city", label: "City",
            value: ko.persistentObservable("city", null, true)},
        {name: "country", label: "Country",
            value: ko.persistentObservable("country", null, true)}
    ]
};
...
```

The values of the `City` and `Country` elements are handled using session storage while the `Name` element remains with local storage. If you load the example into the browser, you will find that reloading the document doesn't clear any of the values you have entered. However, only the `Name` value remains if you close and reopen the document.

Using Local Storage with Offline Web Applications

Part of the benefit that comes from using local storage is that it is available offline. This means that we can use local data to address the problems arising from Ajax GET requests when the browser is offline. Listing 6-9 shows the cached CheeseLux web app from the previous chapter, updated to take advantage of local storage.

Listing 6-9. Using Local Storage for Offline Web Apps That Use Ajax

```
<!DOCTYPE html>
<html manifest="cheeselux.appcache">
<head>
    <title>CheeseLux</title>
    <link rel="stylesheet" type="text/css" href="styles.css"/>
    <script src="jquery-1.7.1.js" type="text/javascript"></script>
```

```
<script src="jquery-ui-1.8.16.custom.js" type="text/javascript"></script>
<script src='knockout-2.0.0.js' type='text/javascript'></script>
<script src='utils.js' type='text/javascript'></script>
<script src='signals.js' type='text/javascript'></script>
<script src='hasher.js' type='text/javascript'></script>
<script src='crossroads.js' type='text/javascript'></script>
<link rel="stylesheet" type="text/css" href="jquery-ui-1.8.16.custom.css"/>
<noscript>
    <meta http-equiv="refresh" content="0; noscript.html"/>
</noscript>
<script>
    var cheeseModel = {
        cache: {
            status: ko.observable(window.applicationCache.status),
            online: ko.observable(window.navigator.onLine)
        }
    };

    $.getJSON("products.json", function(data) {
        cheeseModel.products = data;
        localStorage["jsondata"] = JSON.stringify(data);
    }).error(function() {
        if (localStorage["jsondata"]) {
            cheeseModel.products = JSON.parse(localStorage["jsondata"]);
        }
    }).complete(function() {
        $(document).ready(function() {
            if (cheeseModel.products) {
                enhanceViewModel();
                ko.applyBindings(cheeseModel);

                hasher.initialized.add(crossroads.parse, crossroads);
                hasher.changed.add(crossroads.parse, crossroads);
                hasher.init();

                crossroads.addRoute("category/:cat:", function(cat) {
                    cheeseModel.selectedCategory(cat ||
                                                cheeseModel.products[0].category);
                });

                $('#buttonDiv input:submit').button();
                $('div.navSelectors').buttonset();
                $(window).bind("online offline", function() {
                    cheeseModel.cache.online(window.navigator.onLine);
                });

                $(window.applicationCache).bind("checking noupdate downloading " +
                    "progress cached updateready", function(e) {
                        cheeseModel.cache.status(window.applicationCache.status);
                });

                $('div.tagcontainer a').button().filter(':not([href])')
```

```
                    .click(function(e) {
                        e.preventDefault();
                        if ($(this).attr("data-action") == "update") {
                            window.applicationCache.update();
                        } else {
                            window.applicationCache.swapCache();
                            window.location.reload(false);
                        }
                    });
            } else {
                var dialogHTML = '<div>Try again later</div>';
                $(dialogHTML).dialog({
                    modal: true,
                    title: "Ajax Error",
                    buttons: [{text: "OK",
                               click: function() {$(this).dialog("close")}}]
                });
            }
        });
    });
    </script>
</head>
<body>
    <div id="logobar">
        <img src="cheeselux.png">
        <div class="tagcontainer">
            <span id="tagline">Gourmet European Cheese</span>
            <div>
                <span data-bind="visible: cheeseModel.cache.online()">
                    <a data-bind="visible: cheeseModel.cache.status() != 4"
                       data-action="update" class="cachelink">Check for Updates</a>
                    <a data-bind="visible: cheeseModel.cache.status() == 4"
                       data-action="swapCache" class="cachelink">Apply Update</a>
                    <a class="cachelink" href="/news.html">News</a>
                </span>
                <span data-bind="visible: !cheeseModel.cache.online()">
                    (Offline)
                </span>
            </div>
        </div>
    </div>

    <div class="cheesegroup">
        <div class="navSelectors" data-bind="foreach: products">
            <a data-bind="formatAttr: {attr: 'href', prefix: '#category/',
               value: category},
            css: {selectedItem: (category == cheeseModel.selectedCategory())}">
                <span data-bind="text: category">
            </a>
        </div>
    </div>
```

```
    <form action="/shipping" method="post">
        <div data-bind="foreach: products">
            <div class="cheesegroup"
                data-bind="fadeVisible: category == cheeseModel.selectedCategory()">
                <div class="grouptitle" data-bind="text: category"></div>
                <!-- ko foreach: items -->
                <div class="groupcontent">
                    <label data-bind="attr: {for: id}" class="cheesename">
                        <span data-bind="text: name">
                        </span> $(<span data-bind="text:price"></span>)</label>
                    <input data-bind="attr: {name: id}, value: quantity"/>
                    <span data-bind="visible: subtotal" class="subtotal">
                        ($<span data-bind="text: subtotal"></span>)
                    </span>
                </div>
                <!-- /ko -->
                <div class="groupcontent">
                    <label class="cheesename">Total:</label>
                    <span class="subtotal" id="total">
                        $<span data-bind="text: cheeseModel.total()"></span>
                    </span>
                </div>
            </div>
        </div>
        <div id="buttonDiv">
            <input type="submit" value="Submit Order"/>
        </div>
    </form>
</body>
</html>
```

In this listing, I use the JSON.stringify method to store a copy of the view model data when the Ajax request is successful:

```
$.getJSON("products.json", function(data) {
    cheeseModel.products = data;
    localStorage["jsondata"] = JSON.stringify(data);
})
```

I added the products.json URL to the NETWORK section of the manifest for this web app, so I have a reasonable expectation that the data will be available and that the Ajax request will succeed.

If, however, the request fails, which will definitely happen if the browser is offline, then I try to locate and restore the serialized data from local storage, like this:

```
}).error(function() {
    if (localStorage["jsondata"]) {
        cheeseModel.products = JSON.parse(localStorage["jsondata"]);
    }
})
```

Assuming the initial request works, I will have a good fallback position if subsequent requests fail. The effect that this technique creates is similar to the way that Firefox handles Ajax requests when the browser is offline because I end up using the last version of the data I was able to obtain from the server.

Notice that I have restructured the code so that the rest of the web app setup occurs in the `complete` handler function, which is triggered irrespective of the outcome of the Ajax request. The success or failure of Ajax no longer determines how I processed it; now it is all about whether or not I have data, either fresh from the server or restored from local storage.

Using Local Storage with Offline Forms

I mentioned in Chapter 5 that the only way of dealing with POST requests in a cached application is to prevent the user from initiating the request when the browser is offline. This remains true, but you can improve the experience that you deliver to the user by using local storage to create persistent values. To demonstrate this approach, I first need to update the enhanceViewModel function in the `utils.js` file to use local storage to persist the form values, as shown in Listing 6-10.

Listing 6-10. Updating the enhanceViewModel Function to Use Local Storage

```
...
function enhanceViewModel() {

    cheeseModel.selectedCategory
        = ko.persistentObservable("selectedCategory", cheeseModel.products[0].category);

    mapProducts(function(item) {
        item.quantity = ko.persistentObservable(item.id + "_quantity", 0);
        item.subtotal = ko.computed(function() {
            return this.quantity() * this.price;
        }, item);
    }, cheeseModel.products, "items");

    cheeseModel.total = ko.computed(function() {
        var total = 0;
        mapProducts(function(elem) {
            total += elem.subtotal();
        }, cheeseModel.products, "items");
        return total;
    });
};
...
```

This is a pretty simple change, but there are a couple of points to note. I want to make the view model quantity property persistent for each cheese product, so I use the value of the item id property to avoid key collision in local storage:

```
item.quantity = ko.persistentObservable(item.id + "_quantity", 0);
```

The second point to note is that when I load values from local storage, I will be putting strings, and not numbers, in the view model. However, JavaScript is clever enough to convert strings when performing multiplication operations, like this:

```
return this.quantity() * this.price;
```

Everything works as I would like it to work. However, JavaScript uses the same symbol to denote string concatenation and numeric addition, so if I had been trying to sum values in the view model, I would have had to take the extra step of parsing the value, like this:

```
return Number(this.quantity()) + someOtherValue;
```

Using Persistence in the Offline Application

Now that I have modified the view model, I can change the main document to improve the way that I handle the form element when the browser is offline. Listing 6-11 shows the changes to the HTML markup.

Listing 6-11. Adding Buttons That Handle the Form When the Browser Is Offline

```
...
<form action="/shipping" method="post">
    <div data-bind="foreach: products">
        <div class="cheesegroup"
            data-bind="fadeVisible: category == cheeseModel.selectedCategory()">
            <div class="grouptitle" data-bind="text: category"></div>
            <!-- ko foreach: items -->
            <div class="groupcontent">
                <label data-bind="attr: {for: id}" class="cheesename">
                    <span data-bind="text: name">
                    </span> $(<span data-bind="text:price"></span>)</label>
                <input data-bind="attr: {name: id}, value: quantity"/>
                <span data-bind="visible: subtotal" class="subtotal">
                    ($<span data-bind="text: subtotal"></span>)
                </span>
            </div>
            <!-- /ko -->
            <div class="groupcontent">
                <label class="cheesename">Total:</label>
                <span class="subtotal" id="total">
                    $<span data-bind="text: cheeseModel.total()"></span>
                </span>
            </div>
        </div>
    </div>
    <div id="buttonDiv">
        <input type="submit" value="Submit Order"
            data-bind="visible: cheeseModel.cache.online()"/>
        <input type="button" value="Save for Later"
            data-bind="visible: !cheeseModel.cache.online()"/>
    </div>
</form>
...
```

I have added a Save for Later button to the document, which is visible when the browser is offline. I have also changed the submit button so that it is visible only when the browser is online. Listing 6-12 shows the corresponding changes to the script element.

Listing 6-12. Changes to the script Element to Support Offline Forms

```
<script>
    var cheeseModel = {
```

```
    cache: {
        status: ko.observable(window.applicationCache.status),
        online: ko.observable(window.navigator.onLine)
    }
};

$.getJSON("products.json", function(data) {
    cheeseModel.products = data;
    localStorage["jsondata"] = JSON.stringify(data);
}).error(function() {
    if (localStorage["jsondata"]) {
        cheeseModel.products = JSON.parse(localStorage["jsondata"]);
    }
}).complete(function() {
    $(document).ready(function() {
        if (cheeseModel.products) {
            enhanceViewModel();
        ko.applyBindings(cheeseModel);

        hasher.initialized.add(crossroads.parse, crossroads);
        hasher.changed.add(crossroads.parse, crossroads);
        hasher.init();

        crossroads.addRoute("category/:cat:", function(cat) {
            cheeseModel.selectedCategory(cat ||
                                    cheeseModel.products[0].category);
        });

        $('#buttonDiv input').button().click(function(e) {
            if (e.target.type == "button") {
                createDialog("Basket Saved for Later");
            } else {
                localStorage.clear();
            }
        });

        $('div.navSelectors').buttonset();
        $(window).bind("online offline", function() {
            cheeseModel.cache.online(window.navigator.onLine);
        });

        $(window.applicationCache).bind("checking noupdate downloading " +
            "progress cached updateready", function(e) {
                cheeseModel.cache.status(window.applicationCache.status);
        });

        $('div.tagcontainer a').button().filter(':not([href])')
            .click(function(e) {
                e.preventDefault();
                if ($(this).attr("data-action") == "update") {
                    window.applicationCache.update();
                } else {
```

```
                            window.applicationCache.swapCache();
                            window.location.reload(false);
                    }
                });
            } else {
                createDialog("Try again later");
            }
        });
    });
</script>
```

This is a simple change, and you'll quickly realize that I am doing some mild misdirection. When the browser is online, the user can submit the form as normal, and any data in local storage is cleared. The misdirection comes when the browser is offline and the user clicks the Save for Later button. All I do is call the createDialog function, telling the user that the form data has been saved. However, I don't actually need to save the data because I am using persistent observable data items in the view model. The user doesn't need to know about this; they just get the benefit of the persistence and a clear signal from the web application that the form data has not been submitted. When the browser is online again, the user can submit the data. Using local storage all of the time means that the user won't lose their data if they close and later reload the application before being able to submit the form to the server. For completeness, Listing 6-13 shows the createDialog function, which I defined in the utils.js file. This is the same approach I used to create an error dialog in the original example, and I moved the code into a function because I needed to create the same kind of dialog box at multiple points in the application.

Listing 6-13. The createDialog Function

```
function createDialog(message) {
    $('<div>' + message + '</div>').dialog({
        modal: true,
        title: "Message",
        buttons: [{text: "OK",
            click: function() {$(this).dialog("close")}}]
    });
};
```

I have taken a very simple and direct approach to dealing with form data when the browser is offline, but you can easily see how a more sophisticated approach could be created. You might, for example, respond to the online event by prompting the user to submit the data or even submit it automatically using Ajax. Whatever approach you take, you must ensure that the user understands and approves of what your web app is doing.

Storing Complex Data

Storing name/value pairs is perfectly suited to storing form data, but for anything more sophisticated, such a simple approach starts to break down. There is another browser feature, called *IndexedDB*, which you can use to store and work with more complex data.

■ **Note** IndexedDB is only one of two competing standards for storing complex data in the browser. The other is WebSQL. As I write this, the W3C is supporting IndexedDB, but it is entirely possible that WebSQL will make a comeback or, at least, become a de facto standard. I have not included WebSQL in this chapter because support for it is limited at present, but this is an area of functionality that is far from settled, and you should review the support for both standards before adopting one of them for your projects.

It is still early days for IndexedDB, and as I write this, the functionality is available only through vendor-specified prefixes, signifying that the browser implementations are still experimental and may deviate from the W3C specification. Currently, the browser that adheres most closely to the W3C specification is Mozilla Firefox, so this is the browser I have used to demonstrate IndexedDB.

■ **Caution** The examples in this chapter may not work with browsers other than Firefox. In fact, they may not work even with versions of Firefox other than the one I used in this chapter (version 10). That said, you should still be able to get a solid understanding of how IndexedDB works, even if the specification or implementations change.

The IndexedDB feature is organized around *databases* that, like local and session storage, are isolated on a per-origin basis so that they can be shared between applications from the same origin. IndexedDB doesn't follow the SQL-based table structure that is common in relational databases. An IndexedDB database is made up of *object stores*, which can contain JavaScript objects. You can add JavaScript objects to object stores, and you can query those stores in different ways, some of which I demonstrate shortly.

The result of this approach is a storage mechanism that is more in keeping with the style of the JavaScript language but that ends up being slightly awkward to use. Almost all operations in IndexedDB are performed as asynchronous requests to which functions can be attached so that they are executed when the operation completes. To demonstrate how IndexedDB works, I am going to create a Cheese Finder application. I will put the cheese product data into an IndexedDB database and provide the user with some different ways of searching the data for cheeses they might like. Figure 6-2 shows the finished web app to help provide some context for the code that follows.

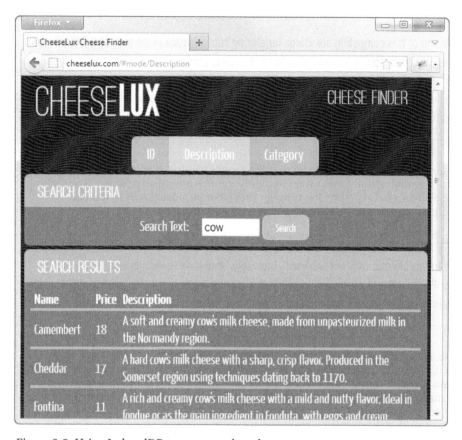

Figure 6-2. Using IndexedDB to query product data

The figure shows the option to search the description of each product in use. I have searched for the term *cow*, and those products whose descriptions contain this term are listed at the bottom of the page. (There are several matches because many of the descriptions explain that the cheese is made from cows' milk.)

Creating the IndexedDB Database and Object Store

The code for this example is split between the utils.js file and the main example.html document. I'll be jumping between these files to demonstrate the core features that IndexedDB offers. To begin, I have defined a DBO object and the setupDatabase function in utils.js, as shown in Listing 6-14.

Listing 6-14. Setting Up the IndexedDB Database

```
var DBO = {
    dbVersion: 31
}

function setupDatabase(data, callback) {
    var indexDB = window.indexedDB || window.mozIndexedDB;
    var req = indexDB.open("CheeseDB", DBO.dbVersion);

    req.onupgradeneeded = function(e) {
        var db = req.result;

        var existingStores = db.objectStoreNames;
        for (var i = 0; i < existingStores.length; i++) {
            db.deleteObjectStore(existingStores[i]);
        }

        var objectStore = db.createObjectStore("products", {keyPath: "id"});
        objectStore.createIndex("category", "category", {unique: false});

        $.each(data, function(index, item) {
            var currentCategory = item.category;
            $.each(item.items, function(index, item) {
                item.category = currentCategory;
                objectStore.add(item);
            });
        });
    };

    req.onsuccess = function(e) {
        DBO.db = this.result;
        callback();
    };
};
```

I have defined an object called DBO that performs two important tasks. First, it defines the version of the database that I am expecting to work with. Each time I make a change to the database schema, I increment the value of the dbVersion property, and as you can see, it took me 31 changes until I got the result I wanted for this example. This was largely because of the differences between the current draft of the specification and the implementation in Firefox.

■ **Tip** The version number is an important mechanism in ensuring I am working with the right version of the schema for my app. I'll show you how to check the schema version and, if needed, upgrade the schema, shortly.

In the setupDatabase function, I begin by locating the object that acts as the gateway to the IndexedDB databases, like this:

```
var indexDB = window.indexedDB || window.mozIndexedDB;
```

The IndexedDB feature is available in Firefox only through the window.mozIndexedDB object at the moment, but that will change to window.indexedDB once the implementation converges on the final specification. To give you the greatest chance of making the examples in this part of the chapter work, I try to use the "official" IndexedDB object first and fall back to the vendor-prefixed alternative if it isn't available. The next step is to open the database:

```
var req = indexDB.open("CheeseDB", DBO.dbVersion);
```

The two arguments are the name of the database and the expected schema version. IndexedDB will open the specified database if it already exists and create it if it doesn't. The result from the open method is an object that represents the request to open the database. To get anything done in IndexedDB, you must supply handler functions for one or more of the possible outcomes from a request.

Responding to the Upgrade-Needed Outcome

I care about two possible outcomes when I open the database. First, I want to be notified if the database already exists and the schema version doesn't match the version I am expecting. When this happens, I want to delete the object stores in the database and start over. I receive notification of a schema mismatch by registering a function through the onupgradeneeded property:

```
req.onupgradeneeded = function(e) {
    var db = req.result;

    var existingStores = db.objectStoreNames;
    for (var i = 0; i < existingStores.length; i++) {
        db.deleteObjectStore(existingStores[i]);
    }

    var objectStore = db.createObjectStore("products", {keyPath: "id"});
    objectStore.createIndex("category", "category", {unique: false});

    $.each(data, function(index, item) {
        var currentCategory = item.category;
        $.each(item.items, function(index, item) {
            item.category = currentCategory;
            objectStore.add(item);
        });
    });
};
```

The database object is available through the result property of the request returned by the open method. I get a list of the existing object stores through the objectStoreNames property and delete each in turn using the deleteObjectStore method. In deleting the object stores, I also delete the data they contain. This is fine for such a simple web app where all of the data is coming from the server and is easily replaced, but you may need to take a more sophisticated approach if your databases contain data that has been generated as a result of user actions.

■ **Caution** The function assigned to the onupgradeneeded property is the only opportunity you have to modify the schema of the database. If you try to add or delete an object store elsewhere, the browser will generate an error.

Once the existing object stores are out of the way, I can create some new ones using the createObject store method. The arguments to this method are the name of the new store and an optional object containing configuration settings to be applied to the new store. I have used the keyPath configuration option, which lets me set a default key for objects that are added to the store. I have specified the id property as the key. I have also created an index using the createIndex method on the newly created object store. An index allows me to perform searches in the object store using a property other than the key, in this case, the category property. I'll show you how to use an index shortly.

Finally, I add objects to the data store. When I use this function in the main document, I'll be using the data I get from an Ajax request for the products.json file. This is in the same format as the data I have been using throughout this book. I use the jQuery each function to enumerate each category and the items it contains. I have added a category property to each item so that I can find all of the products that belong to the same category more easily.

■ **Tip** The objects you add to an object store are cloned using the HTML5 *structured clone* technique. This is a more comprehensive serialization technique than JSON, and the browser will generally manage to deal with complex objects, just as long as none of the properties is a function or DOM API object.

Responding to the Success Outcome

The second outcome I care about is *success*, which I handle by assigning a function to the onsuccess property of the request to open the database, as follows:

```
req.onsuccess = function(e) {
    DBO.db = this.result;
    callback();
};
```

The first statement in this function assigns the opened database to the db property of the DBO object. This is just a convenient way to keep a handle on the database so that I can use it in other functions, something that I'll demonstrate shortly.

The second statement invokes the callback function that was passed as the second argument to the setupDatabase function. It isn't safe to assume that the database is open until the onsuccess function is executed, which means I need to have some mechanism for signaling the function caller that the database has been successfully opened and data-related operations can be started.

■ **Tip** IndexedDB requests have a counterpart outcome property called `onerror`. I won't be doing any error handling in these examples because, as I write this, trying to deal with IndexedDB errors causes more problems than it solves. Ideally, this will have improved by the time you read this chapter, and you will be able to write more robust code.

Incorporating the Database into the Web Application

Listing 6-15 shows the markup and inline JavaScript for the example application. With the exception of the database-specific functions, everything in this example relies on topics covered in earlier chapters.

Listing 6-15. The Database-Consuming Web Application

```
<!DOCTYPE html>
<html>
<head>
    <title>CheeseLux Cheese Finder</title>
    <link rel="stylesheet" type="text/css" href="styles.css"/>
    <script src="jquery-1.7.1.js" type="text/javascript"></script>
    <script src="jquery-ui-1.8.16.custom.js" type="text/javascript"></script>
    <script src='knockout-2.0.0.js' type='text/javascript'></script>
    <script src='utils.js' type='text/javascript'></script>
    <script src='signals.js' type='text/javascript'></script>
    <script src='hasher.js' type='text/javascript'></script>
    <script src='crossroads.js' type='text/javascript'></script>
    <link rel="stylesheet" type="text/css" href="jquery-ui-1.8.16.custom.css"/>
    <noscript>
        <meta http-equiv="refresh" content="0; noscript.html"/>
    </noscript>
    <script>

        var viewModel = {
            searchModes: ["ID", "Description", "Category"],
            selectedMode: ko.observable("ID"),
            selectedItems: ko.observableArray()
        };

        function handleSearchResults(resultData) {
            if (resultData) {
                viewModel.selectedItems.removeAll();
                if ($.isArray(resultData)) {
                    for (var i = 0; i < resultData.length; i++) {
                        viewModel.selectedItems.push(resultData[i]);
                    }
                } else {
                    viewModel.selectedItems.push(resultData);
                }
            }
        }
```

```
        }
        $.getJSON("products.json", function(data) {
            setupDatabase(data, function() {
                $(document).ready(function() {

                    hasher.initialized.add(crossroads.parse, crossroads);
                    hasher.changed.add(crossroads.parse, crossroads);
                    hasher.init();

                    crossroads.addRoute("mode/:mode:", function(mode) {
                        viewModel.selectedMode(mode || viewModel.searchModes[0]);
                        viewModel.selectedItems.removeAll();
                        $('#textsearch').val("");
                    });
                    crossroads.parse(location.hash.slice(1));

                    ko.applyBindings(viewModel);
                    $('div.navSelectors').buttonset();
                    $('div.groupcontent a').button().click(function() {
                        var sText = $('#textsearch').val();
                        switch (viewModel.selectedMode()) {
                            case "ID":
                                getProductByID(sText, handleSearchResults)
                                break;
                            case "Description":
                                getProductsByDescription(sText, handleSearchResults);
                                break;
                            case "Category":
                                getProductsByCategory(sText, handleSearchResults);
                                break;
                        };
                    });
                });
            });
        });
    </script>
</head>
<body>
    <div id="logobar">
        <img src="cheeselux.png">
        <div class="tagcontainer">
            <span id="tagline">Cheese Finder</span>
        </div>
    </div>

    <div class="cheesegroup">
        <div class="navSelectors" data-bind="foreach: searchModes">
            <a data-bind="formatAttr: {attr: 'href', prefix: '#mode/', value: $data},
                css: {selectedItem: $data == $root.selectedMode()}">
                <span data-bind="text: $data">
            </a>
```

```
            </div>
        </div>

        <div class="cheesegroup">
            <div class="grouptitle">Search Criteria</div>
            <div class="groupcontent centered">
                <label class="cheesename">Search Text:</label>
                <input id="textsearch" class="stwin"/>
                <a id="textsearch" class="smallbutton">Search</a>
            </div>
        </div>

        <div class="cheesegroup">
            <div class="grouptitle">Search Results</div>
            <div class="groupcontent centered">
                <table id="resultTable" data-bind="visible: selectedItems().length > 0">
                    <thead>
                        <tr><th>Name</th><th>Price</th><th>Description</th></tr>
                        <tr><td colspan=3 class="sumline"></td></tr>
                    </thead>
                    <tbody>
                        <!-- ko foreach: viewModel.selectedItems() -->
                        <tr>
                            <td data-bind="text: name"></td>
                            <td data-bind="text: price"></td>
                            <td data-bind="text: description"></td>
                        </tr>
                        <tr><td colspan=3 class="sumline"></td></tr>
                        <!-- /ko -->
                    </tbody>
                </table>
                <div data-bind="visible: selectedItems().length == 0">
                    No matches
                </div>
            </div>
        </div>
    </div>
</body>
</html>
```

As you might expect by now, I have used a view model to bind the state of the application to the HTML markup. Most of the document is taken up defining and controlling the view given to the user and supporting user interactions.

When the user clicks the search button, one of three functions in the utils.js file is called, depending on the selected search mode. If the user has elected to search by product ID, then the getProductByID function is called. The getProductsByDescription function is used when the user wants to search the product descriptions, and the getProductsByCategory function is used to find all the products in a specific category. Each of these functions takes two arguments: the text to search for and a callback function to which the results should be dispatched (even searching an object store is an asynchronous operation with IndexedDB). The callback function is the same for all three search modes: handleSearchResults. The result from the search functions will be a single product object or an array of objects. The job of the handleSearchResults function is to clear the contents of the selectedItems observable array in the view model and replace them with the new results; this causes the elements to be updated and the results to be displayed to the user.

Notice that I place most of the code statements in my inline `script` element inside the callback for the `setupDatabase` function. This is the function that is called when the database has successfully been opened.

Locating an Object by Key

The first of the search functions is `getProductByID`, which locates an object based on the value of the `id` property. You will recall that I specified this property as the key for the object store when I created the database:

```
var objectStore = db.createObjectStore("products", {keyPath: "id"});
```

Getting an object using its key is pretty simple. Listing 6-16 shows the `getProductByID` function, which I defined in the `utils.js` file.

Listing 6-16. Locating an Object Using Its Key

```
function getProductByID(id, callback) {
    var transaction = DBO.db.transaction(["products"]);
    var objectStore = transaction.objectStore("products");
    var req = objectStore.get(id);
    req.onsuccess = function(e) {
        callback(this.result);
    };
}
```

This function shows the basic pattern for querying an object store in a database. First, you must create a transaction, using the `transaction` method, declaring the objects stores that you want to work with. Only then can you open an object store, using the `objectStore` method on the transaction you just created.

⬛ **Tip** You don't need to explicitly close your object store or your transactions; the browser closes them for you when they are out of scope. There is no benefit in trying to explicitly force the store or transactions to close.

I obtain the object with the specified key using the get method, which matches at most one object (if there are multiple objects with the same key, then the first matching object is matched). The method returns a request, and I must supply a function for the `onsuccess` property to be notified when the search has completed. The matched object is available in the `result` property of the request, which I pass back to the main part of the web app by invoking the callback function passed to the `getProductByID` function (which, as you will recall, is the `handleSearchResults` function).

The (eventual) result from the get method is a JavaScript object or, if there is no match, `null`. I don't have to worry about re-creating an object from the serialized data stored by the database or use any kind of object-relational mapping layer. The IndexedDB database works on JavaScript objects throughout, which is a nice feature.

It is a little frustrating to have to use callbacks every time you want to perform a simple operation, but it quickly becomes second nature. The result is a storage mechanism that fits nicely into the JavaScript world and that doesn't tie up the main thread of execution when long operations are being performed but that requires careful thought and application design to be properly used.

Locating Objects Using a Cursor

I have to take a different approach when the user wants to search for products by their description. Descriptions are not a key in my object store, and I want to be able to look for partial matches (otherwise the user would have to exactly type in all of the description to make a match). Listing 6-17 shows the getProductsByDescription function, which is defined in utils.js.

Listing 6-17. Locating Objects Using a Cursor

```
function getProductsByDescription(text, callback) {
    var searchTerm = text.toLowerCase();
    var results = [];
    var transaction = DBO.db.transaction(["products"]);
    var objectStore = transaction.objectStore("products");
    objectStore.openCursor().onsuccess = function(e) {
        var cursor = this.result;
        if (cursor) {
            if (cursor.value.description.toLowerCase().indexOf(searchTerm) > -1) {
                results.push(cursor.value);
            }
            cursor.continue();
        } else {
            callback(results);
        }
    };
};
```

My technique here is to use a *cursor* to enumerate all of the objects in the object store and look for those whose products property contains the search term provided by the user. A cursor simply keeps track of my progress as I enumerate through a sequence of database objects.

IndexedDB doesn't have a text search facility, so I have to handle this myself. Calling the openCursor method on an object store creates a request whose onsuccess callback is executed when the cursor is opened. The cursor itself is available through the result property of the this context object. (It should also be available through the result property of the event passed to the function, but the current implementation doesn't always set this reliably.)

If the cursor isn't null, then there is an object available in the value property. I check to see whether the description property of the object contains the term I am looking for, and if it does, I push the object into a local array. To move the cursor to the next object, I call the continue method, which executes the onsuccess function again.

The cursor is null when I have read all of the objects in the object store. At this point, my local array contains all of the objects that match my search, and I pass them back to the main part of the web application using the callback supplied as the second argument to the getProductsByDescription function.

Locating Objects Using an Index

Enumerating all of the objects in an object store isn't an efficient way of finding objects, which is why I created an index for the category property when I set up the object store:

```
objectStore.createIndex("category", "category", {unique: false});
```

The arguments to the createIndex method are the name of the index, the property in the objects that will be indexed, and a configuration object, which I have used to tell IndexedDB that the values for the category property are not unique.

The getProductsByCategory function, which is shown in Listing 6-18, uses the index to narrow the objects that are enumerated by the cursor.

Listing 6-18. Using an IndexedDB Index

```
function getProductsByCategory(searchCat, callback) {
    var results = [];
    var transaction = DBO.db.transaction(["products"]);
    var objectStore = transaction.objectStore("products");
    var keyRange = IDBKeyRange.only(searchCat);
    var index = objectStore.index("category");
    index.openCursor(keyRange).onsuccess = function(e) {
        var cursor = this.result;
        if (cursor) {
            results.push(cursor.value);
            cursor.continue();
        } else {
            callback(results);
        }
    };
};
```

The IDBKeyRange object has a number of methods for constraining the key values that will match objects in the object store. I have used the only method to specify that I want exact matches only.

I open the index by calling the index method on the object store and pass in the IDBKeyRange object as an argument when I open the cursor. This has the effect of narrowing the set of objects that are available through the cursor, meaning that the results I pass via the callback contain only the cheese products in the specified category. There is no partial matching in this example; the user must enter the entire category name, such as French Cheese.

Summary

In this chapter, I showed you how to use local storage to persistently store name/value pairs in the browser and how this feature can be used in an offline web app to deal with HTML forms. I also showed you the IndexedDB features, which is far less mature but shows promise as a foundation for storing and querying more complex data using natural JavaScript objects and language idioms.

IndexedDB isn't yet ready for production use, but I find that local storage is very robust and helpful in a wide range of situations. I find it especially useful in making forms more useful and less annoying, much as I demonstrated in this chapter. The local storage feature is very easy to use, especially when it is embedded within your application view model.

In the next chapter, I show you how to create responsive web apps that adapt and respond to the capabilities of the devices on which they run.

CHAPTER 7

Creating Responsive Web Apps

There are two approaches to targeting multiple platforms with a web app. The first is to create a different version of the app for each kind of device you want to target: desktop, smartphone, tablet, and so on. I'll give you some examples of how to do this in Chapter 8.

The other approach, and the topic of this chapter, is to create a *responsive web app*, which simply means that the web app adapts to the capabilities of the device it is running on. I like this approach because it doesn't draw a hard distinction between mobile and "normal" devices.

This is important because the capabilities of smartphones, tablets, and desktops blur together. Many mobile browsers already have good HTML5 support, and desktop machines with touchscreens are becoming more common. In this chapter, I'll show you techniques that you can use to create web applications that are flexible and fluid.

Setting the Viewport

I need to address one issue that is specific to the browsers running on smartphones and tablets (which I'll start referring to as *mobile browsers*). Mobile browsers typically start from the assumption that a website will have been designed for a large-screened desktop device and that, as a consequence, the user will need some help to be able to view it. This is done through the *viewport*, which scales down the web page so that the user gets a sense of the overall page structure. The user then zooms in to a particular region of the page in order to read or use it. You can see the effect in Figure 7-1.

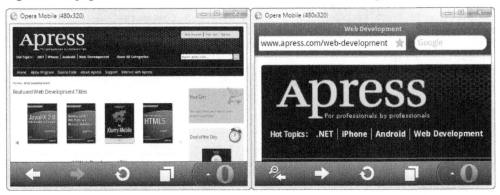

Figure 7-1. The effect of the default viewport in a mobile browser

---

■ **Note** The screenshots in Figure 7-1 are of the Opera Mobile emulator, which you can get from www.opera.com/developer/tools/mobile. Although it has some quirks, this emulator is reasonably faithful to the real Opera Mobile, which is widely used in mobile devices. I like it because it allows me to create emulators with screen sizes ranging from small smartphones to large tablets and to select whether touch events are supported. As a bonus, you can debug and inspect your web app using the standard Opera development tools. An emulator is no substitute for testing on a range of real hardware devices but can be very convenient during the early stages of development.

This is a sensible feature, but you need to disable it for web apps; otherwise, content and controls are displayed at a size that is too small to use. Listing 7-1 shows how to disable this feature using the HTML meta tag, which I have applied to a simplified version of the CheeseLux web app, which will be the foundation example for this chapter.

Listing 7-1. Using the meta Tag to Control the Viewport in the CheeseLux Web App

```
<!DOCTYPE html>
<html>
<head>
    <title>CheeseLux</title>
    <link rel="stylesheet" type="text/css" href="styles.css"/>
    <script src="jquery-1.7.1.js" type="text/javascript"></script>
    <script src="jquery-ui-1.8.16.custom.js" type="text/javascript"></script>
    <script src='knockout-2.0.0.js' type='text/javascript'></script>
    <script src='utils.js' type='text/javascript'></script>
    <script src='signals.js' type='text/javascript'></script>
    <script src='crossroads.js' type='text/javascript'></script>
    <script src='hasher.js' type='text/javascript'></script>
    <script src='modernizr-2.0.6.js' type='text/javascript'></script>
    <link rel="stylesheet" type="text/css" href="jquery-ui-1.8.16.custom.css"/>
    <meta name="viewport" content="width=device-width, initial-scale=1">
    <script>
        var cheeseModel = {};

        $.getJSON("products.json", function(data) {
            cheeseModel.products = data;
        }).success(function() {
            $(document).ready(function() {
                $('#buttonDiv input:submit').button().css("font-family", "Yanone");
                $('div.cheesegroup').not("#basket").css("width", "50%");
                $('div.navSelectors').buttonset();

                enhanceViewModel();
                ko.applyBindings(cheeseModel);

                hasher.initialized.add(crossroads.parse, crossroads);
                hasher.changed.add(crossroads.parse, crossroads);
```

```
                hasher.init();

                crossroads.addRoute("category/:newCat:", function(newCat) {
                    cheeseModel.selectedCategory(newCat ?
                        newCat : cheeseModel.products[0].category);
                });
                crossroads.parse(location.hash.slice(1));
            });
        });
    </script>
</head>
<body>
    <div id="logobar">
        <img src="cheeselux.png">
        <span id="tagline">Gourmet European Cheese</span>
    </div>

    <div class="cheesegroup">
        <div class="navSelectors" data-bind="foreach: products">
            <a data-bind="formatAttr: {attr: 'href', prefix: '#category/',
                value: category},
            css: {selectedItem: (category == cheeseModel.selectedCategory())}">
                <span data-bind="text: category">
            </a>
        </div>
    </div>

    <div id="basket" class="cheesegroup basket">
        <div class="grouptitle">Basket</div>
        <div class="groupcontent">

            <div class="description" data-bind="ifnot: total">
                No products selected
            </div>

            <table id="basketTable" data-bind="visible: total">
                <thead><tr><th>Cheese</th><th>Subtotal</th><th></th></tr></thead>
                <tbody data-bind="foreach: products">
                    <!-- ko foreach: items -->
                        <tr data-bind="visible: quantity, attr: {'data-prodId': id}">
                            <td data-bind="text: name"></td>
                            <td>$<span data-bind="text: subtotal"></span></td>
                        </tr>
                    <!-- /ko -->
                </tbody>
                <tfoot>
                    <tr><td class="sumline" colspan=2></td></tr>
                    <tr>
                        <th>Total:</th><td>$<span data-bind="text: total"></span></td>
                    </tr>
                </tfoot>
            </table>
```

```
        </div>
        <div class="cornerplaceholder"></div>

        <div id="buttonDiv">
            <input type="submit" value="Submit Order"/>
        </div>
    </div>

    <form action="/shipping" method="post">
        <!-- ko foreach: products -->
        <div class="cheesegroup"
            data-bind="fadeVisible: category == cheeseModel.selectedCategory()">
            <div class="grouptitle" data-bind="text: category"></div>
            <div data-bind="foreach: items">
                <div class="groupcontent">
                    <label data-bind="attr: {for: id}" class="cheesename">
                        <span data-bind="text: name">
                        </span> $(<span data-bind="text:price"></span>)</label>
                    <input data-bind="attr: {name: id}, value: quantity"/>
                    <span data-bind="visible: subtotal" class="subtotal">
                        ($<span data-bind="text: subtotal"></span>)
                    </span>
                </div>
            </div>
        </div>
        <!-- /ko -->
    </form>
</body>
</html>
```

Adding the highlighted meta element to the document disables the scaling feature. You can see the effect in Figure 7-2. This particular meta tag tells the browser to display the HTML document using the actual width of the display and without any magnification. Of course, the web app is still a mess, but it is a mess that is being displayed at the correct size, which is the first step toward a responsive app. In the rest of this chapter, I'll show you how to respond to different device characteristics and capabilities.

Figure 7-2. The effect of disabling the viewport for a web app

Responding to Screen Size

Media queries are a useful way of tailoring CSS styles to the capabilities of the device. Perhaps the most important characteristic of a device from the perspective of a responsive web app is screen size, which CSS media queries address very well. As Figure 7-2 shows, the CheeseLux logo takes up a lot of space on a small screen, and I can use a CSS media query to ensure that it is shown only on larger displays. Listing 7-2 shows a simple media query that I added to the styles.css file.

Listing 7-2. A Simple Media Query

```
@media screen AND (max-width:500px) {
    *.largeScreenOnly {
        display: none;
    }
}
```

> **Tip** Opera Mobile aggressively caches CSS and JavaScript files. When experimenting with media queries, the best technique is to define the CSS and script code in the main HTML document and move it to external files when you are happy with the result. Otherwise, you will need to clear the cache (or restart the emulator) to ensure your changes are applied.

The @media tag tells the browser that this is a media query. I have specified that the largeScreenOnly style contained in this query should be applied only if the device is a screen (as opposed to a projector or printed material) and the width is no greater than 500 pixels.

> **Tip** In this chapter, I am going to divide the world into two categories of displays. *Small* displays will be those whose width is no greater than 500 pixels, and *large* displays will be everything else. This is simple and arbitrary, and you may need to devise more categories to get the effect you require for your web app. I am going to ignore the height of the display entirely. My simple categories will keep the examples in this chapter manageable, albeit at the cost of granularity.

If these conditions are met, then a style is defined that sets the CSS display property for any element assigned to the largeScreenOnly class to none, which hides the element from view. With the addition to the style sheet, I can ensure that the CheeseLux logo is shown only on large displays by applying the largeScreenOnly class to my markup, as shown in Listing 7-3.

Listing 7-3. Using CSS Media Queries to Respond to Screen Sizes

```
...
<div id="logobar" class="largeScreenOnly">
    <img src="cheeselux.png">
    <span id="tagline">Gourmet European Cheese</span>
</div>
...
```

CSS media queries are *live*, which means the category of screen size can change if the browser window is resized. This isn't much use on mobile devices, but it means that a responsive web app will adapt to the display size even on a desktop platform. You can see how the layouts alter in Figure 7-3.

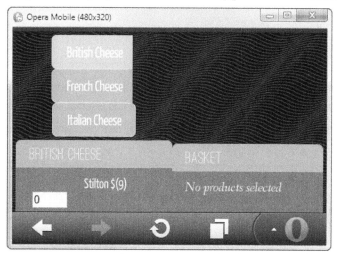

Figure 7-3. Using media queries to manage the visibility of elements

Using Media Queries with JavaScript

To properly integrate media queries into a web app, we need to use the View module of the W3C *CSS Object Model* specification, which brings JavaScript media queries support into the browser. Media queries are evaluated in JavaScript using the window.matchMedia method, as shown in Listing 7-4. I have defined the detectDeviceFeatures function in the utils.js file; at the moment, it detects only the screen size, but I'll detect some additional features later. There is a lot going on in the listing, so I'll break it down and explain the various parts in the sections that follow.

Listing 7-4. Using a Media Query in JavaScript

```
function detectDeviceFeatures(callback) {
    var deviceConfig = {};
    Modernizr.load({
        test: window.matchMedia,
        nope: 'matchMedia.js',
        complete: function() {
```

```
var screenQuery = window.matchMedia('screen AND (max-width:500px)');
deviceConfig.smallScreen = ko.observable(screenQuery.matches);
if (screenQuery.addListener) {
    screenQuery.addListener(function(mq) {
        deviceConfig.smallScreen(mq.matches);
    });
}

deviceConfig.largeScreen = ko.computed(function() {
    return !deviceConfig.smallScreen();
});

setInterval(function() {
    deviceConfig.smallScreen(window.innerWidth <= 500);
}, 500);

callback(deviceConfig);
        }
    });
};
```

Loading the Polyfill

I need to use a polyfill to make sure I can use the `matchMedia` method. Support for this feature is good in desktop browsers but spotty in the mobile world. The polyfill I use is called `matchMedia.js` and is available from http://github.com/paulirish/matchMedia.js.

I want to load the polyfill only if the browser doesn't support the `matchMedia` feature natively. To arrange this, I have used the `Modernizr.load` method, which is a flexible resource loader. I pass the `load` method an object whose properties tell Modernizr what to do.

■ **Tip** The `Modernizr.load` feature is available only when you create a custom Modernizr build; it is *not* included in the uncompressed development version of the Modernizr library. The Modernizr load method is a wrapper around a library called *YepNope*, which is available at http://yepnopejs.com. You can use YepNope directly if you don't want to use a compressed Modernizr build for any reason. The http://yepnopejs.com site also contains details of all of the loader features; the syntax doesn't change when the library is included with Modernizr. Be careful when using a resource loader in external JavaScript files. There are serious issues that can arise, which I describe in Chapter 9. You will see a link to create a custom download on the Modernizr web page. For the custom build that I used in this chapter, I simply checked all of the options to include as much Modernizr functionality as possible in the download.

The `test` property, as the name suggests, specifies the expression that I want Modernizr to evaluate. In this case, I want to see whether the `window.matchMedia` method is defined by the browser. You can use any JavaScript expression with the `test` property, including Modernizr feature detection checks.

The nope property tells Modernizr what resources I want to load if test evaluates false. In this example, I have specified the matchMedia.js file, which contains the polyfill code. There is a corresponding property, yep, which tells Modernizr what resources are required if test is true, but I don't need to use that in this example because I will be relying on the built-in support for matchMedia if test is true. The complete property specifies a function that will be executed when the resources specified by the yep or nope property have all been loaded and executed.

Modernizr.load gets and executes JavaScript scripts asynchronously, which is why the detectDeviceFeatures function takes a callback function as an argument. I invoke this callback at the end of the complete function, passing in an object that contains details of the features that have been detected.

Detecting the Screen Size

I can now turn to working out whether the device's screen falls into my large or small category. To do this, I pass a media query, just the like the one I used in CSS, to the matchMedia method, like this:

```
var screenQuery = window.matchMedia('screen AND (max-width:500px)');
```

I determine whether my media query has been matched by reading the matches property of the object I get back from matchMedia. If matches is true, then I am dealing with a screen that is in my small category (500 pixels and smaller). If it is false, then I have a large screen. I assign the result to an observable data item in the object that I pass to the callback function:

```
var deviceConfig = {
    smallScreen: ko.observable(screenQuery.matches)
};
```

If the browser implements the matchMedia feature, then I can use the addListener method to be notified when the status of the media query changes, like this:

```
if (screenQuery.addListener) {
    screenQuery.addListener(function(mq) {
        deviceConfig.smallScreen(mq.matches);
    });
}
```

The status of a media query changes when one of the conditions it contains changes. The two conditions in my query are that we are working on a screen and that it has a maximum width of 500 pixels. A change notification, therefore, indicates that the width of the display has changed. This means that the browser window has been resized or that the screen orientation has changed (see the "Responding to Screen Orientation" section later in this chapter for more details).

The matchMedia.js polyfill doesn't support change notifications, so I have to test for the existence of the addListener method before I use it. My function is executed when the status of the media query changes and I update the value of the observable data item. The last thing I do is create a computed observable data item, like this:

```
deviceConfig.largeScreen = ko.computed(function() {
    return !deviceConfig.smallScreen();
});
```

This is just to help tidy up my syntax when I want to refer to the screen size in the rest of my web app so that I can refer to smalllScreen and largeScreen to figure out what I am working with, as opposed to smallScreen and !smallScreen. It is a small thing, but I create fewer typos this way.

Some browsers are inconsistent in the way that status changes in media queries are handled. For example, the version of Google Chrome that is current as I write this doesn't always update media queries when the screen size changes. As a belt-and-braces measure, I have added a simple check on the screen size, which is set up using the setInterval function:

```
setInterval(function() {
    deviceConfig.smallScreen(window.innerWidth <= 500);
}, 500);
```

The function is executed every 500 milliseconds and updates the screen size item in the view model. This isn't ideal, but it is important that a responsive web app is able to adapt to device changes, and this can mean taking some undesirable precautions, including polling for status changes.

■ **Tip** Notice that I use the window.innerWidth property to try to figure out the size of the screen. The problem I am working around is that the media queries don't work properly in all browsers, so I need to find a substitute mechanism for assessing screen size.

Integrating Capability Detection into the Web App

I want to detect the capabilities of the device before I do anything else in the web app, which I why I added a callback to the detectDeviceFeatures function. You can see how I have integrated the use of this function to the web app script element in Listing 7-5.

Listing 7-5. Calling the detectDeviceFeatures Function from the Inline script Element

```
<script>
    var cheeseModel = {};

    detectDeviceFeatures(function(deviceConfig) {
        cheeseModel.device = deviceConfig;
        $.getJSON("products.json", function(data) {
            cheeseModel.products = data;
        }).success(function() {
            $(document).ready(function() {
                $('#buttonDiv input:submit').button().css("font-family", "Yanone");
                $('div.cheesegroup').not("#basket").css("width", "50%");
                $('div.navSelectors').buttonset();

                enhanceViewModel();
                ko.applyBindings(cheeseModel);

                hasher.initialized.add(crossroads.parse, crossroads);
                hasher.changed.add(crossroads.parse, crossroads);
                hasher.init();

                crossroads.addRoute("category/:newCat:", function(newCat) {
                    cheeseModel.selectedCategory(newCat ?
```

```
                              newCat : cheeseModel.products[0].category);
                });
            });
        });
    });
</script>
```

I assign the object that the detectDeviceFeatures function passes to the callback to the device property in the view model. By using an observable data item, I disseminate changes into the application from the view model when the media query changes.

The last step is to take advantage of the enhancements to the view model in the web app markup. Listing 7-6 shows how I can control the visibility of the CheeseLux logo through a data binding.

Listing 7-6. Controlling Element Visibility Based on Screen Capability Expressed Through the View Model

```
...
<div id="logobar" data-bind="visible: device.largeScreen()">
    <img src="cheeselux.png">
    <span id="tagline">Gourmet European Cheese</span>
</div>
...
```

The result is to re-create the effect of using the CSS media query in JavaScript. The CheeseLux logo is visible only on large screens. You might be wondering why I have gone to all the effort of re-creating a simple and elegant CSS technique in JavaScript. The reason is simple: pushing information about the capabilities of the device through my web app view model gives me a foundation for creating responsive web apps that are far more capable and flexible than would be possible with CSS alone. The following section gives an example.

Deferring Image Loading

The problem with simply hiding an img element is that the browser still loads it; it just never shows it to the user. This is a ridiculous situation because it is costing me *and* the user bandwidth to download a resource that won't ever be shown on a device with a small screen. To fix this, I have defined a new data binding called ifAttr in the utils.js file, as shown in Listing 7-7. This binding adds and removes an attribute based on evaluating a condition.

Listing 7-7. A Data Binding for Conditionally Setting an element Attribute

```
ko.bindingHandlers.ifAttr = {
    update: function(element, accessor) {
        if (accessor().test) {
            $(element).attr(accessor().attr, accessor().value);
        } else {
            $(element).removeAttr(accessor().attr);
        }
    }
}
```

This binding expects a data object that contains three properties: the attr property specifies which attribute I want to apply, the test property determines whether the attribute is added to the element, and the value attribute specifies the value that will be assigned to the attribute if test is true. Listing 7-8 shows how I can apply this binding to my CheeseLux logo markup to defer loading the image until it is required.

Listing 7-8. Using the ifAttr Binding to Prevent Image Loading

```
<div id="logobar" data-bind="visible: device.largeScreen()">
    <img data-bind="ifAttr: {attr: 'src', value: 'cheeselux.png',
                             test: device.largeScreen()}">
    <span id="tagline">Gourmet European Cheese</span>
</div>
```

The browser can't load an image when the img element doesn't have a src attribute. To take advantage of this, I use the ifAttr attribute with the largeScreen view model item so that the src attribute is set only when the image will be displayed. In this way, I am able to prevent the image from loading unless it will be shown. This is a pretty simple trick but demonstrates the kind of flexibility that you should look for when creating a responsive web app.

■ **Tip** It is important to distinguish between resources that you don't want to use immediately from resources that you are unlikely to want at all. If you have a reasonable expectation that the user will require an image in the normal use of your application, then you should let the browser download it so that it is immediately available when required. Use the ifAttr technique to avoid a wasted download if it is unlikely that the user will require a resource.

Adapting the Web App Layout

From this point on, I simply have to adapt each part of the web app to the two categories of screen that I am interested in. Listing 7-9 shows the changes that are required.

■ **Tip** Don't try to load this listing in the browser until you have also applied the changes in Listing 7-10. If you do, you'll get an error because the view model data and the data bindings are out of sync.

Listing 7-9. Adapting the Web App to Large and Small Screens

```
<!DOCTYPE html>
<html>
<head>
    <title>CheeseLux</title>
    <link rel="stylesheet" type="text/css" href="styles.css"/>
    <script src="jquery-1.7.1.js" type="text/javascript"></script>
    <script src="jquery-ui-1.8.16.custom.js" type="text/javascript"></script>
```

```
<script src='knockout-2.0.0.js' type='text/javascript'></script>
<script src='utils.js' type='text/javascript'></script>
<script src='signals.js' type='text/javascript'></script>
<script src='crossroads.js' type='text/javascript'></script>
<script src='hasher.js' type='text/javascript'></script>
<script src='modernizr-2.0.6.js' type='text/javascript'></script>
<link rel="stylesheet" type="text/css" href="jquery-ui-1.8.16.custom.css"/>
<meta name="viewport" content="width=device-width, initial-scale=1">
<script>
    var cheeseModel = {};

    detectDeviceFeatures(function(deviceConfig) {
        cheeseModel.device = deviceConfig;
        $.getJSON("products.json", function(data) {
            cheeseModel.products = data;
        }).success(function() {
            $(document).ready(function() {

                function performScreenSetup(smallScreen) {
                    $('div.cheesegroup').not("#basket")
                        .css("width", smallScreen ? "" : "50%");
                };
                cheeseModel.device.smallScreen.subscribe(performScreenSetup);
                performScreenSetup(cheeseModel.device.smallScreen());

                $('div.buttonDiv input:submit').button();
                $('div.navSelectors').buttonset();

                enhanceViewModel();
                ko.applyBindings(cheeseModel);

                hasher.initialized.add(crossroads.parse, crossroads);
                hasher.changed.add(crossroads.parse, crossroads);
                hasher.init();

                crossroads.addRoute("category/:newCat:", function(newCat) {
                    cheeseModel.selectedCategory(newCat ?
                        newCat : cheeseModel.products[0].category);
                });
                crossroads.parse(location.hash.slice(1));
            });
        });
    });
</script>
</head>
<body>
    <div id="logobar" data-bind="visible: device.largeScreen()">
        <img data-bind="ifAttr: {attr: 'src', value: 'cheeselux.png',
                                 test: device.largeScreen()}">
        <span id="tagline">Gourmet European Cheese</span>
    </div>
```

```
<div class="cheesegroup">
    <div class="navSelectors" data-bind="foreach: products">
        <a data-bind="formatAttr: {attr: 'href', prefix: '#category/',
            value: category},
        css: {selectedItem: (category == cheeseModel.selectedCategory())}">
            <span data-bind="text: cheeseModel.device.smallScreen() ?
                shortName : category"></span>
        </a>
    </div>
</div>

<div id="basket" class="cheesegroup basket"
        data-bind="visible: cheeseModel.device.largeScreen()">
    <div class="grouptitle">Basket</div>
    <div class="groupcontent">

        <div class="description" data-bind="ifnot: total">
            No products selected
        </div>

        <table id="basketTable" data-bind="visible: total">
            <thead><tr><th>Cheese</th><th>Subtotal</th><th></th></tr></thead>
            <tbody data-bind="foreach: products">
                <!-- ko foreach: items -->
                    <tr data-bind="visible: quantity, attr: {'data-prodId': id}">
                        <td data-bind="text: name"></td>
                        <td>$<span data-bind="text: subtotal"></span></td>
                    </tr>
                <!-- /ko -->
            </tbody>
            <tfoot>
                <tr><td class="sumline" colspan=2></td></tr>
                <tr>
                    <th>Total:</th><td>$<span data-bind="text: total"></span></td>
                </tr>
            </tfoot>
        </table>
    </div>
    <div class="cornerplaceholder"></div>

    <div class="buttonDiv">
        <input type="submit" value="Submit Order"/>
    </div>
</div>

<form action="/shipping" method="post">
    <div data-bind="foreach: products">
        <div class="cheesegroup"
            data-bind="fadeVisible: category == $root.selectedCategory()">
            <div class="grouptitle" data-bind="text: category"></div>
            <!-- ko foreach: items -->
            <div class="groupcontent">
```

```
                <label data-bind="attr: {for: id}" class="cheesename">
                    <span data-bind="text: name">
                    </span> $(<span data-bind="text:price"></span>)</label>
                <input data-bind="attr: {name: id}, value: quantity"/>
                <span data-bind="visible: subtotal" class="subtotal">
                    ($<span data-bind="text: subtotal"></span>)
                </span>
            </div>
            <!-- /ko -->
            <div class="groupcontent" data-bind="if: $root.device.smallScreen()">
                <label class="cheesename">Total:</label>
                <span class="subtotal" id="total">
                    $<span data-bind="text: cheeseModel.total()"></span>
                </span>
            </div>
        </div>
    </div>
    <div class="buttonDiv" data-bind="visible: $root.device.smallScreen()">
        <input type="submit" value="Submit Order"/>
    </div>
    </form>
</body>
</html>
```

The joy of this approach is how few changes are required to make a web app responsive to screen size (and how simple those changes are). That said, there are a small number of changes that require explanation, which I provide in the following sections. You can see how my responsive web app appears on large and small screens in Figure 7-4.

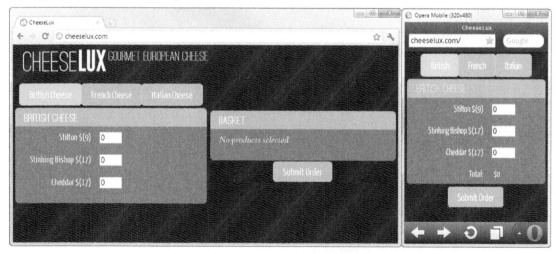

Figure 7-4. The same web app displayed on a large and small screen

These small changes have a big impact, and for the most part, the changes are cosmetic. The underlying features and structure of my web app remain the same. I don't have to forgo my view model or routing just to support a device with a smaller screen.

Adapting the Source Data

The category buttons are a problem on a small screen, so I want to display something to the user that is meaningful but requires less screen space. To do this, I made some additions to the products.json file so that each category contains a name to be used when space is limited. Listing 7-10 shows the addition for one of the categories.

Listing 7-10. Adding Screen-Specific Information to the Product Data

```
...
[{"category": "British Cheese",
  "shortName": "British",
    "items" : [
        {"id": "stilton", "name": "Stilton", "price": 9,
        "description": "A semi-soft blue cow's milk cheese produced in the
          Nottinghamshire region. A strong cheese with a distinctive smell
          and taste and crumbly texture."},
...
```

I have applied a similar change to all of the other categories in the products.json file. I could have arrived at the short name by splitting the category value string on the space character, but I want to make the point that it is not just the script and markup in a web app that can be responsive; you can also support this concept in the data that drives your application.

In Listing 7-9, I modified the data binding for the navigation buttons to take advantage of the shorter categories names, like this:

```
<div class="cheesegroup">
    <div class="navSelectors" data-bind="foreach: products">
        <a data-bind="formatAttr: {attr: 'href', prefix: '#category/',
            value: category},
        css: {selectedItem: (category == cheeseModel.selectedCategory())}">
            <span data-bind="text: cheeseModel.device.smallScreen() ?
                shortName : category"></span>
        </a>
    </div>
</div>
```

I still use the full category name for the formatAttr binding. This allows me to use the same set of navigation routes irrespective of the screen size (see Chapter 4 for details of using routing in a web app).

Applying Conditional jQuery UI Styling

In the large screen layout, I resize the product list elements to make room for the basket. In the small screen layout, I replace the dedicated basket with a one-line total at the end of each section. I like to take advantage of the matchMedia.addListener feature if it is available, which means I must be able to toggle between the small and large screen layouts as needed. To accommodate this, I treat those script statements that drive the individual layouts in their own function and register that function as a subscriber to changes in the view model:

```
function performScreenSetup(smallScreen) {
    $('div.cheesegroup').not("#basket").css("width", smallScreen ? "" : "50%");
};
cheeseModel.device.smallScreen.subscribe(performScreenSetup);
```

The function will be called only when the value changes, so I call the function explicitly to get the right behavior when the document is first loaded, like this:

```
performScreenSetup(cheeseModel.device.smallScreen());
```

In effect, I toggle the CSS width property of the div elements in the cheesegroup class based on the size of the screen. You could ignore this approach and just leave the layout in its initial state, but I think that is a lost opportunity to provide a nice experience for desktop users.

Removing Elements from the Document

For the most part, I simply hide and show elements in the document based on the size of the screen. However, there are occasions when the if and ifnot bindings are required to ensure that elements are completely removed from the document. A simple example of this can be seen in the listing where I use the if binding for the one-line total summary:

```
<div class="groupcontent" data-bind="if: $root.device.smallScreen()">
    <label class="cheesename">Total:</label>
    <span class="subtotal" id="total">
        $<span data-bind="text: cheeseModel.total()"></span>
    </span>
</div>
```

I have used the if binding here because tucked away in the styles.css file is a CSS style that applies rounded corners:

```
div.groupcontent:last-child {
    border-bottom-left-radius: 8px;
    border-bottom-right-radius: 8px;
}
```

The browser doesn't take into account the visibility of elements when working out which is the last child of its parent. If I had used the visible binding, then I don't get the rounded corners I want in the large screen layout. The if binding forces the behavior I want by removing the elements entirely, ensuring that the rounded corners are applied correctly.

Responding to Screen Orientation

Many mobile devices respond to the way that the user is holding the device by changing the screen orientation between landscape and portrait modes. Keeping informed of the display mode turns out to be quite tricky, but it is worth doing to make sure that your web app responds appropriately when the orientation changes. There are several ways to approach this issue.

Some devices support a window.orientation property and an orientationchange event to make it easier to keep track of the screen orientation, but this feature isn't universal, and even when it is implemented, the event tends to be fired when it shouldn't be (and isn't fired when it should be).

Other devices support orientation as part of a media query. This is useful if the addListener feature is supported as part of matchMedia, but most mobile browsers don't support this feature, and these are the devices whose orientation is most likely to change.

Almost all browsers support a resize event, which is triggered when the window is resized or the orientation is changed. However, some implementations introduce delays between orientation changes and the event being triggered, which makes for a web app that is slow to respond and that may change its layout or behavior after the user has started interacting in the new orientation.

The final approach is to periodically check screen dimensions and work out the orientation manually. This is crude but effective and works only if the frequency of the check is high enough to make for a rapid response but low enough not to overwhelm the device.

The only reliable way to make sure you detect orientation changes is to apply all four techniques. Listing 7-11 shows the required additions to the detectDeviceFeatures function.

Listing 7-11. Detecting Screen Orientation Changes

```
function detectDeviceFeatures(callback) {
    var deviceConfig = {};

    deviceConfig.landscape = ko.observable();
    deviceConfig.portrait = ko.computed(function() {
        return !deviceConfig.landscape();
    });

    var setOrientation = function() {
        deviceConfig.landscape(window.innerWidth > window.innerHeight);
    }
    setOrientation();

    $(window).bind("orientationchange resize", function() {
        setOrientation();
    });

    setInterval(setOrientation, 500);

    if (window.matchMedia) {
        var orientQuery = window.matchMedia('screen AND (orientation:landscape)')
        if (orientQuery.addListener) {
            orientQuery.addListener(setOrientation);
        }
    }

    Modernizr.load({
        test: window.matchMedia,
        nope: 'matchMedia.js',
        complete: function() {
            var screenQuery = window.matchMedia('screen AND (max-width:500px)');
            deviceConfig.smallScreen = ko.observable(screenQuery.matches);
            if (screenQuery.addListener) {
                screenQuery.addListener(function(mq) {
                    deviceConfig.smallScreen(mq.matches);
                });
```

```
        }
        deviceConfig.largeScreen = ko.computed(function() {
            return !deviceConfig.smallScreen();
        });

        setInterval(function() {
            deviceConfig.smallScreen(window.innerWidth <= 500);
        }, 500);

        callback(deviceConfig);
    }
    });
};
```

I have set up two view model data items, landscape and portrait, following the same pattern that I used for smallScreen and largeScreen. I don't want to duplicate my code for testing the orientation of the device, so I have created a simple inline function called setOrientation that sets the value of the landscape data item:

```
var setOrientation = function() {
    deviceConfig.landscape(window.innerWidth > window.innerHeight);
}
```

I have found comparing the innerWidth and innerHeight values of the window object to be the most reliable way of figuring out the screen orientation. The screen.width and screen.height values *should* work, but some browsers don't change these values when the device is reoriented. The window.orientation property provides good information, but it isn't universally implemented. This is an undoubted compromise, and I recommend you test the efficacy of this approach on your target devices.

The rest of the additions implement the various means by which the setOrientation will be called: via the orientationchange and resize events, via a media query, and via polling. Judging the right frequency to poll the orientation is difficult, but I usually use 500 milliseconds. It isn't always as responsive as I would like, but it strikes a reasonable balance.

▪ **Tip** I could have used a single setInterval call to poll for both the screen size and the orientation, but I prefer to keep the regions of code functionality as separate as possible.

Integrating Screen Orientation into the Web App

I can make the web app respond to the screen orientation now that the view model has the portrait and landscape items. To demonstrate this, I am going to fix a problem: the web app currently requires the user to scroll down to see all of the elements in landscape mode on a device that has a small screen. Figure 7-5 shows the problem and the result after I have modified the web app layout.

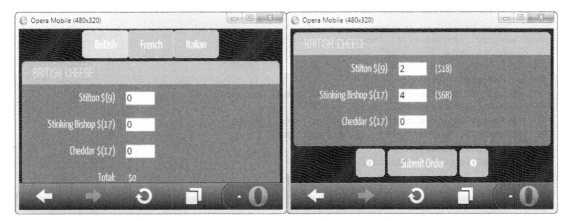

Figure 7-5. Responding to the landscape orientation on small screens

To respond to this orientation for small screens, I have removed the category navigation elements and replaced them with left and right buttons that page through the categories. This isn't the most elegant approach, but it makes good use of limited screen space while preserving the basic nature of the web app. Listing 7-12 shows the addition of the data binding to control visibility for the navigation items.

Listing 7-12. Binding Element Visibility to the Screen Size and Orientation

```
<div class="cheesegroup"
    data-bind="ifnot: cheeseModel.device.smallScreen() &&
        cheeseModel.device.landscape()">
    <div class="navSelectors" data-bind="foreach: products">
        <a data-bind="formatAttr: {attr: 'href', prefix: '#category/',
            value: category},
        css: {selectedItem: (category == cheeseModel.selectedCategory())}">
            <span data-bind="text: cheeseModel.device.smallScreen()?
                shortName : category"></span>
        </a>
    </div>
</div>
```

I remove the elements from the DOM if the device has a small screen and is in the landscape orientation. The buttons I add are as follows:

```
<div class="buttonDiv" data-bind="visible: $root.device.smallScreen()">
    <button id="left">Prev</button>
    <input type="submit" value="Submit Order"/>
    <button id="right">Next</button>
</div>
```

The elements themselves are not interesting, but the code that handles the navigation that arises when clicked is worth looking at:

```
...
function performScreenSetup(smallScreen) {
    $('div.cheesegroup').not("#basket")
        .css("width", smallScreen ? "" : "50%");
    $('button#left').button({icons:
        {primary: "ui-icon-circle-triangle-w"},text: false});
    $('button#right').button({icons:
        {primary: "ui-icon-circle-triangle-e"},text: false});
    $('button#left, button#right').click(function(e) {
        e.preventDefault();
        advanceCategory(e, this.id);
    });
};
...
```

This is an example of when using routing for navigation doesn't work. I want the user to be able to repeatedly click these buttons, and as I mentioned already, the browser won't respond to an attempt to navigate to the same URL that is already being displayed. With this in mind, I have used the jQuery click method to handle the regular JavaScript event by calling the advanceCategory function. I defined this function in utils.js, and it is shown in Listing 7-13.

Listing 7-13. The advanceCategory Function

```
function advanceCategory(e, dir) {
    var cIndex = -1;
    for (var i = 0; i < cheeseModel.products.length; i++) {
        if (cheeseModel.products[i].category == cheeseModel.selectedCategory()) {
            cIndex = i;
            break;
        }
    }
    cIndex = (dir == "left" ? cIndex - 1 : cIndex + 1) % (cheeseModel.products.length);
    if (cIndex < 0) {
        cIndex = cheeseModel.products.length -1;
    }
    cheeseModel.selectedCategory(cheeseModel.products[cIndex].category)
}
```

There is no neat ordering of categories in the view model, so I enumerate through the data to find the index of the currently selected category and increment or decrement the value based on which button has been clicked. The result is a more compact layout that better suits the small-screen landscape orientation. The way I have categorized devices is pretty crude, and I recommend you take a more granular approach in real projects, but it serves to demonstrate the techniques you need in order to respond to screen orientation.

Responding to Touch

The final feature that a responsive web app needs to deal with is touch support. The idea of touch-based interaction is firmly established in the smartphone and tablet markets, but it is also making its way to the desktop, mostly through Microsoft Windows 8.

To support touch interaction, we need two things: a touch screen and a browser that emits touch events. These two don't always come together; plugging a touch-enabled monitor into a desktop machine doesn't automatically enable touch in the browser, for example. Equally, you should not assume that if a device supports touch that this will be the only model for interactions. Many devices will support mouse and keyboard interactions alongside touch, and the user should be able to pick whichever model suits them when using your web app and switch freely between them.

Devices that don't have a regular mouse and keyboard synthesize events such as click in response to touch events. This means you don't need to make changes to your web app to support basic touch interactions. However, to create a truly response web app, you should consider supporting the navigation gestures that are common on touch devices, such as swiping. I demonstrate how to do this shortly.

Detecting Touch Support

There is a W3C specification for touch events, but it is low-level, and a lot of work is required to figure out what gestures the user is making. As I have said before, part of the joy of web app development is the availability of high-quality JavaScript libraries that make development simpler. One such example is *touchSwipe*, which builds on jQuery and transforms the low-level touch events into events that represent gestures. I included the touchSwipe library in the source code download that accompanies this book and that is available from Apress.com. The website for the library is http://labs.skinkers.com/touchSwipe.

The simplest and most reliable approach to detecting touch support is to rely on the Modernizr test. Listing 7-14 shows the additions to the detectDeviceFeatures function in the utils.js file to detect and report on touch support and shows the use of touchSwipe to respond to touch events.

Listing 7-14. Detecting Support for Touch Events

```
function detectDeviceFeatures(callback) {
    var deviceConfig = {};

    deviceConfig.landscape = ko.observable();
    deviceConfig.portrait = ko.computed(function() {
        return !deviceConfig.landscape();
    });

    var setOrientation = function() {
        deviceConfig.landscape(window.innerWidth > window.innerHeight);
    }
    setOrientation();

    $(window).bind("orientationchange resize", function() {
        setOrientation();
    });

    setInterval(setOrientation, 500);

    if (window.matchMedia) {
        var orientQuery = window.matchMedia('screen AND (orientation:landscape)')
        if (orientQuery.addListener) {
            orientQuery.addListener(setOrientation);
        }
    }
}
```

```
Modernizr.load([{
    test: window.matchMedia,
    nope: 'matchMedia.js',
    complete: function() {
        var screenQuery = window.matchMedia('screen AND (max-width:500px)');
        deviceConfig.smallScreen = ko.observable(screenQuery.matches);
        if (screenQuery.addListener) {
            screenQuery.addListener(function(mq) {
                deviceConfig.smallScreen(mq.matches);
            });
        }
        deviceConfig.largeScreen = ko.computed(function() {
            return !deviceConfig.smallScreen();
        });
    }
}, {
    test: Modernizr.touch,
    yep: 'jquery.touchSwipe-1.2.5.js',
    callback: function() {
        $('html').swipe({
            swipeLeft: advanceCategory,
            swipeRight: advanceCategory
        });
    }
},{
    complete: function() {
        callback(deviceConfig);
    }
}]);
};
```

When you pass an array of objects to the Modernizr.load method, each test is performed in turn. I have added a test that uses the Modernizr.touch check and that loads the touchSwipe library if touch support is present.

■ **Tip** Make sure you included the touch tests if you downloaded your own version of Modernizr. The version I included in the source code for this chapter contains all of the available tests.

Notice that I used the callback property to set up support for handling swipes. Functions set using the callback property are executed when the specified resources are loaded, whereas functions specified using complete are executed at the end of the test, irrespective of the test result. I want to handle swipe events only if touchSwipe has been loaded (which itself indicates that touch support is present), so I have used callback to give Modernizr my function.

The touchSwipe library is applied using the swipe method. In this example, I have selected the html element as the target for detecting swipe gestures. Some browsers limit the body element size so that it doesn't fill the entire window when the content is smaller than the available space. This isn't usually a problem, but it creates dead spots on the screen when dealing with gestures, which may not be targeted at individual elements. The simplest way to get around this is to work on the html element.

The touchSwipe library is able to differentiate between different kinds of touch events and swipes in a range of directions. I care about swipes only to the left and the right in this example, which is why I have defined a function for the swipeLeft and swipeRight properties in the object I passed to the swipe method. In both cases I have specified the advanceCategory function, which is the same function I used to change selected categories earlier. The result is that swiping left moves to the previous category and swiping right goes to the next category. The last point to note about this listing is the last item in the array passed to the Modernizr.load method:

```
{
    complete: function() {
        callback(deviceConfig);
    }
}
```

I don't want to invoke the callback function until I have set up all of the device details in the result object that will be added to the view model. The easiest way to ensure this happens is to create an additional test that contains just a complete function. Modernizr won't execute this function until all of the other tests have been performed, the required resources have been loaded, and the callback and complete functions for all of the previous tests have been performed.

Using Touch to Navigate the Web App History

In the previous example, I respond to swipe gestures by looping through the available product categories. In this section, I show you how to respond to these gestures in a more useful way.

The temptation is to use the browser's history to respond to swipes. The problem is that there is no way to peek at the previous or next entry in the history and see whether it is one that belongs to the web app. If it isn't, then you end up making the user navigate away from your web app, potentially to a URL that they had no intention of visiting. Listing 7-15 shows the changes required to the enhanceViewModel function in the utils.js file to set up the basic support for tracking the user's category selections.

■ **Tip** You could elect to use local storage and make the swipe-related history persistent. I prefer not to do this, since I think it makes more sense for the history to be limited to the current life of the web app.

Listing 7-15. Adding Application-Specific History Using Session Storage

```
function enhanceViewModel() {

    cheeseModel.selectedCategory = ko.observable(cheeseModel.products[0].category);

    mapProducts(function(item) {
        item.quantity = ko.observable(0);
        item.subtotal = ko.computed(function() {
            return this.quantity() * this.price;
        }, item);
    }, cheeseModel.products, "items");
```

```
cheeseModel.total = ko.computed(function() {
    var total = 0;
    mapProducts(function(elem) {
        total += elem.subtotal();
    }, cheeseModel.products, "items");
    return total;
});

var history = cheeseModel.history = {};
history.index = 0;
history.categories = [cheeseModel.selectedCategory()];
cheeseModel.selectedCategory.subscribe(function(newValue) {
    if (newValue != history.categories[history.index]) {
        history.index++;
        history.categories.push(newValue);
    }
})
};
```

The additions are simple. I have added an index and an array to the view model and subscribed to the selectedCategory observable data item so that I can build up the user's history as they change categories. I have not worried about managing the size of the array since I think it is unlikely that enough category changes will be made to cause a capacity problem. Listing 7-16 shows the changes to the ad.

Listing 7-16. Taking Advantage of the App-Specific History

```
function advanceCategory(e, dir) {
    if (cheeseModel.device.smallScreen() && cheeseModel.device.landscape()) {
        var cIndex = -1;
        for (var i = 0; i < cheeseModel.products.length; i++) {
            if (cheeseModel.products[i].category == cheeseModel.selectedCategory()) {
                cIndex = i;
                break;
            }
        }
        cIndex = (dir == "left" ? cIndex-1 : cIndex + 1) % (cheeseModel.products.length);
        if (cIndex < 0) {
            cIndex = cheeseModel.products.length -1;
        }
        cheeseModel.selectedCategory(cheeseModel.products[cIndex].category)

    } else {
        var history = cheeseModel.history;
        if (dir == "left" && history.index > 0) {
            cheeseModel.selectedCategory(history.categories[--history.index]);
        } else if (dir == "right" && history.index < history.categories.length -1) {
            cheeseModel.selectedCategory(history.categories[++history.index]);
        }
    }
}
```

I have to be careful not to apply the swipe history when the web app is displayed on a small screen in the landscape orientation. I removed the category buttons in this device configuration, meaning that there is no way for the user to generate a history for me to navigate through. In all other device configurations, I am able to respond to the swipe by changing the value of the index and selecting the corresponding historic category. The result is that the user can navigate between categories using the navigation buttons and swiping moves backward or forward through the recent selections.

Integrating with the Application Routes

The last tweak I want to make is to respond to the swipe events through the web app's URL routes. In the last listing, I took the shortcut of changing the observable data item directly, but this means I will bypass any code that is generated as a result of a URL change, including integration with the HTML5 History API (which I describe in Chapter 4). The changes are shown in Listing 7-17.

Listing 7-17. Responding to Swipe Events Through the Application Routes

```
function advanceCategory(e, dir) {
    if (cheeseModel.device.smallScreen() && cheeseModel.device.landscape()) {
        var cIndex = -1;
        for (var i = 0; i < cheeseModel.products.length; i++) {
            if (cheeseModel.products[i].category == cheeseModel.selectedCategory()) {
                cIndex = i;
                break;
            }
        }
        cIndex = (dir == "left" ? cIndex-1 : cIndex + 1) % (cheeseModel.products.length);
        if (cIndex < 0) {
            cIndex = cheeseModel.products.length -1;
        }
        cheeseModel.selectedCategory(cheeseModel.products[cIndex].category)

    } else {
        var history = cheeseModel.history;
        if (dir == "left" && history.index > 0) {
            location.href = "#category/" + history.categories[--history.index];
        } else if (dir == "right" && history.index < history.categories.length -1) {
            location.href = "#category/" + history.categories[++history.index];
        }
    }
}
```

I have used the browser `location` object to change the URL that the browser displays. Since I have specified relative URLs, the browser will not navigate away from the web app, and my routes will be able to match the URLs. By doing this, I ensure that my response to swipe events is consistent with other forms of navigation.

Summary

In this chapter, I have shown you the three characteristics that you must adapt to in order to create a responsive web app: screen size, screen orientation, and touch interaction. By detecting and adapting to different device configurations, you can create one web app that can seamlessly and elegantly adapt its layout and interaction model to suit the user's device. The advantages of such an approach are obvious when you consider the proliferation of smartphones and tablets and the blurring of the distinctions between these devices and desktops. In the next chapter, I show you a different approach to supporting different types of devices: creating a platform-specific web app.

CHAPTER 8

Creating Mobile Web Apps

An alternative to creating a web app that adapts to the capabilities of different devices is to create a version that is specifically targeted to mobile devices. Choosing between a responsive web app and a mobile-specific implementation can be difficult, but my rule of thumb is that a mobile version makes sense when I want to offer a radically different experience to mobile and desktop users or when dealing with device constraints in a responsive implementation becomes unwieldy and overly complex. Your decision will, of course, depend on the specifics of your project, but this chapter is for when you decide that one version of your web app, however responsive, won't cater to your mobile users' needs.

Detecting Mobile Devices

The first step is to decide how you are going to direct users of mobile devices to the mobile version of your web app. The decision you make at this stage will shape a lot of the assumptions you will have when you come to build the mobile web app. There are a couple of broad approaches, which I describe in the following sections.

Detecting the User Agent

The traditional approach is to look at the user agent string that the browser uses to describe itself. This is available through the `navigator.userAgent` property, and the value that it returns can be used to identify the browser and, usually, the platform the browser is running on. As an example, here is the value of `navigator.userAgent` that Chrome returns on my Windows system:

```
"Mozilla/5.0 (Windows NT 6.1; WOW64) AppleWebKit/535.7 (KHTML, like Gecko) Chrome/16.0.912.77
Safari/535.7"
```

And, for contrast, here is what I get from the Opera Mobile emulator:

```
Opera/9.80 (Windows NT 6.1; Opera Mobi/23731; U; en) Presto/2.9.201 Version/11.50"
```

You can identify mobile devices by building a list of user agent values and keeping track of which ones represent mobile browsers. You don't have to create and manage these lists yourself, however — there are some good sources of information available online. (A very comprehensive database called *WURFL* can be found at `http://wurfl.sourceforge.net`, but this requires integration into your server-side code, which is not ideal for this book.)

A less-comprehensive client-side solution can be found at `http://detectmobilebrowsers.com`, where you can download a small jQuery library that matches the user agent against a known list of mobile browsers. This approach isn't as complete as WURFL, but it is simpler to use, and it detects the most widely used mobile browsers. To demonstrate this kind of mobile device detection, I downloaded the jQuery code to my Node.js content directory in a file called `detectmobilebrowser.js` (you can find this file in the source code download for this book, available from Apress.com). Listing 8-1 shows how to use this plugin to detect mobile devices.

Listing 8-1. Detecting Mobile Devices at the Client

```
<!DOCTYPE html>
<html>
<head>
    <title>CheeseLux</title>
    <link rel="stylesheet" type="text/css" href="styles.css"/>
    <script src="jquery-1.7.1.js" type="text/javascript"></script>
    <script src="jquery-ui-1.8.16.custom.js" type="text/javascript"></script>
    <script src='knockout-2.0.0.js' type='text/javascript'></script>
    <script src='utils.js' type='text/javascript'></script>
    <script src='signals.js' type='text/javascript'></script>
    <script src='crossroads.js' type='text/javascript'></script>
    <script src='hasher.js' type='text/javascript'></script>
    <script src='modernizr-2.0.6.js' type='text/javascript'></script>
    <script src='detectmobilebrowser.js' type='text/javascript'></script>
    <link rel="stylesheet" type="text/css" href="jquery-ui-1.8.16.custom.css"/>
    <meta name="viewport" content="width=device-width, initial-scale=1">
    <script>

        if ($.browser.mobile) {
            location.href = "mobile.html";
        }

        var cheeseModel = {};
        ...
```

Once I have added the library to my document with a `script` element, I can check to see whether my web app is running on a mobile browser by reading the `$.browser.mobile` property, which returns true if the user agent is recognized as belonging to a mobile browser. In this case, I redirect mobile users to the `mobile.html` document, which I will use to build my mobile web app later in this chapter.

The main problem with using the user agent is that it isn't always accurate, and as I mentioned in the previous chapter, the distinctions between mobile and desktop devices are becoming blurred. In essence, you rely on someone else's decision about what defines *mobile*, and that won't always line up with the way you want to segment your user base. And, although the lists of browser are generally accurate, it can take a while for new models to be properly identified and categorized, especially from niche hardware providers.

A related problem is that many browsers allow the user to change the user agent so that another browser is identified. Not many users make this change, but it does mean you cannot entirely rely on the user agent reported through the `navigator.userAgent` property.

Detecting Device Capabilities

I prefer to classify a device as mobile by detecting its capabilities, much as I did in Chapter 7. This allows me to decide what defines *mobile* in the context of the way my web app works. For the CheeseLux web app, I have decided that devices that are touch enabled and that have screens that are narrower than 500 pixels will be given the mobile version of my web app. You can see how I have implemented this policy in Listing 8-2, which shows the changes to the `detectDeviceFeatures` function from the `utils.js` file.

Listing 8-2. Detecting Mobile Devices Based on Their Capabilities

```
function detectDeviceFeatures(callback) {
    var deviceConfig = {};

    ...code removed for brevity...

    Modernizr.load([{
        test: window.matchMedia,
        nope: 'matchMedia.js',
        complete: function() {
            var screenQuery = window.matchMedia('screen AND (max-width: 500px)');
            deviceConfig.smallScreen = ko.observable(screenQuery.matches);
            if (screenQuery.addListener) {
                screenQuery.addListener(function(mq) {
                    deviceConfig.smallScreen(mq.matches);
                });
            }
            deviceConfig.largeScreen = ko.computed(function() {
                return !deviceConfig.smallScreen();
            });
        }
    }, {
        test: Modernizr.touch,
        yep: 'jquery.touchSwipe-1.2.5.js',
        callback: function() {
            $('html').swipe({
                swipeLeft: advanceCategory,
                swipeRight: advanceCategory
            })
        }
    },{
        complete: function() {
            deviceConfig.mobile = Modernizr.touch && deviceConfig.smallScreen();
            callback(deviceConfig);
        }
    }]);
};
```

I have added a mobile property to the view model; it returns true if the device meets my criteria for getting the mobile version of my web app. Listing 8-3 shows how I have used this new property in example.html.

Listing 8-3. Using Mobile Device Detection in the Main Web App Document

```
var cheeseModel = {};

detectDeviceFeatures(function(deviceConfig) {
    cheeseModel.device = deviceConfig;
    if (cheeseModel.device.mobile) {
        location.href = "mobile.html";
    }
```

```
$.getJSON("products.json", function(data) {
    cheeseModel.products = data;

}).success(function() {
    $(document).ready(function() {
...
```

I add the capabilities check before the JSON data is loaded so that I can direct the user to mobile.html before I start making network requests and processing the elements in the DOM.

■ **Tip** In this example and the previous one, I placed the mobile detection code outside of the jQuery ready event so that the browser will execute the code as soon as it reaches it in the document. A more thorough approach would be to place the detection code right at the top of the document so that it is executed before any of the JavaScript libraries are loaded. However, since I rely on some of these libraries to actually perform the detection, careful ordering of the script elements is required.

Creating a Simple Mobile Web App

Both of the approaches I showed you assume that the user will *want* to view the mobile version of my web app—but this won't always be the case. I prefer to identify a mobile device and then ask the user what they want to do. This approach puts control into users' hands (which is where it should be), but it does mean that I have to provide a mechanism for letting them choose and remembering the choice they make. So, rather than simply directing mobile devices to the mobile version of the web app, I use an interim document called askmobile.html. I placed this file in the Node.js content directory, and you can see the file content in Listing 8-4. This is a very simple web app that uses jQuery and jQuery Mobile.

Listing 8-4. Asking the User If They Want to Use the Mobile Version of the Web App

```
<!DOCTYPE html>
<html>
<head>
    <title>CheeseLux</title>
    <script src="jquery-1.7.1.js" type="text/javascript"></script>
    <script src="jquery.mobile-1.0.1.js" type="text/javascript"></script>
    <link rel="stylesheet" type="text/css" href="jquery.mobile-1.0.1.css"/>
    <link rel="stylesheet" type="text/css" href="styles.mobile.css"/>
    <meta name="viewport" content="width=device-width, initial-scale=1">
    <script>
        function setCookie(name, value, days) {
            var date = new Date();
            date.setTime(date.getTime()+(days * 24 * 60 * 60 *1000));
            document.cookie = name + "="+ value
                + "; expires=" + date.toGMTString() +"; path=/";
        }
```

```
        $(document).bind("pageinit", function() {
            $('button').click(function(e) {
                var useMobile = e.target.id == "yes";
                var useMobileValue = useMobile ? "mobile" : "desktop";
                if (localStorage) {
                    localStorage["cheeseLuxMode"] = useMobileValue;
                } else {
                    setCookie("cheeseLuxMode", useMobileValue, 30);
                }
                location.href = useMobile ? "mobile.html" : "example.html";
            });
        });
    </script>
</head>
<body>
    <div id="page1" data-role="page" data-theme="a">
        <img class="logo" src="cheeselux.png">
        <span class="para">
            Would you like to use our mobile web app?
        </span>
        <div class="middle">
            <button data-inline="true" data-theme="b" id="yes">Yes</button>
            <button data-inline="true" id="no">No</button>
        </div>
    </div>
</body>
</html>
```

Tip I explain how to get the CSS and JavaScript files referred to in this listing shortly.

This document presents the user with two buttons that they can use to choose the version of the web app they want to use. You can see how the document is displayed in the browser in Figure 8-1.

Figure 8-1. Asking the user which version of the web app they require

This tiny web app gives me a good example with which to introduce jQuery Mobile, which is what I'll be using in this chapter. jQuery Mobile is a toolkit optimized for mobile devices, and it includes widgets that are easy to interact with using touch and built-in support for handling touch events and gestures.

jQuery Mobile is the "official" mobile toolkit from the main jQuery project, and it's pretty good, although there are some rough edges with some layouts that need tweaking with minor CSS. There are other jQuery-based mobile widget toolkits available—and some of them are very good as well. I have chosen jQuery Mobile because it shares a broadly common approach with jQuery UI and it has some design characteristics that are typical of most mobile toolkits and that require special attention when writing complex web apps.

AVOIDING PSEUDONATIVE MOBILE APPS

Another reason that I use jQuery Mobile is that it doesn't try to re-create the appearance of a native smartphone application, which is an approach that some of the other toolkits adopt. I don't like that approach because it doesn't quite work. If you give the user something that looks like a native iOS or Android app, then you need to make sure it behaves exactly the way a native application should—and, at least at the moment, that isn't possible.

The worst possible approach is to try to re-create a native app for just one platform. You often see this, and it is usually iOS that web app developers aim for. This might not be so bad if the re-creation was faithful and all mobile devices ran iOS, but users of Android and other operating systems get something that is totally alien, and iOS users get something that initially appears to be familiar but that turns out to be confusing and inconsistent.

To my mind, it is far better to design a web app that is genuinely obvious and easy to use. The results are better, you users will be happier, and you don't have to contort your web app to fit inside the constraints of platform that you can't properly adhere to anyway.

I am not going to provide a lengthy tutorial on jQuery Mobile, but there are some important characteristics that I need to explain in order to demonstrate how to create a solid mobile web application. I explain the core concepts in the sections that follow. If you want more information about jQuery Mobile, then see the project web site or my *Pro jQuery* book, which is published by Apress and contains a complete reference for using jQuery Mobile.

Installing jQuery Mobile

You can download jQuery Mobile from `http://jquerymobile.com`. jQuery Mobile depends on jQuery, and the `script` element that imports jQuery into the document must come before the one that imports the jQuery Mobile library, like this:

```
<head>
    <title>CheeseLux</title>
    <script src="jquery-1.7.1.js" type="text/javascript"></script>
    <script src="jquery.mobile-1.0.1.js" type="text/javascript"></script>
    <link rel="stylesheet" type="text/css" href="jquery.mobile-1.0.1.css"/>
```

jQuery Mobile relies on its own CSS and images that are different from those used by jQuery UI. When you download jQuery Mobile, copy the CSS file into the Node.js `content` directory along with the JavaScript file, and put the images into the `images` directory along with those from jQuery UI.

Understanding the jQuery Mobile Data Attributes

jQuery Mobile relies on data attributes to configure the layout of the web app. Data attributes allow custom attributes to be applied to elements, just like the `data-bind` attribute that I have been using for data bindings. There is no `data-bind` attribute defined in the HTML specification, but any attribute that is prefixed by `data-` is ignored by the browser and allows you to embed useful information in your markup that you can then access via JavaScript. Data attributes have been used unofficially for a few years and are an official part of HTML5.

jQuery Mobile uses data attributes rather than the code-centric approach that jQuery UI requires. You use the `data-role` attribute to tell jQuery Mobile how it should treat an element—the markup is processed automatically when the document is loaded and the widgets are created.

You don't always need to use the `data-role` attribute. For some elements, jQuery Mobile will assume that it needs to create a widget based on the element type. This has happened for the buttons in the document: jQuery Mobile will create a button widget when it finds a `button` element in the markup. So, this element:

```
<button data-inline="true" id="no">No</button>
```

doesn't need a `data-role` attribute but could have been written like this if you prefer:

```
<button data-role="button" data-inline="true" id="no">No</button>
```

Defining Pages

The most important value for the `data-role` attribute is page. When building mobile web apps, it is good practice to minimize the number of requests made to the server. jQuery Mobile helps in this regard by supporting *single-page apps*, where the markup and script for multiple logical pages is contained within a single document and shown to the user as required. A page is denoted by a `div` element whose `data-role` attribute is page. The content of the `div` element is the content of that page:

```
...
<body>
    <div id="page1" data-role="page" data-theme="a">

        ...page content goes here...

    </div>
</body>
...
```

There is just one page in my `askmobile.html` document, but I'll return to the topic of pages when we build the full mobile CheeseLux app later in the chapter.

Configuring Widgets

jQuery Mobile also uses data attributes to configure widgets. By default, jQuery Mobile buttons span the entire page. This gives a large target to hit on a small portrait screen but looks pretty odd in other layouts. To disable this behavior, I have told jQuery Mobile that I want *inline buttons*, where the button is just large enough to contain its content. I did this by setting the `data-inline` attribute to `true` for the button elements, like this:

```
<button data-inline="true" id="no">No</button>
```

A number of element-specific data attributes are available, and you should consult the jQuery Mobile web site for details. One important configuration attribute that I will mention, however, is `data-theme`, which applies a style to the page or widget to which it is applied. A jQuery Mobile theme contains a number of *swatches*, named A, B, C, and so on. I have set the `data-theme` attribute to a for the page element so as to set the theme for the single page in the document and all of its content:

```
<div id="page1" data-role="page" data-theme="a">
```

You can create your own custom themes using the jQuery Mobile ThemeRoller, which is available at jquerymobile.com. I am using the default themes, and swatch A provides the dark style for the web app. For contrast, I have set the swatch on the Yes button to b, like this:

```
<button data-inline="true" data-theme="b" id="yes">Yes</button>
```

Buttons in swatch B are blue, which gives the user a strong suggestion as to the recommended decision.

▪ **Tip** I have defined a new CSS style sheet for use with jQuery Mobile. It is called `http://styles.mobile.css`, and it lives in the Node.js `content` directory along with the other example files. The styles in this file just tweak the layout slightly, allowing me to center elements in the page and make other minor adjustments to the default jQuery Mobile layout. You can find the style sheet in the source code download for this book, which is available from Apress.com.

Dealing with jQuery Mobile Events

Using a widget library that is based on jQuery means we can handle events using familiar techniques. If you look at the script element in the askmobile.html document, you will see that handling the events triggered when the buttons are clicked requires the same basic jQuery code that I have been using throughout this book:

```
<script>
    ...code removed for brevity...

    $(document).bind("pageinit", function() {
        $('button').click(function(e) {
            var useMobile = e.target.id == "yes";
            var useMobileValue = useMobile ? "mobile" : "desktop";
            if (localStorage) {
                localStorage["cheeseLuxMode"] = useMobileValue;
            } else {
                setCookie("cheeseLuxMode", useMobileValue, 30);
            }
            location.href = useMobile ? "mobile.html" : "example.html";
        });
    });
</script>
```

I use jQuery to select the button elements and the standard click method to handle the click event. However, there is one very important difference in the way that jQuery Mobile deals with events . Here it is:

```
$(document).bind("pageinit", function() {
    ...code to handle button click events...
}
```

jQuery Mobile processes the markup for data attributes when the standard jQuery ready event fires. This means I have to bind to the pageinit event if I want to execute code after jQuery Mobile has finished setting up its widgets. There is no convenient method for specifying a function for this event and so I have used the bind method instead. The code in this example would have run in response to the jQuery ready event quite happily, since I am not interacting directly with the widgets that jQuery Mobile creates. This will change when I come to the full jQuery Mobile CheeseLux web app, and it is good practice to use the pageinit event in all jQuery Mobile apps.

Storing the User's Decision

Now that I have described the jQuery Mobile parts of askmobile.html, we can return to the application's function, which is to record and store the user's preference for the version of the web app the user wants to use. I use local storage if it is available and fall back to a regular cookie if it is not. There is no convenient jQuery support for working with cookies, so I have written my own function called setCookie:

```
function setCookie(name, value, days) {
    var date = new Date();
    date.setTime(date.getTime()+(days * 24 * 60 * 60 *1000));
    document.cookie = name + "="+ value
        + "; expires=" + date.toGMTString() +"; path=/";
}
```

If I have to use the cookie, then I set the life to be 30 days, after which the browser will delete the cookie and the user will have to express their preference again. For brevity, I have not set any lifetime when using local storage, but doing so would be good practice.

■ **Tip** It is also good practice to ask the user if they want you to store their choice at all. I haven't taken this step in my simple example, but some users are sensitive to these issues, especially when it comes to cookies.

Detecting the User's Decision in the Web App

The last step is to detect the user's decision in the desktop version of the CheeseLux web app. Listing 8-5 shows a pair of functions I have added to utils.js to support this process.

Listing 8-5. Checking for a Prior Decision Before Performing a Redirect

```
function checkForVersionPreference() {
    var previousDecision;
    if (localStorage && localStorage["cheeseLuxMode"]) {
        previousDecision = localStorage["cheeseLuxMode"];
    } else {
        previousDecision = getCookie("cheeseLuxMode");
    }
    if (!previousDecision && cheeseModel.device.mobile) {
        location.href = "/askmobile.html";
    } else if (location.pathname == "/mobile.html" && previousDecision == "desktop") {
        location.href = "/example.html";
    } else if (location.pathname != "/mobile.html" && previousDecision == "mobile") {
        location.href = "/mobile.html";
    }
}

function getCookie(name) {
    var val;
    $.each(document.cookie.split(';'), function(index, elem) {
        var cookie = $.trim(elem);
        if (cookie.indexOf(name) == 0) {
            val = cookie.slice(name.length + 1);
        }
    })
    return val;
}
```

The checkForVersionPreference function uses the view model values to see whether the user has a mobile device and, if so, tries to recover the result of a previous decision from local storage or a cookie. Cookies are awkward to process, so I have added a getCookie function that finds a cookie by name and returns its value. If there is no stored value, then I direct the user to the askmobile.html document to get their preference. If there *is* a stored value, then I use it to switch to the mobile version if that was the user's preference. All that remains is to incorporate a call to the checkForVersionPreference function into example.html, which contains the desktop version of the web app, like this:

```
...
detectDeviceFeatures(function(deviceConfig) {
    cheeseModel.device = deviceConfig;
    checkForVersionPreference();

    $.getJSON("products.json", function(data) {
        cheeseModel.products = data;

    }).success(function() {
        $(document).ready(function() {
            ... code removed for brevity...
        });
    });
)};
...
```

I have shown the changes as code snippets because I don't want to use pages in a chapter on mobile devices to list the desktop web app code. You can get the complete listing as part of the source code download available free of charge from Apress.com.

■ **Tip** It makes sense to offer the user the chance to change their minds when the effect of the decision is stored and applied automatically. I skipped this step because I want to focus on the mobile app in this chapter, but you should always include some kind of UI cue that allows the user to switch to the other version of the web app, especially if the decision is stored and used persistently.

Building the Mobile Web App

I am going to start with a basic mobile version of the CheeseLux web app and then build on it to show you how to create a better experience for the user. When I create a mobile version of a web app that has a desktop counterpart, I have two goals in mind:

- Reuse as much desktop code as is possible

- Ensure that the mobile responds elegantly to different device capabilities

The first goal is all about long-term maintainability. The more common code I have, the fewer occasions there will be where I have to find and fix a bug in two different places. I like to decide in advance which version of the web app has primacy and which will have to flex to be able to use the code.

In general, I tend to create the desktop version first and make the mobile web app adapt. The exception to this is when the majority of users will be using mobile devices.

WHAT ABOUT MOBILE FIRST?

There is a view (often referred to as *mobile first*) that focuses on the design and development of the mobile platform first, largely because it forces you to work within the most constrained environment you will be targeting and because mobile devices have capabilities, like geolocation, that are not on desktops.

In my projects, I don't want initial constraints—I want to build the richest, deepest, and most immersive experience I can, and, for the moment at least, that is the desktop. Once I have a handle on what is possible with large screens and rich interaction, I begin the process of dealing with device constraints, paring down and tailoring my app until I get something that works well on a mobile device. I am not a believer in the unique capabilities of mobile devices, either. As I mentioned in Chapter 7, the hard and fast distinctions between categories of devices are fading fast. One of my moments of wonder recently was when Google was able to use the Wi-Fi data it collects along with its Street View product to pinpoint my location within a few feet. This was on a machine that would require a forklift truck to be mobile.

But, as I mentioned previously, I am not a pattern zealot, and you should follow whatever approach makes the most sense for you and your projects. Don't let anyone dictate your development style, including me.

The second goal is about ensuring that my mobile web app is responsive and adapts to the wide range of device types that users may have. You cannot afford to make assumptions about screen size and input mechanisms even when targeting just mobile devices.

▪ **Caution** You may be tempted to try to create a web app that switches between jQuery UI and jQuery Mobile (or equivalent libraries) based on the kind of device that is being used. Such a trick is possible but incredibly hard to pull off without creating a lot of very contorted code and markup. The most sensible approach is to create separate versions if you want to take advantage of features that are specific to one library or another.

To get things going, Listing 8-6 shows a first pass at creating the core functionality using jQuery Mobile. This listing depends on some changes in the view model that I'll explain shortly.

Listing 8-6. The Initial Version of the CheeseLux Mobile Web App

```
<!DOCTYPE html>
<html>
<head>
    <title>CheeseLux</title>
    <script src="jquery-1.7.1.js" type="text/javascript"></script>
    <script type="text/javascript">
        $(document).bind("mobileinit", function() {
            $.mobile.autoInitializePage = false;
```

```
        });
    </script>
    <script src="jquery.mobile-1.0.1.js" type="text/javascript"></script>
    <link rel="stylesheet" type="text/css" href="jquery.mobile-1.0.1.css"/>
    <link rel="stylesheet" type="text/css" href="styles.mobile.css"/>
    <script src='knockout-2.0.0.js' type='text/javascript'></script>
    <script src='utils.js' type='text/javascript'></script>
    <script src='signals.js' type='text/javascript'></script>
    <script src='crossroads.js' type='text/javascript'></script>
    <script src='hasher.js' type='text/javascript'></script>
    <script src='modernizr-2.0.6.js' type='text/javascript'></script>
    <meta name="viewport" content="width=device-width, initial-scale=1">
    <script>
        var cheeseModel = {};

        detectDeviceFeatures(function(deviceConfig) {
            cheeseModel.device = deviceConfig;
            checkForVersionPreference();

            $.getJSON("products.json", function(data) {
                cheeseModel.products = data;
                enhanceViewModel();

                $(document).ready(function() {
                    ko.applyBindings(cheeseModel);
                    $('button#left, button#right').live("click", function(e) {
                        e.preventDefault();
                        advanceCategory(e, e.target.id);
                    })
                    $.mobile.initializePage();
                });
            });

            $(document).bind("pageinit", function() {
                function positionCategoryButtons() {
                    setTimeout(function() {
                        $('fieldset:visible').each(function(index, elem) {
                            var fsWidth = 0;
                            $(elem).children().each(function(index, child) {
                                fsWidth+= $(child).width();
                            });
                            if (fsWidth > 0) {
                                $(elem).width(fsWidth);
                            } else {
                                positionCategoryButtons();
                            }
                        });
                    }, 10);
                };
                positionCategoryButtons();
                cheeseModel.device.smallAndPortrait.subscribe(positionCategoryButtons);
            });
```

```
            });
        </script>
    </head>
    <body>
        <div id="page1" data-role="page" data-theme="a">
            <div id="logobar" data-bind="visible: device.largeScreen()">
                <img data-bind="ifAttr: {attr: 'src', value: 'cheeselux.png',
                    test: device.largeScreen()}">
                <span id="tagline">Gourmet European Cheese</span>
            </div>

            <fieldset class="middle" data-role="controlgroup" data-type="horizontal"
                data-bind="foreach:products, visible: device.largeScreen() ||
                    device.smallAndPortrait()">
                <input type="radio" name="category" data-bind="attr: {id: category,
                    value: category}, checked: $root.selectedCategory" />
                <label data-bind="attr: {for: category}">
                    <span data-bind="text: $root.device.smallAndPortrait()?
                        shortName : category"></span>
                </label>
            </fieldset>

            <form action="/basket" method="post">
                <div data-bind="foreach: products">
                    <div data-bind="fadeVisible: category == $root.selectedCategory()">
                        <div data-role="header" >
                            <h1 data-bind="text: category"></h1>
                        </div>
                        <!-- ko foreach: items -->
                        <div class="itemContainer ui-grid-a">
                            <div class="ui-block-a">
                                <label data-bind="attr: {for: id}, formatText: {value: name,
                                    suffix:':'}"></label>
                            </div>
                            <div class="ui-block-b">
                                <input data-bind="attr: {name: id}, value: quantity">
                            </div>
                        </div>
                        <!-- /ko -->
                        <div data-role="footer">
                            <h1>
                                <label>Total:</label>
                                <span data-bind="formatText: {prefix: '$',
                                    value: cheeseModel.total()}"
                            </h1>
                        </div>
                    </div>
                </div>

                <div class="middle" data-role="controlgroup" data-type="horizontal"
                        data-bind="visible: device.smallAndLandscape()">
                    <button id="left" data-icon="arrow-l"> </button>
```

```
                <input type="submit" value="Submit Order"/>
                <button id="right" data-icon="arrow-r"
                        data-iconpos="right"> </button>
            </div>

            <div class="middle" data-role="controlgroup" data-type="horizontal"
                data-bind="visible: !device.smallAndLandscape()">
                <input type="submit" value="Submit Order"/>
            </div>
        </form>
    </div>
</body>
</html>
```

For the most part, this is a straightforward web app that relies on the core functionality of jQuery Mobile, but you need to be aware of some wrinkles and additions that I describe in the following sections. You can see the landscape and portrait layouts for a small-screen device in Figure 8-2. The web app also supports layouts for mobile devices with larger screens. I have not shown these layouts, but they are similar to those shown in the figure, but with the CheeseLux logo and the full category names displayed in the navigation buttons.

Figure 8-2. The basic implementation of the mobile CheeseLux web app

You will notice new data bindings and view model items in this listing. The formatText data binding lets me apply a prefix and suffix to the text content of an element, which simplifies working with

209

composed strings, especially currency amounts. This is one of the set of custom bindings that I generally add to projects and the code, which is included in the utils.js file, as shown in Listing 8-7. The composeString function used by this binding is the same one I showed you in Chapter 4 when I introduced the custom formatAttr binding.

Listing 8-7. The formatText Custom Data Binding

```
ko.bindingHandlers.formatText = {
    update: function(element, accessor) {
        $(element).text(composeString(accessor()));
    }
}
```

The other additions are some helpful shortcuts added to the device capabilities information in the view model. Although KO can deal with expressions in data bindings, I don't like defining code in this way, and I generally create computed data items that allow me to determine the state of the device through a single view model item. For this chapter, I defined a pair of computed values that let me easily read the combinations of screen size and orientation that I am interested in for the mobile web app. These shortcuts are defined in the detectDeviceFeatures function in the utils.js file, as shown in Listing 8-8.

Listing 8-8. Creating Shortcuts in the View Model to Avoid Expressions in Bindings

```
...
function detectDeviceFeatures(callback) {
    var deviceConfig = {};

    deviceConfig.landscape = ko.observable();
    deviceConfig.portrait = ko.computed(function() {
        return !deviceConfig.landscape();
    });

    var setOrientation = function() {
        deviceConfig.landscape(window.innerWidth > window.innerHeight);
    }
    setOrientation();

    $(window).bind("orientationchange resize", function() {
        setOrientation();
    });

    setInterval(setOrientation, 500);

    if (window.matchMedia) {
        var orientQuery = window.matchMedia('screen AND (orientation:landscape)')
        if (orientQuery.addListener) {
            orientQuery.addListener(setOrientation);
        }
    }

    Modernizr.load([{
        test: window.matchMedia,
```

```
        nope: 'matchMedia.js',
        complete: function() {
            var screenQuery = window.matchMedia('screen AND (max-width: 500px)');
            deviceConfig.smallScreen = ko.observable(screenQuery.matches);
            if (screenQuery.addListener) {
                screenQuery.addListener(function(mq) {
                    deviceConfig.smallScreen(mq.matches);
                });
            }
            deviceConfig.largeScreen = ko.computed(function() {
                return !deviceConfig.smallScreen();
            });

            setInterval(function() {
                deviceConfig.smallScreen(window.innerWidth <= 500);
            }, 500);
        }
    }, {
        test: Modernizr.touch,
        yep: 'jquery.touchSwipe-1.2.5.js',
        callback: function() {
            $('html').swipe({
                swipeLeft: advanceCategory,
                swipeRight: advanceCategory
            })
        }
    },{
        complete: function() {
            deviceConfig.mobile = Modernizr.touch && deviceConfig.smallScreen();

            deviceConfig.smallAndLandscape = ko.computed(function() {
                return deviceConfig.smallScreen() && deviceConfig.landscape();
            });
            deviceConfig.smallAndPortrait = ko.computed(function() {
                return deviceConfig.smallScreen() && deviceConfig.portrait();
            });

            callback(deviceConfig);
        }
    }]);
};
...
```

Managing the Event Sequence

As I demonstrated in the askmobile.html document, jQuery Mobile will process a document automatically and create widgets based on element types and the value of the data-role attribute. This is a nice feature, and it significantly reduces the amount of code required for simple web apps. Unfortunately, it gets in the way when you are using the view model to generate or format elements, especially if the data in the view model is obtained via Ajax. jQuery Mobile will process the document before the view model is populated with the data bindings, which means that widgets are not created properly.

This is the same problem I encountered previously with jQuery UI, but the issue is worse with jQuery Mobile because it assumes that it has sole control of elements in a page and makes it very difficult to create bindings that can negotiate the extra elements that jQuery Mobile uses when it sets up a widget. (This is a problem I'll return to for different reasons later in this chapter.)

Disabling Automatic Processing

The best approach is to prevent jQuery Mobile from automatically processing the document. To do this, I need to handle the mobileinit event, which is emitted by jQuery Mobile when the library is first loaded. I need to register my handler function before jQuery Mobile is loaded, which means I have to insert a new script element after the one that imports jQuery and before the one that imports jQuery Mobile, like this:

```
...
<sript src="jquery-1.7.1.js" type="text/javascript"></script>
<script type="text/javascript">
    $(document).bind("mobileinit", function() {
        $.mobile.autoInitializePage = false;
    });
</script>
<script src="jquery.mobile-1.0.1.js" type="text/javascript"></script>
...
```

By setting the $.mobile.autoInitializePage property to false, I disable the jQuery Mobile feature that processes the markup in the document automatically.

■ **Tip** To be fair, I need to insert my script element after jQuery only if I want to use the bind method, but I prefer to do this rather than use the clunky DOM API for handling events.

Disabling the automatic processing stops the race between the view model and jQuery Mobile and allows me to make my Ajax request, populate the view model, and do any other tasks I need without worrying about premature widget creation. When I am done setting up, I explicitly tell jQuery Mobile that it should process the page, like this:

```
$.getJSON("products.json", function(data) {
    cheeseModel.products = data;
    enhanceViewModel();

    $(document).ready(function() {
        ko.applyBindings(cheeseModel);
        $('button#left, button#right').live("click", function(e) {
            e.preventDefault();
            advanceCategory(e, e.target.id);
        })
        $.mobile.initializePage();
```

```
        });
});
```

The `mobile` object provides access to the jQuery Mobile API, and the `initializePage` method starts page processing.

Responding to the pageinit Event

Now that I have the main events under control, I can use the `pageinit` to perform tasks after jQuery Mobile has processed the pages in the document. jQuery Mobile is generally very solid, but it has some layout quirks. One in particular is that groups of buttons are not centered in the page. For the buttons at the bottom of the page, I have been able to fix this issue with CSS (which is what the `centered` style is for in the `styles.mobile.css` file). But the size of the navigation buttons changes, and that requires a JavaScript solution, which is as follows:

```
...
$(document).bind("pageinit", function() {
    function positionCategoryButtons() {
        setTimeout(function() {
            $('fieldset:visible').each(function(index, elem) {
                var fsWidth = 0;
                $(elem).children().each(function(index, child) {
                    fsWidth+= $(child).width();
                });
                if (fsWidth > 0) {
                    $(elem).width(fsWidth);
                } else {
                    positionCategoryButtons();
                }
            });
        }, 10);
    };
    positionCategoryButtons();
    cheeseModel.device.smallAndPortrait.subscribe(positionCategoryButtons);
});
...
```

I want to center the buttons after jQuery Mobile has finished creating them, which is an ideal use for the `pageinit` event. In the function, I add up the width of the children of each `fieldset` element and then use the total value to set the width of the `fieldset`. jQuery Mobile leaves the `fieldset` to be the width of the window, and the sequence of elements required to create a set of buttons makes it hard to center the buttons by other means.

◼ **Tip** I use the jQuery `each` method so that I can be sure that the `children` method returns only the children of one `fieldset` element. This means my code won't break if I add another `fieldset` element later. Element selectors are greedy, and if I just call `$('fieldset').children()`, I will get the children of all `fieldset` elements in the document, which will throw out the width calculations.

I wrapped the code that sets the width inside a call to the setTimeout function because I want to correctly resize the fieldset element when the content of the navigation buttons change, which happens when the size and orientation are altered.

The content of the elements is changed by data bindings, which are executed when observable data items in the view model are updated. Since I am using the subscribe method to receive the same kind of notifications, I need to make sure that my code to resize the fieldset isn't executed before the button content is changed, which I achieve by introducing a small delay using the setTimeout function.

Preparing for Content Changes

jQuery Mobile assumes that it has control of the elements that are used as the foundation for widgets. In the case of buttons, jQuery Mobile wraps the button contents (or label contents when using radio buttons) in a span element so that styling can be applied.

This is the same problem that jQuery UI creates, and the solution is the same for jQuery Mobile: wrap the content in a span element yourself so that you have a target for data bindings. Once you have an element that you can attach data bindings to, you don't need to worry about how jQuery Mobile transforms the element into a widget. You can see how I have done this for the navigation buttons:

```
<fieldset class="middle" data-role="controlgroup" data-type="horizontal"
    data-bind="foreach:products, visible: device.largeScreen() ||
        device.smallAndPortrait()">
    <input type="radio" name="category" data-bind="attr: {id: category,
        value: category}, checked: $root.selectedCategory" />
    <label data-bind="attr: {for: category}">
        <span data-bind="text: $root.device.smallAndPortrait()?
            shortName : category"></span>
    </label>
</fieldset>
```

This may seem like a simple trick, but a lot of mobile web app programmers get caught by this issue and end up trying to resolve it through some tortured and unreliable alternative. This simple approach resolves the problem rather neatly. All of the mobile widget toolkits that I have used clash with data bindings in a similar way. In the case of jQuery Mobile, you know that the problem has occurred when the formatting of buttons is lost when a data binding changes the button content, as shown in Figure 8-3.

Figure 8-3. Problems caused by jQuery Mobile adding elements for styling

Duplicating Elements and Using Templates

Not all conflicts between widget libraries and data bindings can be resolved so easily. In Listing 8-6, I created duplicate sets of the buttons that are displayed at the bottom of the page, like this:

```
<div class="middle" data-role="controlgroup" data-type="horizontal"
        data-bind="visible: device.smallAndLandscape()">
    <button id="left" data-icon="arrow-l"> </button>
    <input type="submit" value="Submit Order"/>
    <button id="right" data-icon="arrow-r"
            data-iconpos="right"> </button>
</div>

<div class="middle" data-role="controlgroup" data-type="horizontal"
        data-bind="visible: !device.smallAndLandscape()">
    <input type="submit" value="Submit Order"/>
</div>
```

One set has additional buttons that the user can click to navigate through the product categories. The problem that I am working around is that jQuery Mobile creates a set of buttons without taking into account the visibility of the elements it is working with. That means the outer buttons are given rounded corners even if they are invisible, which means that using the `visible` binding doesn't create well-formatted groups of buttons.

The `if` binding has its own issues because jQuery Mobile won't automatically update the styling of buttons when new elements are added to the container, and asking jQuery Mobile to refresh the content doesn't address this issue. So, the simplest approach is to create duplicate sets of elements.

Using Two-Pass Data Bindings

Duplicating elements is OK for simple situations, but it becomes problematic when you are working with complex sets of elements that have a lot of bindings and formatting. At some point, a change will be applied to one set of elements and not the other. Tracking down this kind of issue when it happens can be time-consuming. An alternative approach is to generate duplicate sets of elements from a single template. This is an elegant, but fiddly, technique—you can see the changes required in Listing 8-9.

Listing 8-9. Using a Template to Create Duplicate Sets of Elements

```
<!DOCTYPE html>
<html>
<head>
    <title>CheeseLux</title>
    <script src="jquery-1.7.1.js" type="text/javascript"></script>
    <script type="text/javascript">
        $(document).bind("mobileinit", function() {
            $.mobile.autoInitializePage = false;
        });
    </script>
    <script src="jquery.mobile-1.0.1.js" type="text/javascript"></script>
    <link rel="stylesheet" type="text/css" href="jquery.mobile-1.0.1.css"/>
    <link rel="stylesheet" type="text/css" href="styles.mobile.css"/>
    <script src='knockout-2.0.0.js' type='text/javascript'></script>
```

```html
<script src='utils.js' type='text/javascript'></script>
<script src='signals.js' type='text/javascript'></script>
<script src='crossroads.js' type='text/javascript'></script>
<script src='hasher.js' type='text/javascript'></script>
<script src='modernizr-2.0.6.js' type='text/javascript'></script>
<meta name="viewport" content="width=device-width, initial-scale=1">
<script>
    var cheeseModel = {};

    detectDeviceFeatures(function(deviceConfig) {
        cheeseModel.device = deviceConfig;
        checkForVersionPreference();

        $.getJSON("products.json", function(data) {
            cheeseModel.products = data;
            enhanceViewModel();

            $(document).ready(function() {
                ko.applyBindings(cheeseModel);
                $('*.deferred').each(function(index, elem) {
                    ko.applyBindings(cheeseModel, elem);
                });
                $('button#left, button#right').live("click", function(e) {
                    e.preventDefault();
                    advanceCategory(e, e.target.id);
                })
                $.mobile.initializePage();
            });
        });

        $(document).bind("pageinit", function() {
            function positionCategoryButtons() {
                setTimeout(function() {
                    $('fieldset:visible').each(function(index, elem) {
                        var fsWidth = 0;
                        $(elem).children().each(function(index, child) {
                            fsWidth+= $(child).width();
                        });
                        if (fsWidth > 0) {
                            $(elem).width(fsWidth);
                        } else {
                            positionCategoryButtons();
                        }
                    });
                }, 10);
            };
            positionCategoryButtons();
            cheeseModel.device.smallAndPortrait.subscribe(positionCategoryButtons);
        });
    });
</script>
<script id="buttonsTemplate" type="text/html">
```

```html
        <div class="deferred middle" data-role="controlgroup" data-type="horizontal"
            data-bind="attr: {'data-bind': 'visible: ' + ($data ? '' : '!')
                + 'device.smallAndLandscape()' }">
            <!-- ko if: $data -->
            <button id="left" data-icon="arrow-l"> </button>
            <!-- /ko -->
            <input type="submit" value="Submit Order"/>
            <!-- ko if: $data -->
            <button id="right" data-icon="arrow-r" data-iconpos="right"> </button>
            <!-- /ko -->
        </div>
    </script>
</head>
<body>
    <div id="page1" data-role="page" data-theme="a">
        <div id="logobar" data-bind="visible: device.largeScreen()">
            <img data-bind="ifAttr: {attr: 'src', value: 'cheeselux.png',
                test: device.largeScreen()}">
            <span id="tagline">Gourmet European Cheese</span>
        </div>

        <fieldset class="middle" data-role="controlgroup" data-type="horizontal"
            data-bind="foreach:products, visible: device.largeScreen() ||
                device.smallAndPortrait()">
            <input type="radio" name="category" data-bind="attr: {id: category,
                value: category}, checked: $root.selectedCategory" />
            <label data-bind="attr: {for: category}">
                <span data-bind="text: $root.device.smallAndPortrait()?
                    shortName : category"></span>
            </label>
        </fieldset>

        <form action="/basket" method="post">
            <div data-bind="foreach: products">
                <div data-bind="fadeVisible: category == $root.selectedCategory()">
                    <div data-role="header" >
                        <h1 data-bind="text: category"></h1>
                    </div>
                    <!-- ko foreach: items -->
                    <div class="itemContainer ui-grid-a">
                        <div class="ui-block-a">
                            <label data-bind="attr: {for: id}, formatText: {value: name,
                                suffix:':'}"></label>
                        </div>
                        <div class="ui-block-b">
                            <input data-bind="attr: {name: id}, value: quantity">
                        </div>
                    </div>
                    <!-- /ko -->
                    <div data-role="footer">
                        <h1>
                            <label>Total:</label>
```

217

```
                            <span data-bind="formatText: {prefix: '$',
                                value: cheeseModel.total()}"
                        </h1>
                    </div>
                </div>
            </div>

            <!-- ko template: {name: 'buttonsTemplate', foreach: [true, false] } -->
            <!-- /ko -->
        </form>
    </div>
</body>
</html>
```

This technique has three parts, and to show how the parts fit together, I need to explain them in reverse order from how they appear in the document.

Invoking a Template with Custom Data

I have used the template binding to generate elements from a Knockout.js template, a technique that I described in Chapter 3:

```
<!-- ko template: {name: 'buttonsTemplate', foreach: [true, false] } -->
<!-- /ko -->
```

The twist is that I am not using the view model to drive the template. Instead, I have created an array that contains true or false values. I am applying this technique in a very simple situation, and I need to know only if I am creating the set of buttons that allow for category navigation (represented by the true value) or the set that doesn't (represented by the false value). The point is that you can use the foreach binding with data that is not part of the view model. You can use more complex data structures for more complex sets of elements.

Using a Template to Generate Bindings

The second step is a little odd. I use the attr data bindings to set the value of the data-bind attribute on the elements that are generated by the template, like this:

```
<script id="buttonsTemplate" type="text/html">
    <div class="deferred middle" data-role="controlgroup" data-type="horizontal"
        data-bind="attr: {'data-bind': 'visible: ' + ($data ? '' : '!')
            + 'device.smallAndLandscape()' }">
        <!-- ko if: $data -->
        <button id="left" data-icon="arrow-l"> </button>
        <!-- /ko -->
        <input type="submit" value="Submit Order"/>
        <!-- ko if: $data -->
        <button id="right" data-icon="arrow-r" data-iconpos="right"> </button>
        <!-- /ko -->
    </div>
</script>
```

The simplest part of the template is the use of the `if` binding to figure out when the category navigation buttons should be generated. My template will be used twice: once each for the `true` and `false` values that I passed to the `foreach` binding. When the value is `true`, the button elements are included in the DOM, and they are omitted when the value is `false`.

The more complex part is where I have used the `attr` binding to specify a value that I want for the `data-bind` attribute in the elements that are generated by the template. Here is the value of the `data-bind` attribute in the template:

```
data-bind="attr: {'data-bind': 'visible: ' + ($data ? '' : '!') +
    'device.smallAndLandscape()'}"
```

There is a lot going on in this binding. The most important thing to understand is that I am specifying the `data-bind` value I want the generated elements to have as a string, and this string won't be processed at the moment. I'll return to the processing shortly.

I use `$data` to refer to the values I passed to the `foreach` binding when I called the template. The value of `$data` will be either `true` or `false`. First, Knockout will resolve this part of the binding, so when I am dealing with the `true` value, the generated `div` element will have a binding like this:

```
data-bind="attr: {'data-bind': 'visible: device.smallAndLandscape()'}"
```

and the `false` value will cause a binding like this:

```
data-bind="attr: {'data-bind': 'visible: !device.smallAndLandscape()'}"
```

Then, once the data values have been resolved, Knockout will process the entire `attr` binding, which has the rather neat effect of replacing itself in the generated element, like this:

```
data-bind="visible: device.smallAndLandscape()"
```

Reapplying the Data Bindings

Knockout processes the data-bind attribute only once, which means that my template generates elements with the data bindings that I want, but these bindings are not live. Changes in the view model won't affect them because the `data-bind` attributes were not defined when I called the `ko.applyBindings` method.

To fix this, I simply call `applyBindings` again, but this time I use the optional argument that allows me to specify which elements are processed:

```
$(document).ready(function() {
    ko.applyBindings(cheeseModel);
    $('*.deferred').each(function(index, elem) {
        ko.applyBindings(cheeseModel, elem);
    });
    $('button#left, button#right').live("click", function(e) {
        e.preventDefault();
        advanceCategory(e, e.target.id);
    })
    $.mobile.initializePage();
});
```

I added my button container element to the `deferred` class. I now select all members of this class and use the each method to call the `applyBindings` method on each element in turn. This makes

Knockout.js process the bindings that I generated from the template and make them live. This final step means that my bindings will respond to changes in the view model.

There are a couple of points to note about this technique. First, I am not trying to prevent duplication of elements in the DOM. There is no easy way to deal with the jQuery Mobile formatting issues without duplicate element sets. My goal is to generate the duplicates from a single set of source elements so that I make changes in one place and have them take effect in all of the duplicates when they are generated.

Second, when using this technique, you must ensure that you don't refer to view model items except within a pair of quote characters (i.e., within a string). If you refer to a variable outside of a string, then Kockout.js will try to find a value to resolve the reference, and you will get an error. View model values are resolved in the second call to the applyBindings method and not when the template is used to create elements.

■ **Caution** It can be difficult to get the string properly set up, but the effort is worthwhile for complex sets of elements. For simpler situations, I suggest you simply duplicate what you need inside the document and skip the templates altogether. The source code download for this book contains the full listings for this example.

Adopting the Multipage Model

My mobile web app is shaping up, but I am still missing URL routing, which means there is a significant difference between the mobile and desktop versions. The first step in adding support for routing is to embrace the multipage model. As I explained earlier, jQuery Mobile supports the idea of having multiple pages in a single HTML document. I will use this feature to provide the user with the means to navigate between categories. Listing 8-10 shows the changes that are required.

Listing 8-10. Adding Support for the Multipage Model

```
<!DOCTYPE html>
<html>
<head>
    <title>CheeseLux</title>
    <script src="jquery-1.7.1.js" type="text/javascript"></script>
    <script type="text/javascript">
        $(document).bind("mobileinit", function() {
            $.mobile.autoInitializePage = false;
        });
    </script>
    <script src="jquery.mobile-1.0.1.js" type="text/javascript"></script>
    <link rel="stylesheet" type="text/css" href="jquery.mobile-1.0.1.css"/>
    <link rel="stylesheet" type="text/css" href="styles.mobile.css"/>
    <script src='knockout-2.0.0.js' type='text/javascript'></script>
    <script src='utils.js' type='text/javascript'></script>
    <script src='signals.js' type='text/javascript'></script>
    <script src='crossroads.js' type='text/javascript'></script>
    <script src='hasher.js' type='text/javascript'></script>
    <script src='modernizr-2.0.6.js' type='text/javascript'></script>
```

```html
<meta name="viewport" content="width=device-width, initial-scale=1">
<script>
    var cheeseModel = {};

    detectDeviceFeatures(function(deviceConfig) {
        cheeseModel.device = deviceConfig;
        checkForVersionPreference();

        $.getJSON("products.json", function(data) {
            cheeseModel.products = data;
            enhanceViewModel();

            $(document).ready(function() {
                ko.applyBindings(cheeseModel);
                $('*.deferred').each(function(index, elem) {
                    ko.applyBindings(cheeseModel, elem);
                });
                $('button.left, button.right').live("click", function(e) {
                    e.preventDefault();
                    advanceCategory(e, $(e.target).hasClass("left")
                        ? "left" : "right");
                    $.mobile.changePage($('div[data-category="'
                        + cheeseModel.selectedCategory() + '"]'));
                })


                $.mobile.initializePage();

                hasher.initialized.add(crossroads.parse, crossroads);
                hasher.changed.add(crossroads.parse, crossroads);
                hasher.init();

                crossroads.addRoute("category/:newCat:", function(newCat) {
                    cheeseModel.selectedCategory(newCat ||
                        cheeseModel.products[0].category);
                });

                crossroads.addRoute("{shortCat}", function(shortCat) {
                    $.each(cheeseModel.products, function(index, item) {
                        if (item.shortName == shortCat) {
                            crossroads.parse("category/" + item.category);
                        }
                    });
                });
                crossroads.parse(location.hash.slice(1));
            });
        });
    });
</script>
<script id="buttonsTemplate" type="text/html">
    <div class="deferred middle" data-role="controlgroup" data-type="horizontal"
        data-bind="attr: {'data-bind': 'visible: ' + ($data ? '' : '!')
```

221

```
                                + 'device.smallAndLandscape()'}">
                    <!-- ko if: $data -->
                    <button class="left" data-icon="arrow-l"> </button>
                    <!-- /ko -->
                    <input type="submit" value="Submit Order"/>
                    <!-- ko if: $data -->
                    <button class="right" data-icon="arrow-r"
                        data-iconpos="right"> </button>
                    <!-- /ko -->
                </div>
        </script>
    </head>
    <body>
        <!-- ko foreach: products -->
            <div data-role="page" data-theme="a"
                    data-bind="attr: {'id': shortName, 'data-category': category}">
                <div id="logobar" data-bind="visible: $root.device.largeScreen()">
                    <img data-bind="ifAttr: {attr: 'src', value: 'cheeselux.png',
                        test: $root.device.largeScreen()}">
                    <span id="tagline">Gourmet European Cheese</span>
                </div>

                <fieldset class="middle" data-role="controlgroup" data-type="horizontal"
                        data-bind="foreach: $root.products,
                            visible: $root.device.largeScreen() ||
                                $root.device.smallAndPortrait()">
                    <a data-role="button" data-bind="formatAttr: {attr: 'href',
                        prefix: '#', value: shortName},
                        css: {'ui-btn-active': (category == $root.selectedCategory())}">
                        <span data-bind="text: $root.device.smallAndPortrait()? shortName :
                            category"></span>
                    </a>
                </fieldset>

                <form action="/basket" method="post">
                    <div>
                        <div>
                            <div data-role="header" >
                                <h1 data-bind="text: category"></h1>
                            </div>
                            <!-- ko foreach: items -->
                            <div class="itemContainer ui-grid-a">
                                <div class="ui-block-a">
                                    <label data-bind="attr: {for: id},
                                        formatText: {value: name, suffix:':'}">
                                    </label>
                                </div>
                                <div class="ui-block-b">
                                    <input data-bind="attr: {name: id}, value: quantity">
                                </div>
                            </div>
```

```
                <!-- /ko -->
                <div data-role="footer">
                    <h1>
                        <label>Total:</label>
                        <span data-bind="formatText: {prefix: '$',
                            value: cheeseModel.total()}"
                    </h1>
                </div>
            </div>
        </div>
        <!-- ko template: {name: 'buttonsTemplate', foreach: [true, false] } -->
        <!-- /ko -->
    </form>
</div>
<!-- /ko -->
</body>
</html>
```

I have highlighted the most important changes (and I'll describe them in a moment), but the basic approach is to create one page per category. Each page contains a duplicate set of navigation items, and only the details of individual products differ. For the most part, the changes are to the data bindings to create this effect. Some changes, however, require more explanation.

Reworking Category Navigation

jQuery Mobile uses the same URL-fragment-based approach I employed in the desktop version to navigate between pages. For example, if there is a div element whose data-role attribute is set to page and whose id attribute is set to mypage, I can get jQuery Mobile to display that page by navigating to the #mypage fragment.

The difference from the desktop web app is that jQuery Mobile places some constraints on the names that can be used for pages. I used the full category name before (such as British Cheese), but spaces are a problem for jQuery Mobile, so I have used the short category name instead (British, for example). Here is the binding that sets the page ID:

```
<div data-role="page" data-theme="a"
    data-bind="attr: {'id': shortName, 'data-category': category}">
```

Notice that I have added a data-category attribute that contains the full category name. I'll return to this attribute shortly.

Replacing Radio Buttons with Anchors

The page navigation model means that I can replace my radio buttons with a elements. jQuery Mobile will create button widgets from an a element if the data-role attribute is set to button, and the value of the href attribute can be used for navigation within the document:

```
<a data-role="button" data-bind="formatAttr: {attr: 'href',
    prefix: '#', value: shortName},
    css: {'ui-btn-active': (category == $root.selectedCategory())}">
    <span data-bind="text: $root.device.smallAndPortrait()? shortName :
        category"></span>
</a>
```

When the data bindings are resolved, I get a navigation element whose purpose is a lot easier to divine:

```
<a data-role="button" href="#British"
    <span>British</span>
</a>
```

Clicking one of the buttons that jQuery Mobile creates from this kind of element will navigate to the appropriate category page. As an added bonus, jQuery Mobile properly centers groups of buttons created from a elements, so I don't have to worry about explicitly setting the width of the containing fieldset element.

■ **Tip** Notice that I have used the `css` binding to apply the `ui-btn-active` class to the button when the selected category matches the category that button represents. This is the jQuery Mobile CSS class that is used when a button is active, and applying this class creates the blue highlighting that I had in the previous version of the mobile web app. Digging around in the toolkit CSS isn't ideal, but sometimes there is no alternative.

Mapping Page Names to Routes

So that I can reuse my JavaScript code for handling routes, I want to use the same route names as in the desktop version. This is a problem because of the restrictions on page names that jQuery Mobile enforces. To get around this, I have added a route that maps between the routes that jQuery Mobile requires and the routes I really want:

```
...
hasher.initialized.add(crossroads.parse, crossroads);
hasher.changed.add(crossroads.parse, crossroads);
hasher.init();

crossroads.addRoute("category/:newCat:", function(newCat) {
    cheeseModel.selectedCategory(newCat ||
        cheeseModel.products[0].category);
});

crossroads.addRoute("{shortCat}", function(shortCat) {
    $.each(cheeseModel.products, function(index, item) {
        if (item.shortName == shortCat) {
            crossroads.parse("category/" + item.category);
        }
    });
});

crossroads.parse(location.hash.slice(1));
...
```

The URL fragment changes when the user clicks one of the a elements to navigate to a new category. The hasher library detects this change and passes on the new hash to the crossroads routing engine. The jQuery Mobile URL matches the highlighted route, and I enumerate the products in the view model to find the one that has a matching shortName value. I use the category property of the product to create the kind of URL that the desktop version uses and call the crossroads.parse method to have it matched against the application routes. This technique allows me to bridge between the jQuery Mobile URLs and routes I want, allowing me to preserve route consistency across all versions of my web app. This isn't a big deal with my simple example routes, but this becomes a useful trick if you have an external JavaScript file full of JavaScript code that is executed when URLs are matched.

Explicitly Changing Pages

The last change relates to the data-category attribute that I added to the page div elements. When the user swipes the screen or uses one of the landscape navigation buttons, the advanceCategory function is called, and the value of the selectedCategory item in the view model is updated. However, updating the view model doesn't automatically cause jQuery Mobile to navigate to the page for the selected category. To address this, I have added a call to the mobile.changePage method. This method will accept a URL to navigate to or a jQuery object as the element to display:

```
$('button.left, button.right').live("click", function(e) {
    e.preventDefault();
    advanceCategory(e, $(e.target).hasClass("left") ? "left" : "right");
    $.mobile.changePage($('div[data-category="'
        + cheeseModel.selectedCategory() + '"]'));
})
```

I use the data-category item to select the page element for the new selectedCategory value without having to iterate through the products. With this small addition, I can rely on the same advanceCategory code that I use in the desktop version of the web app but get the benefits of the jQuery Mobile page model.

Adding the Final Chrome

There is just one final change that I want to make to the CheeseLux mobile app. At one level, it is an entirely trivial change, but it does also allow me to demonstrate an important behavioral quirk that jQuery Mobile displays.

jQuery Mobile plays a sliding animation when a new page is displayed. By default, the page slides in from the right. The change that I want to make is to have the new page slide in from the left when the user presses the left landscape navigation button or presses one of the portrait/large screen buttons for a category that appears in the view model before the current category.

The jQuery Mobile changePage method accepts an optional configuration object. One of the object properties that jQuery Mobile recognizes is reverse. When the value of this property is true, the page appears from the left. The default value, false, causes the new page to appear from the right.

For the portrait navigation buttons, I have added a function to utils.js called getIndexOfCategory. This function, which is shown in Listing 8-11, enumerates through the view model data to find the index of a specified full or short category name.

Listing 8-11. The getIndexOfCategory Function

```
function getIndexOfCategory(category) {
    var result = -1;
    for (var i = 0; i < cheeseModel.products.length; i++) {
        if (cheeseModel.products[i].category == category ||
                cheeseModel.products[i].shortName == category) {
            result = i;
            break;
        }
    }
    return result;
}
```

Listing 8-12 shows the changes in mobile.html to make use of this function.

Listing 8-12. Managing Page Transition Animation Direction

```
<script>
    var cheeseModel = {};

    detectDeviceFeatures(function(deviceConfig) {
        cheeseModel.device = deviceConfig;
        checkForVersionPreference();

        $.getJSON("products.json", function(data) {
            cheeseModel.products = data;
            enhanceViewModel();

            $(document).ready(function() {
                ko.applyBindings(cheeseModel);
                $('*.deferred').each(function(index, elem) {
                    ko.applyBindings(cheeseModel, elem);
                });
                $('button.left, button.right').live("click", function(e) {
                    e.preventDefault();
                    advanceCategory(e, $(e.target).hasClass("left") ? "left" : "right");
                    $.mobile.changePage($('div[data-category="'
                        + cheeseModel.selectedCategory() + '"]'),
                        {reverse: $(e.target).hasClass("left")});
                })

                $('a[data-role=button]').click(function(e) {
                    e.preventDefault();
                    var cIndex = getIndexOfCategory(cheeseModel.selectedCategory());
                    var newIndex = getIndexOfCategory(this.hash.slice(1));
                    $.mobile.changePage(this.hash, {reverse: cIndex > newIndex});
                });

                $.mobile.initializePage();
```

```
                hasher.initialized.add(crossroads.parse, crossroads);
                hasher.changed.add(crossroads.parse, crossroads);
                hasher.init();

                crossroads.addRoute("category/:newCat:", function(newCat) {
                    cheeseModel.selectedCategory(newCat ||
                        cheeseModel.products[0].category);
                });

                crossroads.addRoute(":shortCat:", function(shortCat) {
                    $.each(cheeseModel.products, function(index, item) {
                        if (item.shortName == (shortCat ||
                            cheeseModel.products[0].shortName)) {
                                crossroads.parse("category/" + item.category);
                        }
                    });
                });

                crossroads.parse(location.hash.slice(1));
            });
        });
    });
</script>
```

I just needed to provide the optional argument to the changePage method to make the horizontal buttons work. For the a elements, I decided to handle the click event, figure out the transition direction, and call the changePage method directly. There are other ways of doing this in jQuery Mobile, but this is the simplest and most direct.

The important jQuery Mobile characteristic I wanted to demonstrate relates to the way that internal URLs are managed. jQuery Mobile will navigate to the URL for the entire document rather than the specific page if you use the changePage method to navigate to the URL that represents the first page in the document. For example, if you call changePage('#British'), jQuery Mobile will navigate to cheeselux.com/mobile.html and not cheeselux.com/mobile.html#British.

To cater for this, I need to change the route that maps between the jQuery Mobile–friendly fragment URLs and the routes shared with the desktop version of the web app, like this:

```
crossroads.addRoute(":shortCat:", function(shortCat) {
    $.each(cheeseModel.products, function(index, item) {
        if (item.shortName == (shortCat || cheeseModel.products[0].shortName)) {
                crossroads.parse("category/" + item.category);
        }
    });
});
```

I made the segment optional, rather than variable (I explain the difference in Chapter 4), and if there is no category name provided as part of the URL, I assume that the first category in the view model should be used. This is a simple change for my web app, but if you are mapping complex sets of routes, you must ensure that you set defaults for all of the route segments that are expected and would usually be provided by the desktop version.

Summary

In this chapter, I created a solid mobile implementation of my CheeseLux web app. I showed you the importance of adopting the navigation model provided by the mobile toolkit you are using and various approaches for integrating the core features of a professional-level web app, such as routing, view models, and data bindings. Mobile widget toolkits usually require some tweaks and tricks to get them to play nicely with pro web apps, but the result is worth figuring out solutions to the wrinkles that arise. In the next chapter, I show you different techniques for improving the way you write and package your JavaScript code.

CHAPTER 9

Writing Better JavaScript

In this chapter, I explain some of the techniques I use to create better JavaScript. This is not a language guide, and I won't be demonstrating any code hacks or tweaks. My coding preferences are your maintenance nightmares, and vice versa. I have seen otherwise mild-mannered people end up in a screaming match over the "right" way to code, and I don't see the point in lecturing you when I have a fair few bad habits myself.

Instead, I am going to show you some of the techniques I use to make my code easier for other programmers and projects to use. Most large-scale web apps have a team of programmers, and sharing code becomes important.

I have been dumping useful functions into the utils.js file throughout this book. This is how I tend to work, with a general kitchen-sink file where I put functions that I expect to repeatedly use. For this book, using utils.js let me spend more time in each chapter on the topics at hand without having to spend pages listing code that I defined in a previous chapter. It also let me demonstrate the idea of using a core set of common functions when creating desktop and mobile versions of the same web app.

The problem with just dumping functions into a file in this way is that they become hard to manage and maintain and, as I'll explain shortly, difficult for others to integrate into their projects. For this reason, I revisit my kitchen-sink file when I have reached a point in a project where the basic functionality is stable and I have a good feel for the way that different features fit together. At this point, and not before, I start to rework the code into modules so that it plays nicely with other libraries. In this chapter, I show you the techniques I use for this.

Once I have tidied up and modularized the code, I begin unit testing. Testing is a very personal thing, and many testing proselytizers will insist that testing must begin as soon as you start coding, if not sooner. I understand that point of view, but I also know that I don't even *think* about testing until I have made a certain amount of progress with a project. There naturally comes a point where I have enough progress and my mind starts to turn toward consolidating and improving what I have.

Testing is another topic on which I am not going to lecture. My only advice is that you should be honest with yourself. Test when it feels right, test until you are happy with your code, and use the techniques and tools that work for you. Do what is right for your project, and accept that testing later will require more coding changes and that not testing at all means your users will have to find your bugs for you.

Managing the Global Namespace

One of the biggest problems with large JavaScript projects is the likelihood of a *naming collision*, where two regions of code use the same *global variable* names for different purposes. A global variable is one that exists outside a function or object. JavaScript makes these available throughout your web application so that a global function defined in an inline script element or external JavaScript file is available to every other `script` element and JavaScript file you use. When a global function or variable is created, it is said to reside in the *global namespace.*

For small applications, this is a useful feature; it means that you can just partition your code and rely on the browser to merge it together when the application is loaded. This is what allows my `utils.js` file to work: the browser loads all of the functions in my file and makes them available via global variables. I don't need to know where the `mapProducts` function is defined to use it; it is automatically available.

The problem comes when you use code that has functions and variables with the same names that you have used. All sorts of problems will arise if I use a JavaScript library that defines a `mapProducts` function. The `mapProducts` contained in the file that is loaded last is the one that will win, and any code that was expecting the other version is going to be surprised.

What can be a useful trick in a small web app becomes a maintenance nightmare as a web application grows in size and complexity. It soon becomes hard to think up meaningful names that are not already in use, and the likelihood of collision increases sharply. In the sections that follow, I describe some useful techniques that will help you avoid naming collisions by structuring your code and reducing the number of global variables that are created as a consequence.

AVOIDING IMPLIED GLOBAL VARIABLES

A common cause of global variables is to assign values to variables that have not been defined using the `var` keyword. JavaScript interprets this as a request to create a global variable:

```
...
(function() {
    var var1 = "my local variable";
    var2 = "my global variable";
})();
...
```

In this listing, the variable `var1` exists only within the scope of the function that defines it, but `var2` is defined in the global namespace. This can be a useful feature when used carefully and deliberately, allowing you control over which variables are exported globally, but usually this situation arises through error rather than intention. I have shown this in a self-executing function, but it can happen in any function that defines variables without the `var` keyword.

Defining a JavaScript Namespace

The first technique is to employ *namespaces,* which limit the scope of variables and functions. You will be familiar with namespaces if you have used a language like Java or C#. JavaScript doesn't have a namespace language construct like those languages, but you can create something that solves the problem by relying on the way that JavaScript scopes objects. Listing 9-1 shows how this is done.

Listing 9-1. Defining a JavaScript Namespace

```
var cheeseUtils = {};

cheeseUtils.mapProducts = function(func, data, indexer) {
    $.each(data, function(outerIndex, outerItem) {
        $.each(outerItem[indexer], function(itemIndex, innerItem) {
```

```
                func(innerItem, outerItem);
            });
        });
}

cheeseUtils.composeString = function(bindingConfig ) {
    var result = bindingConfig.value;
    if (bindingConfig.prefix) { result = bindingConfig.prefix + result; }
    if (bindingConfig.suffix) { result += bindingConfig.suffix;}
    return result;
}
```

To create the namespace effect, I create an object and then assign my functions and variables as properties within it. This means that to access these functions elsewhere, I have to use the name of the object as a prefix, like this:

```
cheeseUtils.mapProducts(function(item) {
    if (item.id == id) { item.quantity(0); }
}, cheeseModel.products, "items");
```

To be clear, this isn't a real namespace because JavaScript doesn't support them; it just looks and acts a little bit like one. But it is enough to reduce pollution of the global namespace, in that I have taken two functions out of the shared context and replaced them with a single object name, cheeseUtils.

There is still a risk of name collision, so it is important to select a name for the object that is specific to your project or area of functionality. You can nest namespaces by nesting objects, creating a hierarchy that must be navigated in order to use your code. Listing 9-2 shows an example.

■ **Tip** To save space, I won't list all of the functions that are in the utils.js file. I'll just pick some representative samples to demonstrate the different techniques.

Listing 9-2. Creating Nested Namespaces

```
if (!com) {
    var com = {};
}
com.cheeselux = {};
com.cheeselux.utils = {};

com.cheeselux.utils.mapProducts = function(func, data, indexer) {
    $.each(data, function(outerIndex, outerItem) {
        $.each(outerItem[indexer], function(itemIndex, innerItem) {
            func(innerItem, outerItem);
        });
    });
}

com.cheeselux.utils.composeString = function(bindingConfig ) {
    var result = bindingConfig.value;
```

```
        if (bindingConfig.prefix) { result = bindingConfig.prefix + result; }
        if (bindingConfig.suffix) { result += bindingConfig.suffix;}
        return result;
}
```

In this listing I have used a pretty standard approach to namespaces, which is to use the structure of my domain name but in reverse. However, since com is likely to be used by other libraries following the same approach, then I check to see whether it has been defined already before doing so myself. I don't have to do this for the cheeselux part because I am the owner of the cheeselux.com domain and there is little chance of collision.

Referring directly to functions in a nested namespace can lead to verbose code. When I use the code in a nested namespaces, I tend to alias the innermost object to a local variable, like this:

```
var utils = com.cheeselux.utils;
```

This creates a loose equivalent to the import or using statements defined by Java and C# (albeit without the isolation features that those other languages support).

I like using nested namespaces, probably because I tend to write my server-side code in C#, which encourages the same approach. To make creating the namespaces simpler, I rely on the fact that global variables are actually defined as properties on the window browser object. This makes it easy to create variables by name without relying in the dreaded eval function, as Listing 9-3 shows.

Listing 9-3. Creating Nested Namespaces Using a Function

```
createNamespace("com.cheeselux.utils");

function createNamespace(namespace) {
    var names = namespace.split('.');
    var obj = window;
    for (var i = 0; i < names.length; i++) {
        if (!obj[names[i]]) {
            obj = obj[names[i]] = {};
        } else {
            obj = obj[names[i]];
        }
    }
};

com.cheeselux.utils.mapProducts = function(func, data, indexer) {
    $.each(data, function(outerIndex, outerItem) {
        $.each(outerItem[indexer], function(itemIndex, innerItem) {
            func(innerItem, outerItem);
        });
    });
}

com.cheeselux.utils.composeString = function(bindingConfig) {
    var result = bindingConfig.value;
    if (bindingConfig.prefix) { result = bindingConfig.prefix + result; }
    if (bindingConfig.suffix) { result += bindingConfig.suffix;}
    return result;
}
```

The createNamespace function takes a namespace as an argument and breaks it into segments. The object that represents each segment is created only if it doesn't already exist, which means that I don't collide with anyone else's use of com or with other com.cheeselux.* namespaces that I create in separate JavaScript files for my project.

■ **Tip** Creating separate files is entirely optional. You can define multiple namespaces in a single file if you prefer. The advantage of a single file is that the browser has to make only one request to get all of your code. If you do like using multiple files, then you can simply concatenate them into one when you release your web app.

I can go one step further and make the namespace itself more easily configurable, as Listing 9-4 demonstrates. This makes it much easier to rename my namespace if there is a conflict and means that I can select a shorter name to save myself some typing.

Listing 9-4. Making Namespaces Easily Configurable

```
function createNamespace(namespace) {
    var names = namespace.split('.');
    var obj = window;
    for (var i = 0; i < names.length; i++) {
        if (!obj[names[i]]) {
            obj = obj[names[i]] = {};
        } else {
            obj = obj[names[i]];
        }
    }
    return obj;
};

var utilsNS = createNamespace("cheeselux.utils");

utilsNS.mapProducts = function(func, data, indexer) {
    $.each(data, function(outerIndex, outerItem) {
        $.each(outerItem[indexer], function(itemIndex, innerItem) {
            func(innerItem, outerItem);
        });
    });
}

utilsNS.composeString = function(bindingConfig) {
    var result = bindingConfig.value;
    if (bindingConfig.prefix) { result = bindingConfig.prefix + result; }
    if (bindingConfig.suffix) { result += bindingConfig.suffix;}
    return result;
}
```

I have updated the createNamespace function so that it returns the namespace object it creates. This allows me to create a namespace and assign the result as a variable, which I can then use to add functions to the namespace. If I need to change the name of the namespace, then I have to do it only in the call to the createNamespace method (and, of course, in any code that relies on my functions). In this example, I have shortened my namespace by dropping the com prefix. The odds of there being a conflict are still pretty slim, but if it does arise, it is a simple enough matter to adapt.

Using Self-executing Functions

One drawback of the previous technique is that I end up creating another global variable, utilsNS. This is still a better approach than defining all of my variables globally, but it is somewhat self-defeating.

I can address this by using a *self-executing function*. This technique relies on the fact that a JavaScript variable defined within a function exists only within the scope of that function. The self-executing aspect means that the function runs without being explicitly invoked from another part of the code. The trick is to define a function and have it execute immediately. It is easier to see the structure of a self-executing function when there isn't any other code:

```
(function() {
    ...statements go here...
})();
```

To make a function self-execute, you wrap it in parentheses and then apply another pair of parentheses at the end. This defines and calls the function in a single step. Any variables defined within the function are tidied up after the function has finished executing and don't end up in the global namespace. Listing 9-5 shows how I can apply this to my utility functions.

Listing 9-5. Using a Self-executing Function to Define Namespaces

```
(function() {
    function createNamespace(namespace) {
        var names = namespace.split('.');
        var obj = window;
        for (var i = 0; i < names.length; i++) {
            if (!obj[names[i]]) {
                obj = obj[names[i]] = {};
            } else {
                obj = obj[names[i]];
            }
        }
        return obj;
    };

    var utilsNS = createNamespace("cheeselux.utils");

    utilsNS.mapProducts = function(func, data, indexer) {
        $.each(data, function(outerIndex, outerItem) {
            $.each(outerItem[indexer], function(itemIndex, innerItem) {
                func(innerItem, outerItem);
            });
        });
    }

    utilsNS.composeString = function(bindingConfig) {
        var result = bindingConfig.value;
```

```
        if (bindingConfig.prefix) { result = bindingConfig.prefix + result; }
        if (bindingConfig.suffix) { result += bindingConfig.suffix;}
        return result;
    }
})();
```

The only global variable that is left is the cheeselux namespace object. My functions are defined within the cheeselux.utils namespace, and my utilsNS variable is tidied up by the browser when the self-executing function has finished.

Consuming a function defined in this way is still just a matter of referring to the function via the namespace, like this:

```
cheeselux.utils.mapProducts(function(item) {
    if (item.id == id) { item.quantity(0); }
}, cheeseModel.products, "items");
```

Creating Private Properties, Methods, and Functions

In JavaScript, every property, method, and function is available for use from any other part of the code that creates or can access them. This makes it difficult to indicate which members are intended for use by others and which are the internal implementations of features.

The difference is important; you want to be able to change the internal implementation to fix bugs or add new features without having to worry if someone has created a dependency that you weren't expecting. Anyone using your code needs to know what properties and methods they can rely on not to change without due notice. JavaScript doesn't have any keywords that control access (such as public and private, which are found in other languages) and so we need to find alternative approaches to address this shortfall.

The simplest solution to this problem is to adopt a naming convention that makes it clear that some properties and methods are not intended for public use. The most widely adopted convention is to prefix private names with an underscore character (_).

My composeString function is an ideal candidate to be private. I use this function only in my custom data bindings, and I want to be free to change every aspect of this function (including its very existence) as my bindings evolve. There is no reason for any other programmer to depend on this function, even if they use my bindings. Listing 9-6 shows the underscore naming style applied to this function and the data bindings that rely on it.

Listing 9-6. Applying a Naming Convention to Denote a Private Function

```
(function() {

    function createNamespace(namespace) {
        var names = namespace.split('.');
        var obj = window;
        for (var i = 0; i < names.length; i++) {
            if (!obj[names[i]]) {
                obj = obj[names[i]] = {};
            } else {
                obj = obj[names[i]];
            }
        }
        return obj;
```

```
    };

    var utilsNS = createNamespace("cheeselux.utils");

    utilsNS.mapProducts = function(func, data, indexer) {
        $.each(data, function(outerIndex, outerItem) {
            $.each(outerItem[indexer], function(itemIndex, innerItem) {
                func(innerItem, outerItem);
            });
        });
    }

    utilsNS._composeString = function(bindingConfig) {
        var result = bindingConfig.value;
        if (bindingConfig.prefix) { result = bindingConfig.prefix + result; }
        if (bindingConfig.suffix) { result += bindingConfig.suffix;}
        return result;
    }
})();

ko.bindingHandlers.formatAttr = {
    init: function(element, accessor) {
        $(element).attr(accessor().attr, cheeselux.utils._composeString(accessor()));
    },
    update: function(element, accessor) {
        $(element).attr(accessor().attr, cheeselux.utils._composeString(accessor()));
    }
}

ko.bindingHandlers.formatText = {
    update: function(element, accessor) {
        $(element).text(cheeselux.utils._composeString(accessor()));
    }
}
...
```

Adopting a naming convention doesn't prevent others from using private members, but it does signal that doing so is against the wishes of the developer and that the property, method, or function is subject to change without notice. It is important to use a naming convention that is widely adopted (such as the underscore) or that is immediately obvious (such as prefixing names with the word private).

An alternative approach is to limit the scope of private functions so that they are not defined as part of the namespace. This prevents the function from being accessed elsewhere in the web app, but it means that all of the dependencies on that function must appear within the same self-executing function, which isn't always practical. Listing 9-7 shows how this approach works.

Listing 9-7. Using a Self-executing Function to Keep a Function Private

```
(function() {

    function createNamespace(namespace) {
        var names = namespace.split('.');
        var obj = window;
        for (var i = 0; i < names.length; i++) {
            if (!obj[names[i]]) {
                obj = obj[names[i]] = {};
            } else {
                obj = obj[names[i]];
            }
        }
        return obj;
    };

    var utilsNS = createNamespace("cheeselux.utils");

    utilsNS.mapProducts = function(func, data, indexer) {
        $.each(data, function(outerIndex, outerItem) {
            $.each(outerItem[indexer], function(itemIndex, innerItem) {
                func(innerItem, outerItem);
            });
        });
    }

    function _composeString(bindingConfig) {
        var result = bindingConfig.value;
        if (bindingConfig.prefix) { result = bindingConfig.prefix + result; }
        if (bindingConfig.suffix) { result += bindingConfig.suffix;}
        return result;
    }

    ko.bindingHandlers.formatAttr = {
        init: function(element, accessor) {
            $(element).attr(accessor().attr, _composeString(accessor()));
        },
        update: function(element, accessor) {
            $(element).attr(accessor().attr, _composeString(accessor()));
        }
    }

    ko.bindingHandlers.formatText = {
        update: function(element, accessor) {
            $(element).text(_composeString(accessor()));
        }
    }

})();
```

The _composeString function is never defined as part of the local or global namespaces and is available only for use in the same enclosing self-executing function. This technique works because JavaScript supports *closures,* which brings variables and functions in scope even when they are defined in this manner.

Managing Dependencies

Packaging up my functions into namespaces makes them more manageable and helps clean up the global namespace, but there is still one major issue: dependencies on other libraries. In the sections that follow, I show you a technique for managing dependencies in libraries that is starting to gain in popularity and that you can use to make your code easier to share and easier to work with.

Understanding Assumed Dependency Problems

There are two kinds of dependency in an external JavaScript file such as utils.js. The first kind is an *assumed dependency,* where I just use the functionality of a library and assume it will be available. I have done this a lot in utils.js, especially with jQuery. An assumed dependency places responsibility on the HTML document that uses a JavaScript file to load the required libraries and to do so before my code is executed. The mapProducts function is a good example of an assumed dependency:

```
utilsNS.mapProducts = function(func, data, indexer) {
    $.each(data, function(outerIndex, outerItem) {
        $.each(outerItem[indexer], function(itemIndex, innerItem) {
            func(innerItem, outerItem);
        });
    });
}
```

This function assumes that the jQuery $.each method will be available. If you want to use this function, then you need to ensure that jQuery is loaded and ready before you call mapProducts. Listing 9-8 shows a very simple jQuery Mobile web app that makes use of the mapProducts function. There is nothing new in this tiny web app, but I am going to use it to demonstrate different dependency issues and solutions in the sections that follow.

Listing 9-8. A Simple Web App That Uses a JavaScript File That Contains an Assumed Dependency

```html
<!DOCTYPE html>
<html>
<head>
    <title>CheeseLux</title>
    <link rel="stylesheet" type="text/css" href="jquery.mobile-1.0.1.css"/>
    <link rel="stylesheet" type="text/css" href="styles.mobile.css"/>
    <script src="jquery-1.7.1.js" type="text/javascript"></script>
    <script type="text/javascript">
        $(document).bind("mobileinit", function() {
            $.mobile.autoInitializePage = false;
        });
    </script>
    <script src="jquery.mobile-1.0.1.js" type="text/javascript"></script>
    <script src='knockout-2.0.0.js' type='text/javascript'></script>
    <script src='modernizr-2.0.6.js' type='text/javascript'></script>
```

```
<script src='utils.js' type='text/javascript'></script>
<meta name="viewport" content="width=device-width, initial-scale=1">
<script>
    var cheeseModel = {
        selectedCount: ko.observable(0)
    };

    $.getJSON("products.json", function(data) {
        cheeseModel.products = data;

        $(document).ready(function() {
            ko.applyBindings(cheeseModel);
            $.mobile.initializePage();

            $('a[data-role=button]').click(function(e) {
                var count = 0;
                cheeselux.utils.mapProducts(function(inner, outer) {
                    if (outer.category == e.currentTarget.id) {
                        count++;
                    }
                }, cheeseModel.products, "items")
                cheeseModel.selectedCount(count);
            });
        });
    });
</script>
</head>
<body>
    <div data-role="page" id="page1" data-theme="a">
        <fieldset class="middle" data-role="controlgroup" data-type="horizontal"
                data-bind="foreach: products">
            <a data-role="button" data-bind="text: category, attr: {id: category}"></a>
        </fieldset>
        <div class="middle results" data-bind="visible: selectedCount">
            There are <span data-bind="text: selectedCount"></span>
            cheeses in this category
        </div>
    </div>
</body>
</html>
```

■ **Note** This is an entirely useless web app in its own right. A button is displayed for each cheese category, and clicking the button displays the number of cheeses within that category. Ignore, if you will, the fact that there are easier ways to obtain this information than using the mapProducts method and that there are three cheeses in every single category. This witless web app is perfect for demonstrating the key aspects of dependency management.

Understanding Directly Resolved Dependencies

The tiny web app works because jQuery has been loaded long before I call the mapProducts function. The situation would be different if I rewrote the web app to use a different toolkit. Most programmers do the same thing when they first understand that assumed dependencies are a problem: they assume control of the situation and take direct action to fix it. Listing 9-9 shows a typical solution.

Listing 9-9. Taking Direct Action to Resolve Assumed Dependencies

```
(function() {

    function createNamespace(namespace) {
        ...code removed for brevity...
    };

    var utilsNS = createNamespace("cheeselux.utils");

    Modernizr.load({
        load: 'jquery-1.7.1.js',
        complete: function() {
            utilsNS.mapProducts = function(func, data, indexer) {
                $.each(data, function(outerIndex, outerItem) {
                    $.each(outerItem[indexer], function(itemIndex, innerItem) {
                        func(innerItem, outerItem);
                    });
                });
            }
        }
    })
    ...code removed for brevity...
})();
```

In this listing, I have taken responsibility for resolving my dependency on jQuery by using Modernizr to load it before creating my mapProducts function. (The load property in a Modernizr.load object specifies that the JavaScript file should always be loaded.)

In doing this, I have transformed an assumed dependency into a *directly resolved dependency*. A directly resolved dependency is when I rely on another JavaScript library and I take direct action to make my code work, usually by loading the library myself.

Understanding the Problems Caused by Resolving a Dependency

Directly resolving a dependency causes a *lot* of problems. First, I created an assumed dependency on Modernizr to ensure that jQuery is loaded, which isn't a huge step forward. But the real damage is that I have made sure that the mapProducts function works; however, in doing so, I have undermined the stability of the web app itself.

To see the problem, load the web app, and reload the page a few times. There are two issues. If the web app works, you have encountered just the least serious one, which is that the jQuery library has been loaded twice. You can see this in the browser developer tools or in the console output from the Node.js server that prints out each URL that is requested. Here is the list of files loaded by the web app as reported by the server, with annotations to highlight the two loads for jQuery:

The "sys" module is now called "util". It should have a similar interface.

```
Ready on port 80
Ready on port 81
GET request for /example.html
GET request for /jquery.mobile-1.0.1.css
GET request for /styles.mobile.css
GET request for /jquery-1.7.1.js              <-- first load
GET request for /jquery.mobile-1.0.1.js
GET request for /knockout-2.0.0.js
GET request for /modernizr-2.0.6.js
GET request for /utils.js
GET request for /products.json
GET request for /jquery-1.7.1.js              <-- second load
GET request for /images/ajax-loader.png
```

You can tell whether you have encountered only the first problem because you will see three buttons, and clicking one of them makes a message appear. You know that you have encountered the second problem if you just get an empty window. Figure 9-1 shows both outcomes.

Figure 9-1. The two outcomes that arise from a directly resolved dependency

The second problem is a race condition, and it won't always manifest itself when you are loading all of the resources from the web app from the local machine. If the Ajax request completes after Modernizr has loaded the jQuery library and executed the callback function, then you will get the blank window, and there will be an error message in the JavaScript console like this:

```
Uncaught TypeError: Cannot call method 'initializePage' of undefined
```

The exact wording will vary from browser to browser, but the problem is that the call to `$.mobile.initializePage` has failed because there is no `$.mobile` object. To help force the problem to appear, I have added a special URL to the Node.js server that introduces a delay in returning the JSON content. To trigger this delay, change the name of the JSON file requested by the `getJSON` method, as shown in Listing 9-10.

Listing 9-10. Deliberately Introducing a Delay in the Ajax Request for the JSON Data

```
...
<script>
    var cheeseModel = {
        selectedCount: ko.observable(0)
    };

    $.getJSON("products.json.slow", function(data) {
        cheeseModel.products = data;

        $(document).ready(function() {
            ko.applyBindings(cheeseModel);
            $.mobile.initializePage();

            ... code removed for brevity...
        });
    });
</script>
...
```

Requesting products.json.slow instead of products.json will add a one-second delay to the Ajax request that will force the Ajax request to take longer than Modernizr requires to load the jQuery library. You can edit the server.js file to add a longer delay if you don't see the problem, but one-second consistently causes the white screen for me.

■ **Tip** This is part of what makes this problem so nasty; it usually won't appear during development because the Ajax request will complete so quickly. Unfortunately, it *does* appear in deployment when requests are made to busy servers over congested networks. If you ever find yourself getting user reports of blank screens that you can't replicate, it is always a good idea to see whether your libraries are self-resolving dependencies.

Here is the sequence of events when the Ajax request completes *before* Modernizr has loaded jQuery:

1. jQuery is loaded by the browser from the script element in example.html and sets up the $ shorthand reference.

2. jQuery Mobile is loaded and adds the mobile property to the jQuery $ shorthand.

3. The Ajax request completes, and the $.mobile.initializePage method is called.

4. Modernizr loads the jQuery library again, which replaces the $ shorthand with an object that doesn't have the jQuery Mobile mobile property.

This is the best-case scenario where jQuery is loaded and executed twice, but at least the web app works. The sequence changes when the Ajax request completes *after* Modernizr has loaded jQuery:

1. jQuery is loaded by the browser from the script element in example.html and sets up the $ shorthand reference.

2. jQuery Mobile is loaded and adds the mobile property to the jQuery $ shorthand.

3. Modernizr loads the jQuery library again, which replaces the $ shorthand with an object that doesn't have the jQuery Mobile mobile property.

4. The Ajax request completes, and the $.mobile.initializePage method is called.

You can see the problem: the call to $.mobile.initialPage is made after the second instance of jQuery has been loaded and the $ shorthand has been redefined, which erases the mobile property. The effect is that loading jQuery a second time has unloaded jQuery Mobile and so the web app dies a horrible death. Even in the best-case scenario, the only reason that the web app works is because it is so simple; *any* call to a jQuery Mobile function will cause a problem once Modernizr has caused the mobile object to be deleted.

■ **Tip** There is a second race condition in this situation. The mapProducts function isn't defined until Modernizr has loaded the jQuery library, which means that a delay in processing the request (because the server or the network is busy) can lead to the code in the inline script element calling mapProducts before it exists. I am not going to demonstrate this issue, but you get the idea: directly resolved dependencies are extremely dangerous.

Making a Bad Problem into a Subtle Bad Problem

Before moving to a real dependency solution, I want to show you a common attempt at fixing the double-loading problem: testing to see whether the library is loaded, like this:

```
...
Modernizr.load({
    test: $.each,
    nope: 'jquery-1.7.1.js',
    complete: function() {
        utilsNS.mapProducts = function(func, data, indexer) {
            $.each(data, function(outerIndex, outerItem) {
                $.each(outerItem[indexer], function(itemIndex, innerItem) {
                    func(innerItem, outerItem);
                });
            });
        }
    }
})
...
```

I have used Modernizr to test some indicator that jQuery has already been loaded and use the nope property to load the JavaScript file if it hasn't. Applying this technique to my tiny example web app will make everything work. But it isn't a real solution, and while the new problem I created occurs less frequently, it is much harder to track down.

The underlying problem is that I am still just trying to make *my* code work. If utils.js is the only file that uses this technique, then everything will be fine, with the exception that the mapProducts function may not be defined in a timely enough manner if the jQuery library does need to be loaded and there is a delay in the request. However, if this technique is used in more than one file, then there is a very subtle race condition. Imagine that there are two files that use Modernizr to test for jQuery: fileA.js and fileB.js. Most of the time, the sequence of events will be this:

1. The browser executes the code in fileA.js, which tests for jQuery. jQuery hasn't been loaded, so Modernizr requests the file and then executes the complete function.

2. The browser executes the code in fileB.js, which tests for jQuery. jQuery has been loaded via fileA.js, and Modernizr executes the complete function without needing to load any files.

However, Modernizr requests are asynchronous, which means that the browser will continue to execute JavaScript code while Modernizr waits for the response from the server. So, if the timing is just right, the sequence will really be as follows:

1. The browser executes the code in fileA.js, which tests for jQuery. jQuery hasn't been loaded, so Modernizr requests the file.

2. The browser continues to execute code while Modernizr is waiting and begins processing fileB.js. The Modernizr request from fileA.js hasn't completed yet, so fileB.js causes Modernizr to make a second request for the jQuery file.

3. The fileA.js request completes, jQuery is loaded, and the fileA.js complete function is executed.

4. The fileB.js request completes, jQuery is loaded for a second time, and the fileB.js complete function is executed.

Any properties that the complete function in fileA.js adds to the jQuery $ shorthand will be lost when Modernizr loads jQuery again. This sequence occurs infrequently, but when it does, it can kill the web app by deleting essential functionality required in at least one of the JavaScript files. You might think that infrequent problems are acceptable, but infrequent can still be a serious issue when your web app has millions of users.

Using the Asynchronous Module Definition

The only real way to eliminate race conditions and duplicated library loading is to deal with dependencies in a coordinated way, and this means taking responsibility for loading dependencies out of individual JavaScript files and consolidating them. The best model for doing this is the *Asynchronous Module Definition* (AMD), which I'll explain and demonstrate in the sections that follow.

Defining an AMD Module

Defining a module is pretty simple and hinges on the use of the `define` function. Listing 9-11 shows how I have created a module in a new file called `utils-amd.js`. You don't have to include amd in the file name; that's just my preference because I like to make it as obvious as possible to the consumers of my code that they are dealing with AMD. Providing the `define` function is the responsibility of the AMD loader. As an author of AMD modules, you can rely on the `define` function being present without having to worry about which loader is being used or how the function is implemented.

Listing 9-11. The utils-amd.js File

```
define(['jquery-1.7.1.js'], function() {
    return {
        mapProducts: function(func, data, indexer) {
            $.each(data, function(outerIndex, outerItem) {
                $.each(outerItem[indexer], function(itemIndex, innerItem) {
                    func(innerItem, outerItem);
                });
            });
        },
        composeString: function(bindingConfig) {
            var result = bindingConfig.value;
            if (bindingConfig.prefix) { result = bindingConfig.prefix + result; }
            if (bindingConfig.suffix) { result += bindingConfig.suffix;}
            return result;
        }
    };
});
```

The `define` function creates an AMD module. The first argument is an array of the libraries that the code in the module depends on. The second argument is a function, known as the *factory function*, that contains the module code. Only one AMD module can be defined in a file, and since I like to keep the functionality defined in a module narrowly focused, my `utils-amd.js` file contains just the `mapProducts` and `composeString` functions. (I'll return to some of the other code from `utils.js` in a while.)

An AMD module can rely on all of the declared dependencies being loaded before the factory function is executed. In this case, I have declared a dependency on `jquery-1.7.1.js`, and I can assume that this JavaScript file will be loaded and jQuery will be available for use when I set up my `mapProducts` and `composeString` functions. The result from the factory function is an object whose properties are the functions I want to export for use elsewhere in the web app. Any variables or functions that I define and that are not part of the result object will be tidied up when the factory function has executed without polluting the global namespace.

■ **Tip** Notice that there is no namespace in my module. One of the nice features of AMD is that it is up to the consumer of my module to decide how to refer to the functionality that I define, as I'll demonstrate in the next section.

Using an AMD Module

AMD solves the dependency issues by having a single resource loader take responsibility for loading libraries. This loader is responsible for executing a module's factory function and ensuring that the libraries it relies on are loaded and ready before this happens. The main means of communication between a module and the loader is through the define function, which the loader is responsible for implementing.

By standardizing the loading process, the decision about which loader to use is left to the consumer of AMD modules, rather than the author. So, I don't have to worry about resolving dependencies when I write an AMD module, and I don't even have to worry about how they will be dealt with.

Although the AMD format is gaining popularity, not all resource loaders support AMD. This includes Modernizr.load, which I have been using to load libraries so far in this book (and to demonstrate why this is a bad idea in this chapter). My favorite AMD-aware loader is requireJS, which you can download from http://requirejs.org. You can see how I have applied requireJS to my tiny web app in Listing 9-12.

Listing 9-12. Using requireJS to Load AMD Modules

```html
<!DOCTYPE html>
<html>
<head>
    <title>CheeseLux</title>
    <link rel="stylesheet" type="text/css" href="jquery.mobile-1.0.1.css"/>
    <link rel="stylesheet" type="text/css" href="styles.mobile.css"/>
    <script src='require.js' type='text/javascript'></script>
    <meta name="viewport" content="width=device-width, initial-scale=1">
    <script>
        var libs = [
            'utils-amd',
            'device-amd',
            'custombindings-amd',
            'jquery-1.7.1.js',
            'knockout-2.0.0.js',
            'modernizr-2.0.6.js'
        ];

        require(libs, function(utils, device) {

            var cheeseModel = {
                selectedCount: ko.observable(0)
            };

            $(document).bind("mobileinit", function() {
                $.mobile.autoInitializePage = false;
            });

            $.getJSON("products.json", function(data) {
                cheeseModel.products = data;
                device.detectDeviceFeatures(function(deviceConfig) {
                    cheeseModel.device = deviceConfig;
                    $(document).ready(function() {
                        ko.applyBindings(cheeseModel);
```

```
                    requirejs(['jquery.mobile-1.0.1.js'], function() {

                        $.mobile.initializePage();

                        $('a[data-role=button]').click(function(e) {
                            var count = 0;
                            utils.mapProducts(function(inner, outer) {
                                if (outer.category == e.currentTarget.id) {
                                    count++;
                                }
                            }, cheeseModel.products, "items")
                            cheeseModel.selectedCount(count);
                        });
                    });
                });
            });
        });
    </script>
</head>
<body>
    <div data-role="page" id="page1" data-theme="a">
        <fieldset class="middle" data-role="controlgroup" data-type="horizontal"
                data-bind="foreach: products">
            <a data-role="button" data-bind="text: category, attr: {id: category}"></a>
        </fieldset>
        <div class="middle results" data-bind="fadeVisible: selectedCount()">
            There are <span data-bind="text: selectedCount"></span>
            cheeses in this category
        </div>
    </div>
</body>
</html>
```

Declaring Dependencies

The first thing to do is remove all of the script elements in the head section of the document and replace them with a single element that imports requireJS. This ensures that requireJS has a complete view of all of the dependencies in the web app and that you don't end up loading script files twice if they are required in dependent libraries.

```
...
<script src='require.js' type='text/javascript'></script>
<meta name="viewport" content="width=device-width, initial-scale=1">
<script>
    var libs = [
        'utils-amd',
        'device-amd',
        'custombindings-amd',
        'jquery-1.7.1.js',
        'knockout-2.0.0.js',
```

```
    'modernizr-2.0.6.js'
];

require(libs, function(utils, device) {
    ...
```

The most important feature of an AMD loader is the require function, which is the counterpart to define. The require function takes two arguments: an array of modules and script files that the web app depends on and a callback function to execute when they are all loaded. I find that defining the dependency array as a variable makes my code more readable, but that is purely a personal preference.

■ **Note** The AMD module takes care of the problems around how dependencies are resolved, but it still requires that the JavaScript files are available from the web server. When sharing your code with others, you will still need to let them know which libraries you depend upon and make it clear that you are using AMD and so they will need an AMD loader.

Notice that some of the items in the dependency array have a .js suffix and others don't. Not all of the dependencies or a web app will be written as AMD modules. If you pass requireJS the name of a JavaScript file (i.e., with a .js suffix), then it will load the file and execute the code inside of it just like any regular resource loader.

If you omit the .js suffix, then requireJS assumes you have specified an AMD module and acts accordingly. It will add the .js suffix when it requests the file from the server, and when it receives the response, it will look for the define function in order to discover the dependencies and the factory function.

■ **Tip** By forcing each file to contain only one module, AMD increases the number of HTTP requests that are required to get the scripts for a web app. In this example, I have gone from one file (utils.js) to three (utils-amd.js, device-amd.js, and custombindings-amd.js). I would have ended up with more if I had properly packaged up all of the functions that utils.js contained. To address this, requireJS supports a server-side optimizer that will concatenate multiple AMD module files into a single response. See http://requirejs.org/docs/optimization.html for details.

Dealing with Callback Arguments

For each AMD module in the list passed to require, there is a corresponding argument passed to the callback function. Each argument is set to the object returned by the factory function in the module. This is a nice alternative to namespaces; the consumer of the module gets to decide how to refer to the module functions rather than the creator.

The first module in my list is utils-amd, and this corresponds to the util argument in my callback function. When I want to use the mapProducts function defined by the module, I make a call like this:

```
utils.mapProducts(function(inner, outer) {
    if (outer.category == e.currentTarget.id) {
        count++;
    }
}, cheeseModel.products, "items")
cheeseModel.selectedCount(count);
```

If I later start using a regular JavaScript library that uses `utils` as a global variable, I can easily change the way that I refer to the code in the `utils-amd` module by renaming the argument for the callback function. And, since the functions are scoped within the context of the callback argument, AMD modules don't pollute the global namespace at all.

So, why are there three AMD modules in the list but only two callback arguments? The answer is that modules are not required to return an object if they don't need to export functions, and this is the approach I have taken with the `custombindings-amd` module, which you can see in Listing 9-13.

Listing 9-13. An AMD Module That Doesn't Export Functions

```
define(['utils-amd', 'jquery-1.7.1.js', 'knockout-2.0.0.js'], function(utils) {

    ko.bindingHandlers.formatAttr = {
        init: function(element, accessor) {
            $(element).attr(accessor().attr, utils.composeString(accessor()));
        },
        update: function(element, accessor) {
            $(element).attr(accessor().attr, utils.composeString(accessor()));
        }
    }

    ko.bindingHandlers.fadeVisible = {

        init: function(element, accessor) {
            $(element)[accessor() ? "show" : "hide"]();
        },

        update: function(element, accessor) {
            if (accessor() && $(element).is(":hidden")) {
                var siblings = $(element).siblings(element.tagName + ":visible");
                if (siblings.length) {
                    siblings.fadeOut("fast", function() {
                        $(element).fadeIn("fast");
                    })
                } else {
                    $(element).fadeIn("fast");
                }
            }
        }
    }
});
```

In this module, I simply add my custom data bindings to the `ko.bindingHandlers` object, and there are no new functions to export directly from the module for use elsewhere.

■ **Tip** Notice that the `custombindings-amd` module depends on the `utils-amd` module. The AMD loader is responsible for ensuring that all the dependencies are resolved, which makes reusing modules very simple.

The `require` callback function does receive an argument when a module that doesn't return an object is loaded, but the value of that argument is `null`. So, I could easily have written my callback function like this:

```
require(libs, function(utils, device, bindings) {
    ...
}
```

But there is little point because the bindings object will be `null`. The order of the arguments always reflects the order of the modules in the `require` list, so I always put the modules that don't return objects at the end of the list so that I can omit the `null` arguments that correspond to them.

Declaring Inline Dependencies

It isn't always possible to declare all of the dependencies at the start of a `script` block. As an example, in order to prevent jQuery Mobile from automatically processing the document, I need to load jQuery and set up an event handler before the jQuery Mobile library is loaded. You can simply call the `requirejs` function to declare dependencies within a require statement, like this:

```
...
requirejs(['jquery.mobile-1.0.1.js'], function() {

    $.mobile.initializePage();

    $('a[data-role=button]').click(function(e) {
        var count = 0;
        utils.mapProducts(function(inner, outer) {
            if (outer.category == e.currentTarget.id) {
                count++;
            }
        }, cheeseModel.products, "items")
        cheeseModel.selectedCount(count);
    });
});
...
```

In this way, I am able to declare my dependencies without having to load all of the code files at once. This grants me space between jQuery and jQuery Mobile being loaded in which I can set up my event handler.

This is also the technique I have used in the `device-amd` module to replace the `Modernizr.load` method. Listing 9-14 shows the code from Chapter 7 where I load a polyfill based on the presence of a browser feature.

Listing 9-14. Loading a Polyfill Using Modernizr

```
...
Modernizr.load([{
    test: window.matchMedia,
    nope: 'matchMedia.js',
    complete: function() {
        var screenQuery = window.matchMedia('screen AND (max-width: 500px)');
        deviceConfig.smallScreen = ko.observable(screenQuery.matches);
        if (screenQuery.addListener) {
            screenQuery.addListener(function(mq) {
                deviceConfig.smallScreen(mq.matches);
            });
        }
        deviceConfig.largeScreen = ko.computed(function() {
            return !deviceConfig.smallScreen();
        });

        setInterval(function() {
            deviceConfig.smallScreen(window.innerWidth <= 500);
        }, 500);
    }
}, {
    complete: function() {
        callback(deviceConfig);
    }
}]);
...
```

The Modernizr syntax is excellent; I love being able to combine the test, loading the dependency and the callback function so elegantly. The requireJS equivalent is shown in Listing 9-15, which shows the device-amd.js file.

Listing 9-15. Loading a Polyfill Using requireJS

```
define(['modernizr-2.0.6.js', 'knockout-2.0.0.js'], function() {

    return {

        detectDeviceFeatures: function(callback) {
            var deviceConfig = {};

            deviceConfig.landscape = ko.observable();
            deviceConfig.portrait = ko.computed(function() {
                return !deviceConfig.landscape();
            });

            var setOrientation = function() {
                deviceConfig.landscape(window.innerWidth > window.innerHeight);
            }
            setOrientation();
```

```
            $(window).bind("orientationchange resize", function() {
                setOrientation();
            });

            setInterval(setOrientation, 500);

            if (window.matchMedia) {
                var orientQuery = window.matchMedia('screen AND (orientation:landscape)')
                if (orientQuery.addListener) {
                    orientQuery.addListener(setOrientation);
                }
            }

            function setupMediaQuery() {
                var screenQuery = window.matchMedia('screen AND (max-width: 500px)');
                deviceConfig.smallScreen = ko.observable(screenQuery.matches);
                if (screenQuery.addListener) {
                    screenQuery.addListener(function(mq) {
                        deviceConfig.smallScreen(mq.matches);
                    });
                }
                deviceConfig.largeScreen = ko.computed(function() {
                    return !deviceConfig.smallScreen();
                });

                setInterval(function() {
                    deviceConfig.smallScreen(window.innerWidth <= 500);
                }, 500);

                callback(deviceConfig);
            }

            if (window.matchMedia) {
                setupMediaQuery();
            } else {
                requirejs(['matchMedia.js'], function() {
                    setupMediaQuery();
                });
            }
        }
    };
});
```

This is a less elegant approach, but it doesn't suffer from the problems I described earlier in the chapter. If you are working on a large project or sharing code with others, then a single, coordinated approach to dependences is essential, even if the code style isn't quite as smooth.

Unit Testing Client-Side Code

The last topic that I want to cover in this book is unit testing. The tools for unit testing web apps are not as sophisticated as those for desktop or server-side code, but they are still pretty good, and you will find it easy to embrace client-side unit testing as part of your development cycle—if you are a believer in unit testing, anyway.

As I said at the beginning of this chapter, I am not going to lecture you about the importance of testing or tell you when you should begin testing your code. From my own experience, I resisted unit testing for a long time, in part because of the number of zealots that kept insisting that testing be done at a certain time and in a certain way. These days, I have come to see the value in unit testing, but when and how unit testing is best applied varies from project to project and programmer to programmer. I am a big believer in writing better-quality code, but I have an intense dislike for rigid approaches that treat every situation in the same way.

With that in mind, I am going to briefly introduce you to the client-side testing tool that I like to use and then leave you to figure out how to apply it. Like all of the techniques in this book, you should pick what works for you, adapt everything to your own needs, and simply ignore anything that doesn't solve any problems you are facing.

Using QUnit

I use QUnit, which is the tool developed by the jQuery team for their unit testing. It is simple and effective and works well. You can get QUnit from http://github.com/jquery/qunit. To install QUnit, download the QUnit package and copy the qunit.js and qunit.css files from the qunit folder in the archive to the Node.js content folder.

QUnit tests are run from an HTML document, and there is a basic structure of elements required in this document so that QUnit can display the test results. Listing 9-16 shows the template that I used when testing AMD modules, which I have created as the file tests.html in the content directory.

Listing 9-16. A QUnit Template Document for AMD Testing

```
<!DOCTYPE html>
<html>
<head>
    <link rel="stylesheet" type="text/css" href="qunit.css"/>
    <script src='require.js' type='text/javascript'></script>
    <script src='jquery-1.7.1.js' type='text/javascript'></script>
    <script src='qunit.js' type='text/javascript'></script>
    <script type="text/javascript">
        $(document).ready(function() {
            require(["utils-amd"], function(utils) {
                module("Utils-AMD Module");
                // tests for utils-amd module will go here
            });
        });
    </script>
</head>
<body>
    <h1 id="qunit-header">AMD Tests</h1>
    <h2 id="qunit-banner"></h2>
    <div id="qunit-testrunner-toolbar"></div>
```

```
    <h2 id="qunit-userAgent"></h2>
    <ol id="qunit-tests"></ol>
    <div id="qunit-fixture">test markup, will be hidden</div>
</body>
</html>
```

To use QUnit, ensure that the script and CSS files you copied into the content directory are imported into the document.

For each module I want to test, I use the QUnit module function to denote the start of a series of tests and use requireJS to load the module code. (The QUnit module function isn't related to AMD modules; it just groups together a set of related tests in the output display.)

The markup added to the template allows QUnit to display the results. You can change the markup to format your results differently, and information about the meaning of each element can be found at http://docs.jquery.com/QUnit, along with the full API documentation.

I have added jQuery to my list of script imports, but QUnit doesn't require jQuery to run. I find jQuery useful for creating more complex tests, as I'll demonstrate shortly.

▪ **Tip** Be careful if you are using requireJS to load QUnit. The QUnit library initializes itself in response to the load event on the window browser object, and this event is usually triggered before requireJS has loaded the jQuery library and executed the callback function. If you absolutely must use requireJS, then you can make a call to QUnit.load() in the requireJS callback function.

Adding Tests for a Module

With the basic structure in place, I can begin to add tests for my module. I am going to keep things simple and perform some argument tests on the composeString function, making sure null arguments don't cause odd results. Listing 9-17 shows the addition of tests to the tests.html file.

Listing 9-17. Adding Tests to the tests.html File

```
<!DOCTYPE html>
<html>
<head>
    <link rel="stylesheet" type="text/css" href="qunit.css"/>
    <script src='require.js' type='text/javascript'></script>
    <script src='jquery-1.7.1.js' type='text/javascript'></script>
    <script src='qunit.js' type='text/javascript'></script>
    <script type="text/javascript">
        $(document).ready(function() {
            require(["utils-amd"], function(utils) {
                module("Utils-AMD Module");
                test("Null prefix and suffix", function() {
                    var config ={
                        prefix: null,
                        suffix: null,
                        value: "value"
```

```
                };
                equal(utils.composeString(config), "value");
            });
            test("Null value", function() {
                var config ={
                    prefix: "prefix",
                    suffix: "suffix",
                    value: null
                };
                equal(utils.composeString(config), "prefixsuffix");
            });
            test("No value property", function() {
                var config ={
                    prefix: "prefix",
                    suffix: "suffix",
                };
                equal(utils.composeString(config), "prefixsuffix");
            });
        });
    });
    </script>
</head>
<body>
    <h1 id="qunit-header">AMD Tests</h1>
    <h2 id="qunit-banner"></h2>
    <div id="qunit-testrunner-toolbar"></div>
    <h2 id="qunit-userAgent"></h2>
    <ol id="qunit-tests"></ol>
    <div id="qunit-fixture">test markup, will be hidden</div>
</body>
</html>
```

Each test is defined with the test function, with arguments for the name of the test and a function that contains the test code. In each of the four tests I have added, I create an object with the prefix, suffix, and value properties that are passed to my function via my custom data bindings and pass this to the composeString function, which I access through the utils argument to my requireJS callback function, like this:

```
equal(utils.composeString(config), "prefixvalue");
```

Like most unit test packages, QUnit provides a series of assertions that test the result of an operation. In this case, I have used the equal function to check that the result from calling the composeString function matches my expectation. A range of different assertions are available, and you can see the full list at http://docs.jquery.com/QUnit.

To run the unit tests, simply load tests.html into the browser. QUnit will perform each test in turn and use the markup as a container for the results. My composeString function passes one of the tests and fails the other two. The results are displayed in the browser, as shown in Figure 9-2.

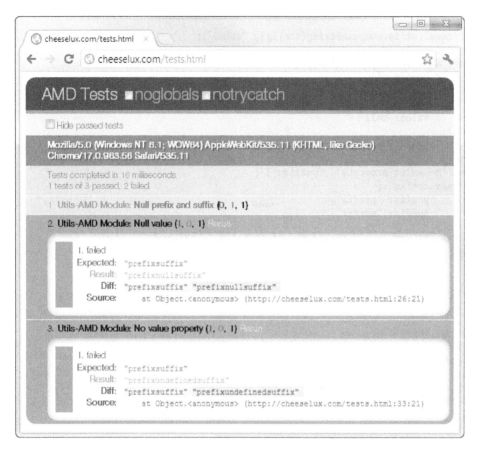

Figure 9-2. Executing unit tests on the composeString function

There is a bug in the composeString function, which doesn't check to see whether the value property of the object passed as the argument exists or has been assigned a value. To fix this problem, I make the change shown in Listing 9-18 and run the tests again.

Listing 9-18. Fixing the composeString Function

```
...
composeString: function(bindingConfig) {
    var result = bindingConfig.value || "";
    if (bindingConfig.prefix) { result = bindingConfig.prefix + result; }
    if (bindingConfig.suffix) { result += bindingConfig.suffix;}
    return result;
}
...
```

I can run individual tests again or, by reloading the document, run all of the tests. My simple fix resolves the problem with the two broken tests, and reloading tests.html gives me the all-clear.

Using jQuery to Perform Tests on HTML

I am not going to write a complete set of tests for my modules because QUnit behaves just like any other unit test package, except it operates on JavaScript in the browser, especially for self-contained functions like composeString where the input and the result are all expressed in JavaScript.

However, a slightly different approach is required when the effect or result of the code being tested is expressed in HTML. This is the reason that I included jQuery in my QUnit test template, and to demonstrate this technique, I will write some tests for the formatAttr binding in the custombindings-amd module, which is shown in Listing 9-19.

Listing 9-19. The formatAttr Binding from the custombindings-amd Module

```
ko.bindingHandlers.formatAttr = {
    init: function(element, accessor) {
        $(element).attr(accessor().attr, utils.composeString(accessor()));
    },
    update: function(element, accessor) {
        $(element).attr(accessor().attr, utils.composeString(accessor()));
    }
}
```

jQuery makes it easy to create, use, and test fragments of HTML without needing to add them to the document. Listing 9-20 shows additions to tests.html for the formatAttr binding.

Listing 9-20. Unit Testing Using HTML Fragments

```
<!DOCTYPE html>
<html>
<head>
    <link rel="stylesheet" type="text/css" href="qunit.css"/>
    <script src='require.js' type='text/javascript'></script>
    <script src='jquery-1.7.1.js' type='text/javascript'></script>
    <script src='qunit.js' type='text/javascript'></script>
    <script type="text/javascript">
        $(document).ready(function() {

            require(["utils-amd"], function(utils) {
                module("Utils-AMD Module");
                // other utils-amd tests removed for brevity
                test("No value property", function() {
                    var config ={
                        prefix: "prefix",
                        suffix: "suffix",
                    };
                    equal(utils.composeString(config), "prefixsuffix");
                });
            });

            require(["custombindings-amd", "knockout-2.0.0.js"], function() {
                module("Custombindings-AMD Module");
                test("Correct attribute applied", function() {
                    var viewModel = {
```

```
                        cat: "British"
            };
            var testElem = $("<a></a>").attr("data-bind",
                "formatAttr: {attr: 'href', prefix: '#', value: cat}")[0];
            ko.applyBindings(viewModel, testElem);

            equal(testElem.attributes.length, 2);
            equal($(testElem).attr("href"), "#British");
        });
    });
});
    </script>
</head>
<body>
    <h1 id="qunit-header">AMD Tests</h1>
    <h2 id="qunit-banner"></h2>
    <div id="qunit-testrunner-toolbar"></div>
    <h2 id="qunit-userAgent"></h2>
    <ol id="qunit-tests"></ol>
    <div id="qunit-fixture">test markup, will be hidden</div>
</body>
</html>
```

I have added a new test that uses jQuery to create an a element and apply a data-bind attribute. If you pass an HTML fragment to the jQuery $ shorthand function, the result is a DOM API element that is not attached to the document. As a bonus, I don't have to make sure that the single and double quotes in the data-bind attribute are properly escaped when using the jQuery attr method:

```
var testElem = $("<a></a>").attr("data-bind",
    "formatAttr: {attr: 'href', prefix: '#', value: cat}")[0];
```

Notice that I used an array-style indexer to get the first element in the object returned by the jQuery $ shorthand function. The ko.applyBindings method works on the DOM API object rather than jQuery objects and so I need to unwrap the a element I have created from the jQuery object. At this point, I can get Knockout.js to apply bindings to my HTML fragment using my test view model:

```
ko.applyBindings(viewModel, testElem);
```

To test the result, I use the QUnit equal function and both the DOM API and jQuery to inspect the result:

```
equal(testElem.attributes.length, 2);
equal($(testElem).attr("href"), "#British");
```

jQuery makes it easy to create and prepare HTML for testing and check the results, and as this example shows, you can use the DOM API to get information about the elements after the test has completed. As you can see, jQuery and QUnit together make testing every aspect of a web app possible and, for the most part, easy to do.

Summary

In this chapter, I showed you the tools and techniques I use to write better JavaScript, not better in the sense of a more complete use of the language features but better in the sense of easier for others to work with, easier for me to maintain, and, with the application of unit testing, so the user will experience fewer problems. These techniques, combined with those from earlier chapters, give you a solid foundation on which to build scalable, dynamic, and flexible web apps that are easy to use and easy to maintain. Good luck on all of your projects, and remember, as I said in Chapter 1, that anything worth doing on the server side is worth considering for the client side, too.

Index

V

W, X, Y, Z

CPSIA information can be obtained at www.ICGtesting.com
Printed in the USA
LVOW02s1951251213

366703LV00008B/341/P